The Lake of Como, its History, art, and Archaeology;

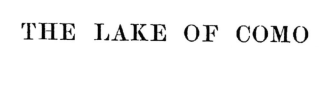

THE LAKE OF COMO

THE LAKE OF COMO

ITS HISTORY, ART, AND ARCHÆOLOGY

BY

REV. T. W. M. LUND, M.A.

CHAPLAIN OF THE CHAPEL OF THE BLESSED VIRGIN MARY, LIVERPOOL

WITH THIRTY-TWO ILLUSTRATIONS

LONDON

KEGAN PAUL, TRENCH, TRÜBNER & CO. LTD

DRYDEN HOUSE, GERRARD STREET, W.

1910

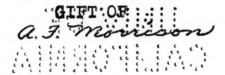

Printed by BALLANTYNE, HANSON & Co.
At the Ballantyne Press, Edinburgh

PREFACE

This volume is that part of my book, "Como and Italian Lakeland," which deals with the Lake of Como alone.

The larger work was found to be too bulky for travellers to carry, so I have adopted the plan of dividing the original volume into parts, which will prove handier for use. Naturally the Lake of Como takes precedence in the first issue. There has been little to exclude or add, but I have tried to revise up to date as thoroughly as possible. I should have felt this reprint superfluous in the face of other publications since mine in 1887, but for the urgency of some of my friends on the Lake, especially the Hôtéliers, who assure me that my book is not superseded, and still has its value for travellers.

I can only say of it what I said in my original Preface, that in its compilation my sole object has been to help English-speaking people to a better use of their opportunities in reaping something of the rich harvest, which lies around them on the shores of the Lake of Como in Scenery, History, Archæology, and Art.

I was first drawn to the task by the want of some book in English to point out the resources of the Lake, and the consequent failure of visitors to see all its charms.

As far as I could, I have given references to my Authorities, in the hope that my readers may go to them for fuller and first-hand information. Original documents have been consulted as far as they were available.

Most of those whom I thanked for their help in 1887, have passed away, and the world is the poorer for their loss.

I am greatly indebted to Messrs. G. E. Thompson and E. H. Gilpin for some of the best illustrations in the book.

T. W. M. Lund.

St. Mary's Lodge, Liverpool,
June, 1910.

CONTENTS

LIST OF ILLUSTRATIONS

THE LAKE OF COMO

CHAPTER I

PONTRESINA TO VARENNA

"Knowledge makes knowledge as money makes money, nor ever perhaps so fast as on a journey."—S. ROGERS.

ACCESS to the Lake of Como is gained by four great gateways,—Como on the S., Lecco on the E., Menaggio on the W., and Colico on the N. We will make our entrance by the northern portal, with that crowd of English people who fly like the swallows to the sunny South with the first chill of winter at Pontresina, S. Moritz, or the huge Maloja Caravanserai. The migration generally begins early in September, so that the autumnal or more popular season on the Lake of Como may be roughly stated as comprising September and the first half of October. There has already been a spring season, fitfully honoured, in April, May, and June. July and August are too hot for such active enjoyment as English people commonly demand, though from personal experience the writer regards these months as among the best for the pure enjoyment of one of the most beautiful phases of the Lake. From November to March, when a stranger is *rara avis* in the land, there is a climate for the most part dry, fresh, and delicious, with almost uninterrupted sunshine and a tranquillity of air, broken now and then by a brief interval of storm, only to be succeeded by a renewed spell of halcyon weather.

The drive of sixty miles between Pontresina and Varenna, leading through the Upper Engadine, over the Maloja Pass, down the Val Bregaglia and the lower part of the Splügen, and along the eastern shore of the Lake of Como, can scarcely be surpassed in Europe for sublimity, beauty, and variety. Nowadays, unfortunately the drive usually ends at Chiavenna, since the completion of the railway from that town to Varenna.

An Italian driver is mostly a picturesque, genial, plausible personage. He drives a hard bargain, game to the last, but sticks to it when made except occasionally in the matter of time, when he always has an excellent excuse for unpunctuality. He directs his horses by sundry strange cries, and warns pedestrians by cracks of his long whip, volleyed out by a succession of clever jerks. In any emergency his repertory of oaths and ejaculations is voluminous. When calm, he swears by two personages only, Christ and Bacchus. When excited, he shows familiarity with the whole calendar of Christian saints and the entire heathen mythology. He is most careful for the comfort of his passengers and the rest of his horses. He plies backwards and forwards over the Alps in summer, and then betakes himself to the Riviera or Naples for winter. He smokes long, rank cigars half the day, and sings snatches of operatic airs, national songs or church music, for the rest of the time. He knows the legends of his locality, and will tell them very prettily and credulously, but his history is slight, and chronology never becomes more definite than "once upon a time." He seems very happy, behaves very well, and would be much less interesting had he learned "extra subjects" in a Government school. Progress will probably lay its hand upon him before long and spoil him, like many other things that it has touched.

A *vetturino* who once brought me by this route, lived at Campo Dolcino on the Splügen. This is worthy of record, if only because he gave that as his sole reason for being Catholic.

It is true courtesy to be careful of other people's feelings. The humblest peasant in the north of Italy seems to be naturally gifted with such grace. This man was convinced of our Protestantism, because we were English, and are not English people proverbially ill at ease in the vicinity of Catholicism? Does it not seem to hurt and offend them?

So, in answer to an inquiry, he announced himself Catholic; yet, with a deprecatory gesture and soft tone of apology, hastened to add—

"But, Signore, Campo Dolcino is Catholic."

His form of religion was quite a matter of geography. For our sakes, he was really sorry at the moment not to be Protestant himself.

The feature which gives its characteristic charm to the whole of the noble scenery, through which the top of the Maloja pass is reached, is the series of lovely lakes, S. Moritz, Silvaplana, Sils; one at least of which is in view the entire distance, while for many miles the road skirts their shores.

The sight that breaks upon the eye at the top of the pass is a startling one. Two thousand feet below us winds the road, so that to one leaning over the rocky battlements at the summit, it seems easy to pitch a stone down upon it over the dark pines, that hang upon the almost perpendicular wall. How the road is carried into the deep valley down those precipices is not so clear. Indeed, the construction is a marvellous piece of engineering skill, which only reveals itself in the descent. Many miles of serpentine windings are traversed to accomplish this short distance from summit to foot of the Maloja precipices. Then, on we go by rock and torrent, forest and glen, ruined abbey and white village, until once more soft meadows spread their sleek carpets, embroidered with the autumn crocus, and the rich foliage of the chestnut begins to supplant the solemn pine.

Below the Maloja pass, the range of mountains which bounds the valley on the left, is remarkable for its gigantic buttresses of grey rock and for ridges splintered into needles sharp and fine, or set with long rows of jagged teeth, or shattered into a variety of fantastic shapes. Here we see the ingenious way in which the winter's supply of fuel is brought from the highest ledges on which the pine-trees grow. A strong wire, perhaps a mile in length, is hung from the point where the wood is being cut, and tightly drawn to a convenient spot in the valley below. The bundles of wood are slung upon it, and with great rapidity traverse the distance.

At Stampa the castle and church of Promontogno come into view between the huge rocks and boulders which guard the Maira torrent. At this point the entire scene can scarcely be surpassed in picturesqueness. But it is at Promontogno that nature seems to have taxed all her wealth of resources to conjure up a scene of the rarest beauty. We move among the colossal, the majestic, the overwhelming. Then we pass between two huge portals of rock, peer down at the swirling stream below, and, as we raise our heads again, before us lies a sunny, opalescent picture, full of warmth and grace and tender hues. It is another world than the one behind that frowning gateway; it is Italy.

The Hotel Bregaglia has a ravishing position. Each window is the frame of some enchanting picture. The rush of two great mountain torrents makes a tuneful lullaby all night for weary walkers, and crisps the air with a delicious coolness. Sojourners in the Val Bregaglia, who seek economy and fine air, will find in Soglio, an hour's walk above Promontogno, all that they need. Returning through the tunnel from the hotel at Promontogno, we cross the bridge on the left, and following a steep cliff path, reach the village of Soglio, perched upon a lofty rock, and commanding a superb view of the Bondasca valley, its white glacier and extraordinary amphitheatre of spiked summits. Here is an old chateau of the De Salis family, built in 1501, and now turned into a pension, where guests are made very comfortable at moderate charges. Antique suits of armour line the hall; the rooms are filled with furniture of three hundred years ago; Damascene tapestry hangs upon the walls; we sleep on bedsteads of quaint, archaic pattern, and behind silken hangings of finest Oriental texture. It is a place to dream in. But there is a legend, which might bring nightmares into the dreams, that Soglio was once a great town, which was overwhelmed by a fall of rock from the mountains above, for proof of which the débris of surrounding stones is adduced. The return to Promontogno is pleasantly varied by taking the carriage road, which leads through shady chestnut groves.

In the Val Bregaglia the Engadiner's custom prevails of affixing inscriptions upon the houses. Racy proverbs and biblical quotations are to be found everywhere north of the Italian frontier, where they suddenly cease.

At Vicosoprano we noted the following :—

"Uomo prudente e pio tiene le mani al lavoro, el cuore a Dio, e pensa alla trave ch'a nel occhio suo pria di tassare il fest (festuco) del frate suo."

"A prudent and pious man keeps his hands to labour and his heart to God, and thinks of the beam which he has in his own eye before blaming his brother's mote."

At Spino the following occurs :—

"Dio è il defensore e G. A. Scartazi il possessore, 1824."

"God is the defender and G. A. S. the possessor."

Bondo yields a rich harvest :—

"Deo, patriae et amicis, 1597."

"To God, fatherland and friends."

"La pratica della verità secundo la pietà è lo soldo stabilimento della renovazione della casa del fedele." 1745.

"The practice of truth, in accordance with piety, is the firm foundation for the rebuilding of the house of a faithful man."

"Non dir di me se di me non sai.
Pensa di te, poi di me dirai." 1770.

"Do not speak of me, if you do not know of me.
Think of yourself, then you shall speak of me."

"D.O.M. 1602. Chi sprezza il suo prosimo è privo di senno; mai uomo prudente sene tace."

"He who depreciates his neighbour is bereft of judgment, but a prudent man keeps silence."

"Ach! Gott, durch Dein Barmherzigkeit
Bewahr diese Haus von Schmerz und Leid."

"O God, by thy loving kindness
Preserve this house from pain and sorrow."

At Promontogno we find :—

"Pensate saviamente, e parlate lealmente." 1827.

"Think wisely and speak truly."

"Nel entrare hai di pensare che non sai se uscirai; nel uscire hai di pensare che non sta a te il ritornare. La casa di giusti stara in pie" (Prov. xii.)

"Upon entering you have to think that you do not know whether you will go out again. Upon going out you have to think that to return does not rest with you. The house of the just shall stand firm."

"D.O.M. 1582. Se il Signore non edifica la casa invano safaticano intorno ad essa quelli che ledeficano. Il fine del ragionamente questo, teme Iddio ed oserva i suoi commandamenti perchè questo è il tutto del uomo."

"If the Lord do not build the house, they labour in vain upon it who build it. The end of the argument is this, Fear God and keep his commandments, for this is the whole of man."

Nothing could be more ideal than the walk from Promontogno to Chiavenna in the early morning. There are shapely mountain forms, a tumultuous river, luxuriant leafage, embowering vines, golden gourds trailing over the brown rocks, quaint houses with sunny balconies, where yellow Indian corn hangs bright against the rich-toned wood, great cataracts foaming over precipices, white graceful campaniles, soaring into the azure from every height; and, embracing and transfiguring all, an atmosphere crystalline, radiant, prismatic; to prodigal nature a glorifying medium; to oneself an intoxicating nectar, reviving for a moment the old belief in a spell for the gift of eternal youth.

What Arcadia could furnish a couch of such velvet sward, under the impenetrable shade of a grove of chestnut and walnut trees, as that on which we cast ourselves before the door of a wayside *osteria?* We only know the modest inn for what it is, by the withered bough that hangs above the door, recalling the obsolete English proverb, "Good wine needs no bush," and by the facetious announcement, laconic and unanswerable, *Si vende cattivo vino*, "Bad wine sold here." This is a favourite piece of irony, presumably found by the trade to be an effective advertisement, if we may judge from the frequency of its use. The wide, gloomy, cavernous interior is empty now of all but a few bare tables and benches, but before nightfall it will be filled with peasants, who will never weary of playing *Mora*, and will always take care to go home sober.

Photo by T. W. M. Lund

THREE GRACES

One seldom passes an *osteria* at night without hearing the quick sharp cries of the players, as they shout out the numbers in their favourite and ancient game. Two take their stand at opposite sides of a small table; one of them places his hand upon it with a certain number of fingers extended, *e.g.* three, simultaneously crying out some other number, say seven, greater than three, but not more than ten, the total number of fingers. His opponent must instantaneously place his hand upon the table with as many fingers extended as make up the difference between three and seven, at the same time crying "four." The game is carried on with lightning speed, the sum being often done almost before the challenge has been fully given. I have seen the correct answer flashed out by the rough digits twenty times in succession. When the number ten is called, the term *Mora* is used instead of ten. The game is often played with sides, and a good deal of small coin changes hands over it.

A black-eyed, bare-legged, sunny girl brings us some of the *cattivo vino* out of a grotto in the rock hard by. It might pass for nectar, so cool, so brilliant, so inspiring it is. The jug in which she bears it, with a nozzle crumpled into a trefoil, is just what has been used in Italy any time these five and twenty centuries. Do not say there is nothing in sentiment. One is drinking there with the old gods. Bacchus and Pan are not far away. Dryads and Naiads are peeping from wood and stream. There is a nymph in that fine, free form before us, so full of the grace that can be bred only of unfettered limbs and unpinched waist.

May she not be Hebe herself, come down in the world a little since Zeus broke up his establishment? There is something odd about Hebe's jug. Near the rim it is pierced with a small hole, through which is passed a bit of lead, flattened out on each side so as to secure it, and stamped with the cross and crown of the Italian kingdom. It is simply the official stamp, attesting the capacity of our pitcher, and safeguarding Hebe from the temptation to use a dishonest measure. The name of this bit of lead is *bollo*. It is the Latin *bulla*. We find ourselves face to face in a wine-shop with an object the like of which has played a mighty part in history. The Pope's Bull gets its name from the leaden boss or seal (*bulla*) which attests the genuineness of his Edicts and gives them their authority. We find the same word in *franco-bollo* or postage-stamp. But there only the name remains. Hebe's pitcher retains the original material, or one of the original materials; for Decrees, both Papal and Imperial, have been attested by seals of gold and wax, as well as the more common lead.

At Castasegna we cross the Italian frontier, a fact made known to us by the Dogana or Custom House, its barrier, guard, and examination. A frank demeanour exempts from vexatious search. The exigency of Law requires the formality of opening at least one package. But rarely does the investigation intrude beyond the surface of portmanteau or trunk. A pocket handkerchief, or a knot of lace, is delicately lifted, replaced, and you are politely permitted to resume your journey. Should you, however, be unfortunate in arousing suspicion, the most rigorous search will be instituted, and if you have packed tightly, the effect on your temper may be serious. Should you be found to carry any contraband article, it will be confiscated, and you will be fined in addition. For the most part you may carry what you please out of a country. But if you try to take old paintings, or even copies of them, out of Italy, without a due permit, they are liable to be detained on the frontier. The Government wisely reserves to itself the right to purchase any works of Art, which the owners wish to sell. They are alive to the folly of allowing their country to be impoverished in its treasures of Art.

At Prosto, shortly before reaching Chiavenna, a great white cliff rises at the head of the ravine, to the right of the road. Some two centuries ago part of the mountain fell and buried Piuro, a prosperous little town of two thousand people, beneath its rocks and débris. The only house which escaped the general ruin was the small chateau of Vertemate Franchi. A walk of fifteen minutes through chestnut woods brings us to its door. It is worth a visit for the sake of a beautiful ceiling of carved wood in a large room frescoed with mythological subjects by the Campi of Cremona. For the ceiling alone forty thousand francs has been offered to the owner, while the beauty of the situation and attractiveness of the house have from time to time provoked many offers of purchase. But though the whole place is rapidly falling into decay, and is only occupied by a servant, who uses the principal rooms for storing farm produce, sale is barred by family jealousies.

From Prosto, Chiavenna can be reached most pleasantly on foot, by crossing the bridge near the church, and following the path by the side of the stream, which leads through shady woods and among rich brown rocks.

Chiavenna, "the key," so called from its commanding position at the junction of the Splügen and Bregaglia valleys, is our first experience of a real Italian town.

The narrow streets, flanked by cavernous shops; the piles of tomatoes—*pome d' oro*, apples of gold, they call them—grapes, figs, pomegranates; the houses of quaint shapes and many colours; their *loggie*, or top stories, with roof supported at back and sides by light walls, but resting in front upon arches and pillars, built for air and shade in the stifling dog days, and often extremely picturesque; the arcades at the sides of the streets; the screaming vendors of hot chestnuts and polenta; the bell towers; the fearless pigeons; the shrines of Christ, Madonna, or Saint, with a lamp hanging in front, and tricked out with paper flowers or a faded bouquet; a cage full of skulls and bones, some of them ticketed with the names of the original owners; here and there a peep into the courtyard of a larger house, green with foliage and cool with its sparkling fountain; the jaunty air of the men; the bright dresses of the women; the gay-plumaged little birds, including a brace of kingfishers, exhibited for sale as articles of food, together with an eaglet and a fox; the primitive carts, drawn by grey, mild-eyed, wide-horned oxen; the army of dogs, one of which gets its tail caught between the brake and the wheel of our carriage, and is sadly punished before the driver can hear the cries to stop above the clatter and rattle twixt hoofs, wheels and paving stones; the urchins, ready to run on any errand and do you any service, yet quite unable to resist the temptation of stealing an inviting strap; by all these tokens, and many more, one knows that this is a town in Italy.

An impressive physical feature around Chiavenna consists in the combination of ferocity and softness. Vast blocks of rock have been dislodged from the precipitous and imminent mountains, and have strewn the whole valley with their colossal ruins. Fragments as big as churches are arrested in positions which a child's finger seems sufficient to disturb. Chiavenna might have suffered bombardment at the hands of Titans. A wild torrent foams and roars in the midst. But groves of chestnut-trees soften the savage face of the scene. Bright lawns smile among the grim, grey boulders. Here a cottage nestles under one of the sheltering giants, and there a gay garden blooms upon a platform of fallen limestone.

Chiavenna abounds in fascinating walks, and is full of work for the artist. There is a fine promenade under plane-trees on the Piano Giano, just outside the town, and a remarkable scene of fantastically shaped rocks on the slope of Uscione, approached by a romantic staircase. The view from the bridge in the centre of the town is almost without a rival in picturesqueness. The Hotel Conradi gives moderate pension and excellent accommodation.

An hour's drive from Chiavenna brings us to the little Lake of Riva. It forms the centre of a scene of rare beauty, as we look back in the direction in which we have come. At one point a wonderfully mirrored precipice seems to carry the eye down into the mysterious depths of the Lake. This sheet of water was once comprised in the Lake of Como, but the river Adda, sweeping in from the Valtelline, built up its deposits, so as to cut off the Lake of Riva from the main body. The marshy flat thus formed is known as the Pian di Spagna. We find our clue to the name in the ruins of the great Castle of Fuentes, so strongly planted on the rock of Montecchio in the midst of the valley. It owes both name and origin to the Count of Fuentes, the Spanish Governor of Milan, who built it in 1603, to overawe the Valtelline. It must have been almost impregnable when the rocks on which it stood were washed by water on every side.

After crossing the Adda, we leave our carriage, and passing under a railway arch, make straight for a cottage on the slope of the hill, in front of which, under some walnut-trees, is a whole family carding, spinning, and knitting wool. One of the boys guides us through the tangled underwood to the ruins of the great fortress above. But little remains of this grim outpost of Spanish dominion in Italy. That little, however, with its peeps into dismal dungeons, its thick walls and solid bastions, is enough to impress upon the beholder a sense of the iron grip of the Spaniard's hand. Now a smooth lawn covers the floor of the great hall, and a few peaceful vines are trained upon parapets which once bristled with guns, while most of the site of the huge fortress is a wilderness of wild shrubs and trailing plants.

Wordsworth's apt words come to mind :—

> "Now gads the wild vine o'er the pathless ascent ;
> O, silence of Nature, how deep is thy sway,
> When the whirlwind of human destruction is spent,
> Our tumults appeased, and our strifes passed away."

There is a splendid view into the broad rich Valtelline, which must have perpetually sharpened the Spanish appetite for its possession.

The juxtaposition of the tiny hamlet of Riva, the ruined Spanish fortress and the prosperous Valtelline, calls up one of those hideous tragedies of history born of religious hatred and unscrupulous statecraft. In the first quarter of the seventeenth century Calvinism was dominant in the Valtelline. No doubt there was truth in the complaint of the Catholics, that they suffered hardship at the hands of their heretical rulers, who certainly had not to go far to find teachers in intolerance. The question of an alliance with the Venetian Republic, at that moment not on speaking terms with the Pope or with the Most Christian King of France, further embittered the relations of the two parties, who were hotly in favour of France or Venice, according to their Catholic or Protestant sympathies. The Catholics secretly carried their grievances to the Duke of Feria, then the Spanish Governor of Milan. The wily statesman fostered their discontent. He not only saw a good chance of striking a pious blow at heresy, but still better, of once more annexing the rich Valtelline to the Milanese Duchy. So he intrigued until, on the 19th of July 1620, the inhabitants of Tirano were early awakened by the clanging of the church bells. Alarmed at the sound, they rushed out to see what the signal portended, when all of the heretical party, of whatever age or sex, were surrounded and cut down by a band of armed men. The head of one aged pastor was cut off and set up in his own pulpit. A little heroine of fourteen years received in her own bosom the blow aimed at her grandfather. Through the long hours of that awful day the red carnage rolled down the valley, and has ever since been known by the anomalous name of *Il sacro macello*, "The Holy Butchery."

The heretics sought aid from their co-religionists in Switzerland. They held Chiavenna and fortified Riva. A war of passion and atrocity ensued. Spaniards and Austrians poured into the country. Mountains echoed to the shrieks of murdered people, and night was lit by blazing homes. Pope Paul V. sent money to help this new crusade. Not until 1623 was the fort of Riva taken, and then by the Pontifical forces of Gregory XV., whose arbitration would have been accepted by all parties as just and impartial, had he not died a few days too soon.[1] When, three years later, a settlement was effected, we find the Spaniards still eager to retain Riva and Chiavenna, but obliged to content themselves with Fuentes. In a curious anonymous epic of the war between Como and Milan in the twelfth century, of which more anon, occurs the following passage, descriptive of the singular wealth of the Valtelline, and the barbarous devastation with which war was carried on in the Middle Ages:—

"Vallis erat formosa satis, nimis apra colonis,
Moribus ornata, est Vallis Tellina vocata,
Arboris est illic, vitum generosa propago,
Fertilis est frugum, satis est ibi copia lactis,
Castaneae multaeque, nuces ibi sunt quoque plures.
Somnia sed faciunt ibi plura papavera nata.
Hac in Valle fures intrant subtiliter hostes,
Depraedant villas, spoliant armentaque multa,
Inde trahunt et ovesque boves, captas quoque vaccas."

In plain English, the Valtelline was beautiful, sunny, and distinguished by the high qualities of its people. It was

[1] *Cf.* Ranke's "Popes of Rome."

rich in vineyards, gardens, and dairies. It boasted a wealth of nuts of various kinds. The poppy, too, was there, parent of sleep and dreams. Into this fruitful vale thievish foes crept stealthily, pillaging the farms, and carrying off the numerous flocks and herds.

Among the many captives who languished in the great fortress, one is worth naming as having been the Mark Tapley of Italian unfortunates.

Anton Maria Stampa, of Gravedona, was a man of eccentric genius, and being on this account deemed dangerous, was shut up in the Castle of Fuentes. We are not surprised at this precaution, when we remember that the reason given by the Sardinian Government for imprisoning Mazzini at Savona was, that "they were not fond of young men of talent, the subject of whose musings was unknown to them." Stampa treated his captivity as an occasion for rallying his spirits, and giving full play to his humour. He employed himself in writing an imaginary history of his illustrious native town in mock heroic style, full of amusing extravagances and rank impossibilities.

At the time of the French Revolution the fortress was no longer a military position. The last governor, Colonel Schreder, bought it from the Austrian Government, and used its environs for the peaceful culture of the mulberry and silkworm. In 1796 General Rambaud and five hundred French soldiers arrived, to find the castle occupied only by a few civilians, sick of slow fever, who of course offered no resistance. The besiegers blew up a portion of the building, but the greater part proved too strong for their powder. This gallant feat is described in certain chronicles of the time as one of the most signal successes ever achieved by the French arms.

The splendid military road constructed by the Austrians leads from Colico to Varenna, and commands some of the most enchanting vistas of the Lake. We pass the beautiful promontory and bay of Piona, the wooded slopes of Legnoncino, the picturesque Castle of Corenno, the busy industrial centre of Bellano, and at last rattle through the streets of Varenna itself.

CHAPTER II

VARENNA

"The Lariano crept
To that fair port, below the castle
Of Queen Theodelind, where we slept;
Or hardly slept, but watched awake
A cypress in the moonlight shake,
The moonlight touching o'er a terrace
One tall agave above the lake."—TENNYSON.

THE Hotel Royal, now an imposing set of buildings since it took in the contiguous Hotel Victoria, built upon a terrace lapped by the rippling water and bristling with cacti and the immemorial aloe, commands the most expansive view of the Lake, looking across its widest part and down two of its three arms. Facing the south, this Hotel might not be a desirable residence in the height of summer, but in spring and autumn no place could be more charming. There is an Italian proverb which contrasts Bellano, swept by icy winds from the Val Sassina in winter, with Varenna, exposed to the full blaze of the sun in summer.

"Che vuol provar pene d'inferno
Vada d'està a Varenna ed a Bellan d'inverno."

"He who would experience the pains of hell, goes in
Summer to Varenna and in winter to Bellano."

Readers of Dante will remember that his southern imagination attributes the extreme of torture in the *Inferno* to the effects of cold and not of heat. These children of the sun seem to suffer intense physical discomfort and profound mental depression under the influence of a searching north wind or a period of sunless rain. It is quite comic to hear the shuddering despair with which they utter their wretched-

Photo by T. W. M. Lund

A SIESTA

ness in the pregnant commonplace, "*Brutto tempo*," "Horrid weather." But with renewed calm and sunshine, gaiety and contentment return to their childish hearts. When the lizard basks and the grasshopper trills, the air is sure to be full of human laughter and song.

The Lake of Como can only be compared to some great master's poem, in which every scene is different from the one which went before, yet all sustain the same supreme level of grandeur and delight. Passion and pathos, energy and repose, light and shadow, the terrible and the tender, in their utmost intensity, enter into the composition, and by the force of their contrasts and the play of their variety give a ceaseless sense of life and beauty, and inspire the soul with indescribable feelings of wonder and of joy.

To-day the bluest of skies repeats itself in the shining mirror of the Lake. The rocky peaks, which frame it in, wear a robe of colour so tender and soft, that they seem to melt away into the ether. Gleaming villages that stud the shores, gleam again in reflected whiteness upon the water. Skimming boats search out the shade of cliff or tree.

To-morrow the sky has veiled itself with cloud splendour which rises from the deep laboratory of the valleys to enthrone itself upon the mountain crests. The solemn purple shadows cast their pall around. The deep ravines grow dark and awful. The air is heavy and stifling. An inky veil is drawn across the sky from east to west. There is a flash, a roll of artillery, and the demon of the storm is loose. Wilder grows the game. The fires of heaven blaze incessantly. We count forty flashes to the minute. One moment there is night, the next brilliant day, lit by the weirdest colours that nature's alchemy can mix. Again the dancing fork gleams. It might be the flash from a cannon, for instantaneously follows a rush of wind, distinct and terrible; it strikes the house like a powerful projectile, shakes it from roof to base; and then succeeds the thunder-clap, that seems to rip and rend and rive the very framework of nature by its violence. Hour after hour the spectacle lasts in unimagined sublimity.

And then the storm-fiend harnesses the wind and rides it

forth in gleeful mischief. Soon the glassy Lake is lashed into a surging sea of billow and foam. Ill-fated is the boat caught in such a gale. The great steamers can play hide-and-seek behind those rolling crests, but one of smaller build founders beneath them. Piers and boat-houses go down before the violence of the storm.

Or yet again, the hot scirocco blows, and heaven empties its reservoirs upon earth. It is the rain of the deluge. Down the steep sides of those vast gathering grounds the water rolls in sheets. Trickling rills grow into raging torrents. Streams rise into rushing rivers. Out of every valley pours a flood. Trees, rocks, houses, bridges, roads are swept away like leaves. The swollen Lake invades the land and lays towns and villages under its waters.

And then once more the cloud rolls off, the sun shines in a blue sky, the Lake smiles its old sweet smile, but the ethereal peaks are wrapped in an ermine mantle of snow, and the forests beneath have turned to crimson and gold.

Such may be the moods of the Lake in one short week; moods so delicately graded that we see a thousand varieties of expression in the face of nature, a thousand vicissitudes of form, colour, and effect, all lifted into the realm of the superlatively beautiful and sublime.

Close to Varenna is a famous stream, issuing like a brilliant mass of sapphire out of a cleft in the mountain side. In its short and steep descent to the Lake it formerly fell in a series of cascades, and from the whiteness into which its water was broken, it was called *Fiume di Latte*, "The Milk Stream." Upon its banks a hamlet had been planted for centuries, and its channel lined by wheels, undershot by the brook, and turning the machinery of certain poor marble cutters. But since the great rainfall of 1882, the picturesqueness of the overhanging houses and the romantic character of the river bed have disappeared. On the morning of the 16th of September in that year the stream rose beyond all precedent. In a few hours it was a raging flood, the more terrible from its precipitous fall, which added enormous force to its great volume. It began its work of ruin by tearing away the two lines of mill wheels. Then it swiftly undermined the houses, which fell wall by wall, floor by floor into the torrent. Next it wrenched out ponderous blocks of stone, and sent them thundering down the stream, ominously shaking the strong bridge of the high road as they ground against its piers. Then it went on to swallow up whole gardens and terraces; but these depredations soon widened the stream and diminished its power. As a house side or a piece of rock or a slice of vineyard fell into the current, the white water turned yellow for a second, a cloud of fresh spray flew upwards, the roar swelled, and then all went on as before. All day long the poor peasants, half naked, were saving what they could of their small possessions, while out on the stormy Lake were boats collecting the floating wreckage.

The priest of the place appealed to the English visitors to raise a small fund for the sufferers among their compatriots on the Lake. He promised to devote to the same purpose one hundred francs destined for music and decorations at the coming festival of the Blessed Virgin. He thought she would feel it no dishonour to have the money transferred to so charitable a use, and that more earnest prayers would compensate her for the loss of the Ceremony to which she had been accustomed.

The beauty of the lower portion of the Fiume di Latte is now quite obliterated.

It is curious that neither of the Plinies, both of whom took so much interest in the physical peculiarities of the Lake, mentions this phenomenon. P. Giovio,[1] however, draws a picture of it, which might serve to-day as well as three and a half centuries ago. He says that the water rises in spring, when the ice and snow begin to melt upon the mountains, and ceases to flow in winter, when all is frozen up. He might have added, that the volume is extremely sensitive to every fall of rain. He describes the stream as gushing from an aperture in the rock, resembling a large window, and lashed into foam so white as to justify the name which it bears, "The Torrent of Milk."

In his day there were people of a curiosity so venturesome (*periculosa curiositate*), that they attempted to explore the cavern from which the water issued, when the bed of the torrent lay dry in winter; but only with the result

[1] *Descriptio Larii Lacus.*

of having their torches extinguished by a gust of wind after they had advanced a considerable distance.

The shepherds of the district, he relates, accounted for the supply of the stream by the hypothesis of a vast hollow, resembling a huge amphitheatre, with the mountains for its walls, into which, as into a cup, the melting snows of spring were drained, and filtering through the porous soil into subterranean reservoirs, fed the torrent in question by a constant overflow.

He assigns peculiar properties to the water, which he makes out to be cold enough to keep dead fish fresh for three days. Live fish, however, though quite recently caught, quickly die in it, when it is low. And so, near the shore, below the corn mills (*molas frumentarias*), turned by the force of the stream, tanks for keeping the dying fish alive (*morientium vivaria*) were built, so that they might be sent fresh to the Lombard markets on the backs of pack animals (*ut inde pisces jumentis ad fora Insubrum exclusa tabe deferantur*).

The majority of people visit the Lake of Como as a small item in a crowded tour. The usual plan of "doing it" is to steam up to Bellagio or Cadenabbia, visit the Villas Carlotta and Melzi, buy a piece of olive wood or a silk dress, and then steam down again *en route* for Milan, Venice, or Rome. I once saw two men "do it" from the cabin of the steamer. They were working so hard at their sight-seeing, that this was their sole chance of snatching a meal; so they ate their dinner on board, and between the mouthfuls plunged to the cabin windows to see what they might of the Lake of Como. But the Queen of Lakes refuses to be so seen. She must be wooed, waited upon, known, to reveal her charms.

There is no greater delight than to walk the entire circuit of the Lake. The most lovely sections are from Nesso to Lezzeno, Menaggio to Dongo, and Bellagio to Vassena by Civenna. What mistaken judgments may be formed, when they are based upon superficial knowledge, is illustrated by a remark of Mr. Thomas Erskine in his Letters in 1823, when the population on the Lake of Como was little less than it is now, and the communication by road or path between place and place almost as complete.

Photo by G. E. Thompson

NEAR VASSENA

"The Lake of Como," he says, "is bounded by its two sides as by two walls, in some cases almost perpendicular. There is not even a mule road on either side! And on one side the steepness of the rocks does not admit even of a footpath the whole way, or even for a considerable way."

Every valley and ravine is worth exploring. Many of them yield a wealth of pleasure and surprise to the lover of scenery, the artist, the botanist, the entomologist, and the geologist. Perhaps the most beautiful are the Val Esino from Varenna to the Cainallo Pass; the Val Sassina from Bellano to Lecco; the Val di Varrone[1] from Dervio to Val Sassina; the Val di Nesso from Nesso to Pian del Tivano and Asso; the Val Intelvi from Argegno to San Fedele and Osteno; the Valle Perlana, or di San Benedetto, behind the Madonna del Soccorso; the Val Sanagra behind Menaggio and under the walls of the Monte Grona; the Val di Dongo and the Val di Gravedona, leading to the San Jorio pass. The great tongue of land which lies between the Como and Lecco arms of the Lake is rich in romantic scenery of the highest order.

Since the completion of the great road on the western side of the Lake, a carriage may now be driven all the way from Como to Lecco by Cadenabbia, Menaggio, Gravedona, Colico, and Varenna. The making of it has effaced some of the pristine picturesqueness of the shores of the Lake, but there is no doubt some countervailing gain for travellers who cannot be pedestrians.

Of high ascents there are enough to reward the efforts of experienced mountaineers. Moncodine or Grigna, above Varenna, and Legnone over Dervio, are the most important, rising to a height of over eight thousand feet. Monte Grona is an interesting expedition, especially in winter. Monte Crocione, behind Cadenabbia; San Primo, above Nesso; and Monte Bisbino, over Carate, present no difficulties. Monte Generoso is one of the mountain excursions that may be made from the Lake, by a good road, on foot, or on horseback, and is unsurpassed in the magnificence of its views.

For those, who are unequal to long expeditions, there are

[1] By this route large stones rolling down from Monte Legnone have to be dodged sometimes.

rambles of great beauty and little exertion upon the lower slopes contiguous to the Lake. A rise of a few feet serves to set one among level terraces, richly cultivated, and thickly planted with the olive, vine, fig, and mulberry. Here we may saunter and lounge with an ever-changing scene of beauty spread out before us. There is no sweeter or more effective setting for a picture than the delicate silver-grey foliage of the olive. The most generous freedom is granted by the tillers of the soil to those, who use their fields and gardens for pleasure grounds. A copper or two makes us welcome to a feast of fat figs. They will probably be gathered for us by a wild-looking man, armed with a *falcetto*, a little sickle or pruning-hook, used for all sorts of gardening operations. He is seen watching us at a distance in statuesque stillness, or starts up behind us like some Elijah, we cannot tell whence or how. He climbs the fig-tree like a squirrel, and picks for us the most luscious fruit, which is only eaten to perfection when fresh gathered. Figs in proper condition are a wholesome fruit; otherwise, they are dangerous, and to be avoided like poison. Shun them for a day or two after rainy or sunless weather, and in selecting them recall the axiom of Marcus Aurelius: "Figs, when they are quite ripe, gape open." Another trifling coin secures for us a fine cluster of grapes of a quality and size not to be despised. Courtesy to these *contadini* receives not only courtesy but devotion in return.

A climb of a few yards more lands us in smooth pastures, green lawns under spreading chestnut-trees, with still more extensive landscapes. We are surprised to find wide spaces stretching out between us and the mountains, which from below seem so imminent. The sweet cyclamen blooms among the grey rocks that begin to break up the sward, and a month or two later the same ground will be starred with countless blossoms of the Christmas rose, white, green, pink, and purple. For these easy but enchanting rambles the lower slopes of Monte Crocione behind Cadenabbia have no rival, unless it be the spur of Moncodine to the E. of Varenna.

The cheap, safe, and comfortable boating provides a far more delightful alternative. The boatmen are courteous and obliging, their boats clean and luxurious, but a plain understanding as to charges is desirable. They are singularly weatherwise, and will avoid exposing their passengers to the danger of those sudden squalls to which the Lake is liable. In settled weather the *Tivano* or North Wind blows steadily down the Lake until noon, when the *Breva* or South Wind regularly takes its place. Any deviation from this rule is a sure sign of change. However fresh the *Breva* may blow, the native scorns the idea of its being wind. It is never more than the harmless, welcome *Breva*, a friend who may be implicitly trusted. Wind, on the contrary, is a malignant demon. Those who prefer to dispense with the services of a boatman should state where they are going, and inquire the weather forecast.

The boating excursions are numberless. If you simply let your boatman row you at will, you can drink in the most ravishing delight on every side. Now you float on the wide expanse of the glowing water, and embrace the whole wondrous vision of the Lake at a glance, the girdle of the dreamy peaks, precipice and forest, purple ravine and wooded headland, crag and castle, white villages and graceful bell-towers. Should it be the hour of sunset, you may see a glory which would move the sternest spirit. You have seen, or you will see, the robes and wings of Angelico's angels. Their colours were no fancy of his own. His reverent eye marked those in which God steeped, for a brief five minutes in a day, cloud, mountain, air; and these he thought the most fitting hues in which to dye the garments of God's incarnate messengers. You may see them all around you in the flames that blaze upon the crest of the Grigna, in the rose that blooms across the heavens, in the shades of amethyst that lie so tenderly upon the distant mountains, in the sapphire and the gold that burn upon the level Lake, in the mist of violet that slowly veils them all.

And then, as though each sense was to be assailed in turn, the Campaniles peal out their evening hymn in rich, deep, solemn melody. Each slowly uttered cadence pauses, as though listening for the answer from some distant tower. No hindering walls check the full tide of the vibrations, since the bells hang almost as much outside the belfry windows as within. Those eloquent tongues fling their voices upon the free air in mellow antiphons. From San Giovanni and Griante, from Bellagio and Varenna, from the far Madonna del Soccorso and Menaggio come the answering chimes. It is a daily confession of the Christian Faith. At midday it is the same. "All through the land, in remembrance of the hour when the true meaning of love and sacrifice was revealed to the human race, there sweeps the music of church bells, bidding the people to pause in their work and pray. Many a peasant raises his thoughts for a moment from sordid cares or hard labour, and realises that there is an unseen world."[1]

But our boat will find us other delights, if we drift along shore by villas buried behind hedges of roses, or smothered among magnolias and the oleander, trees of verbena and heliotrope, groves of myrtle and the golden orange. We pause by great masses of crimson creeper, festooning rock and wall, climbing over the grey olives or streaming in bleeding rivers down the dark green sides of majestic cypresses; or we round a little headland, crowned with the cactus and aloe, the long weepers of its willows trailing in the wave. Perhaps we reach the sunny island of Comacina or San Giovanni, row round it to see some of the choicest views upon the Lake, and sketch the picturesque old tower of Sta. Maria Maddalena di Stabio upon the mainland. Then we may cross to the little grotto opposite the Villa Arconati on the Lavedo promontory, roofed with maidenhair fern, and in its weird effects of light and colour see a miniature of the famous cave at Capri, then saunter home by the rock-bound eastern shore, Grosgalli.

Or we cool ourselves in the shadows of the Serbelloni cliff; mark the points from which many a well-known picture has been painted; watch the becalmed *camballo*, the picturesque barge of Pliny's day, with eccentric rudder and arabesqued gunwale, lazily waiting for the Breva di Lecco to fill its sail; listen to the harmonised song of its crew, now wild, now tender; hang on the last sweet, slowly dying note, and then shudder at the startling maniac laugh with which they wake the echoes and chill one's blood.

Then we may explore the neglected beauties of the Lecco

[1] Edna Lyall.

Photo by T. W. M. Lund

A CAMBALLO IN PORT

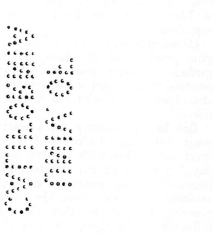

arm. To skirt the southern shore as far as Onno, cross to Lierna and coast up to Varenna, forms a memorable experience.

Or we may seek the cool Bay of Menaggio, float under the grim precipice of the Sasso Rancio, picnic in the smiling gardens of Gaeta near its foot, and drift along, as time permits, by rock and castle, ravines spanned by airy bridges, and shores laden with the wealth of corn, and wine, and silk.

But in enumerating the attractive uses of the boat we must not omit fishing and a moonlight *giro.* Ample sport can be had with the rod under the rocks during the day, but a merrier game is found in choosing a dark night, illuminating the water by a blazing fire suspended in a *scaldino* or brazier from the prow of the boat, and then spearing the fish as they lie still under the paralysing influence of the light. A bad shot sometimes ends in a cool bath.

It has not, however, been my fortune, nor that of any one I have known, to hook, net, or spear a specimen of those royal fish which P. Giovio ascribes to the Lake of Como. In his day,[1] he says, its waters were the haunt of trout weighing one hundred pounds, while carp could be caught double that size. More[2] wonderful and exciting still, he tells of great caves in the rocky coast between San Giovanni and Lezzeno (*Grosgallia Saxa*), where in the heat of summer great monsters (*burburi pisces*), as big as a man, might be descried cooling themselves in the glassy depths; so strong that no net could hold them, and armed with a coat of mail (*gravique squamarum serie thoracati*) which no arrow could pierce. When such fish as these are feeding, let the votaries of the gentle art look well to their tackle. But possibly in three hundred and fifty years these species have become extinct, and P. Giovio would not be too scrupulous when he had undertaken to prove the excellence of the fish of his own Lake above all others. His assurance, that in his brochure upon the Lake of Como no heed has been paid to hearsay (*nihil est tributum fabulis*) must be taken *cum grano salis*.

[1] *De Piscibus Romanis*, c. 38. [2] *Descrip. Lar. Lac.*

The more sentimental will give the palm to the moonlight *passeggiata al batello* or *promenade en bateau*, especially should some fair nightingale choose to sing upon the Lake that evening, or violinist appeal to the panting stars. Fragrant flowers launch their odours on the balmy air. The boat rocks to the liquid ripple. Voice or viol floats out its soul to the infinite silence. A spell lies upon each sense. The thoughts that are too deep for words begin to stir. And then suddenly a strident tongue from a gliding barque breaks the stillness:—

"Waal, I guess this is real slow. Why don't somebody boss a dance at the Bellevue, just to take the creases out of one's knees?"

Nothing could be more ideal than a week spent in a voyage round the entire Lake, like that made by P. Giovio when he wrote his *Descriptio Larii Lacus*, to which repeated reference will have to be made. He followed the coast line, visiting each point of interest and covering a distance of one hundred and twenty miles in six days (*sexto die completo universae navigationis cursu, qui per oram centum et viginti millibus passuum conficitur*).

Nowadays a motor boat may be hired which will achieve the same feat in a few hours, but not with the same results of repose, observation, and enjoyment. And yet in fairness let it be said, that the speed of the motor boat is a godsend to earnest travellers with limited time, since by this aid many points of prime interest can be visited which must otherwise be neglected.

The shoes of the district, made of canvas uppers, with thick soles of string (*scarpe di tela*), and costing about three francs, will be found invaluable for comfort and safety in traversing the steep roads, or *salite*, paved with round and slippery cobbles, or in crossing steep, smooth rocks.

The vicinity of the Lake of Como is rich in shells. Perhaps no district in Europe exhibits such a variety of species and abundance of individuals within so small an area. Mr. G. Jefferies, the eminent English conchologist, was engaged in investigating the mollusca of this region shortly before his death. But there is no need to be a scientific shell-hunter in order to enjoy the beauty and variety of these treasures, scattered so lavishly all around, and often carrying us in their quest into spots of untrodden seclusion and luxuriant loveliness.

The region is as rich in flora as in shells, and the botanist will happily find the most prolific fields of his research among the noblest scenery of the district, as *e.g.* the Val Sassina, the Val di S. Benedetto, Monte Grigna, Monte Campione, and Monte Generoso.

What we miss of Autumnal tints and fruits by visiting the Lake in Spring, we gain in the vividness of the young verdure and the wealth of wild flowers, which carpet every available piece of ground with their brilliant colours and graceful forms. For a full appreciation of the Lake of Como, it should be visited at least in Spring and Autumn, and, if possible, in every month, since its face is as variable as the seasons, and beautiful at all times.

CHAPTER III

THE CONVENTIONAL ROUND OF THE LAKE OF COMO

"O, si bona norint."—VIRGIL.

SOME personal experiences will furnish typical examples of the days that may be spent upon the Lake of Como.

We begin with the conventional round. Our boat glides alongside the marble steps of Villa Carlotta, embosomed in a little paradise of tropical luxuriance. But probably before these words are in print the new road from Como to Colico will have rendered this experience impossible, as it is to be built out into the Lake in front of the Villa, and will have destroyed for ever one of the most beautiful sections of the western shore of the Lake. The Villa, built about the middle of the eighteenth century by the Marchese Clerici, came into the possession of Count Sommariva a century ago, and bore his name. On the extinction of the family, Princess Albrecht of Prussia bought it in 1843 for £27,000, and gave it in 1850 as a wedding present to her daughter Carlotta, on her marriage with the hereditary Prince of Saxe-Meiningen. Hence the name. Several treasures of modern sculpture are found in the entrance-hall, beyond which there is little of interest.

The chief work is a marble frieze by Thorwaldsen, a commission by Napoleon I. in 1811 for the decoration of the Throne Room of the Quirinal Palace at Rome. The Emperor fell while the work was still only modelled in stucco, but Count Sommariva assumed the dethroned monarch's obligation, and had the work completed for himself at a cost of £15,000. The frieze, thirty-seven yards long and more than a yard high, which portrays the Triumph of Alexander of Macedon in Babylonia, makes the entire circuit of this

Photo by G. E. Thompson

BELLAGIO FROM VILLA CARLOTTA

large apartment. The central figure is the youthful conqueror, who heads the victorious procession in a chariot swiftly driven by the Goddess of Victory. His mien bespeaks the pride of conquest, but a touch of *ennui* is thrown into the expression, as befits the man who wept because there were no more fields for his warlike ambition to reap.

Behind him follow warriors in variety of equipment; elephants, bridleless horses laden with Eastern spoils; forlorn captives on foot, less free in their fetters than the victors' beasts of burden; while citizens who seem to be calculating the benefits of victory bring up the rear. The other half of the frieze depicts the conqueror's welcome home. The Genius of Peace meets him with an olive branch and horn of plenty. The people, headed by his own family, strew flowers or offer gifts. Balconies are crowded with eager spectators. A final panel shows the development of commerce through successful war. The many groups in this work deserve much longer study than is usually given to them. The two figures bringing up the rear of the procession, on the left hand as we face the door, are said to be portraits of the artist and his patron, Count Sommariva.

Canova's group of Eros and Psyche, a work of 1800, is a more popular subject, since it appeals to humanity at large. While few sympathise deeply with the ambition of Alexander, most of us know how the birth of passion transfigures life. There is an exquisite *abandon* about Psyche, who is lost in her beautiful lover. We almost hear her say, "I would die a hundred times rather than be deprived of thy sweet usage." Those who have the good fortune to visit Rome and see Raffaelle's rendering of the myth in the Villa Farnesina, will learn how "many waters quench not love" in the heart of faithful Psyche, not even the cruellest waters of neglect, or jealousy, or tyranny, or death.

Psyche, as the old story goes, was a royal child, so lovely that men saw in her an incarnation of divine beauty, and began to desert the shrine of Venus to lay their offerings at the feet of this new goddess.

But Venus could brook no rival, and forthwith summoning her "winged bold boy of evil ways," she pointed out the maiden, and bade him make her the slave of an unworthy love. Meantime an oracle had commanded Psyche to be placed upon a mountain top, as for the bed of marriage or of death, and there await for bridegroom "that evil serpent thing, by reason of whom even the gods tremble, and the shadows of Styx are afraid."

Then Zephyr bore her to a palace, like the beauty of the loveliest dream, and hither Eros came and made her all his own. But he came only in the darkness of the night, and went again before the break of dawn, so that Psyche knew not the face of him she had learnt to love, and of whose sweet usage she could not bear to be deprived. Nor had she hope of seeing him, since he warned her, that if ever in an evil hour curiosity mastered her, so that she espied his bodily form, she would feel his embrace no more.

But the course of true love never ran smooth, and now came her jealous sisters, who contrived to work upon poor Psyche's feelings and credulity, until she believed herself the victim of a dread monster in her unseen lover, whom she resolved to slay. But when, with lamp in one hand and knife in the other, she nerved herself for the fatal blow, the vision that met her eye disarmed her purpose, for there lay Eros, golden-locked and dewy pinioned, all soft and white and lovely. Then Pysche, catching sight of his bow and arrows, drew out a dart, and trying the temper of its point upon her thumb, drove in the barb, and so fell into the love of Love; and in her rapture a drop of scalding oil fell from her lamp upon her lover's shoulder, who awoke, and seeing the failure of her faith, took flight and left her.

And now began many sorrows for Psyche, the bitter penalty of doubt and curiosity. Venus learnt the amour of her boy, and though Juno and Ceres received her overtures for help in the quest of Psyche coldly and with some spiteful taunts, yet from Jupiter she obtained the use of Mercury, the god of speech, who soon tracked out for her the object of her persecution. With insults and hardships, many and cruel, did Venus ply her daughter-in-law, to whose help came in turn the ant, and the reed, and the eagle, and the very stones of the walls, all for the sake of Love. And even to Hades, across Charon's ferry and past Cerberus, the fierce watch-dog of Proserpine, went patient Psyche, since love is stronger than death, and brought away in the casket of Venus what her mistress had told her was the divine beauty itself, but what proved to be the sleep of the dead.

And opening the casket on her way, that she might touch herself with some particle of the precious gift, to enhance her own fair beauty in the eyes of her truant lover and win him back again, she fell into a deadly sleep, until Eros found her, and by the touch of his arrow awoke her once more to life. Then Eros, who had grown love-sick for his sweet bride, sought his father's sympathy; and Jupiter granted his son's desire, and bade Mercury bring Psyche to the court of Heaven, and there he gave her a draught of the immortal wine, saying, "Take it and live for ever; nor shall Eros ever depart from thee."

"And the gods sat down to the marriage-feast. On the first couch lay the bridegroom, and Psyche in his bosom. His rustic serving-boy bore the wine to Jupiter; and Bacchus to the rest. The seasons crimsoned all things with their roses. Apollo sang to the lyre, while little Pan prattled on his reeds, and Venus sweetly danced to the soft music. Thus, with due rites, did Psyche pass into the power of Cupid (Eros); and from them was born the daughter whom men call Voluptas (Pleasure)." [1]

Those who wish to study the myth more minutely will find all they wish in "The Golden Ass" of Apuleius, a quarry out of which material has been dug to enrich the Decameron, Don Quixote, and Gil Blas.

The romance of Apuleius, and its illustration by Canova's chisel, do not lose in interest, if it be true that they are the ultimate evolution of the germ of a solar myth, born in the far East, in times too remote for fancy, among the Aryan ancestry of Europe.

By this theory, what we have come to regard as an allegory of love is but a tale elaborated from the natural phenomena

[1] Quoted from the translation in Pater's "Marius the Epicurean."

of the earth's rotation. It is the drama of sunrise and sunset played before our eyes every day. It is the story of Eos (Dawn or Evening) and Phoibos (the Sun), who are fated to part in the moment when they first look upon each other; yet after the day-long quest of Eos through all lands, among all dangers, against overwhelming difficulties, sustained by the deathless desire to see her lover once again, at eventide her faithful search is rewarded, and she is found face to face with the bright object of her devotion.[1]

Close by, in striking contrast, is a Magdalen by the same artist in 1796. She has sunk upon her knees; her face is full of desolate sorrow; her marble hands and arms are made to utter the physical weakness of grief; her whole attitude is eloquent of pain and penitence, loss, loneliness and love.

In the centre of the room is a group of Mars and Venus, by Acquisti. It may tell more tales than one. Certainly the woman pleads and the man stands irresolute. Perhaps he is caught between the rival claims of love and duty. Perhaps she would win him from the savage passion of war to the softer arts of peace. Anyhow her power is evident. She can inspire, restrain, unman.

In an adjacent room are some designs in plaster for Napoleon's projected Arch of Triumph at Milan. They are singular trophies of the fickleness of fortune.

The Garden of the Villa is famous at once for the great variety of its trees and the beauty of the views that may be seen from it. Among the tangle of tropical and sub-tropical vegetation are no less than seventy different species of acicular leaved conifers.

Abutting on the avenue of broad-leaved plane-trees, which forms a unique feature of the Lake, is the little Sommariva Chapel, which enshrines works of Art worth notice by the passing visitor. Over the altar is a fine Pietà in white marble. The word Pietà means "pity," and is applied to painting or sculpture, in which the subject is the dead body of our Lord, exhibited to the compassion of men and angels The lifeless form sometimes lies across the mother's knees,

[1] *Cf.* "The Mythology of the Aryan Nations," by Sir G. W. Cox, p. 210.

sometimes stands erect as a half-length figure, sometimes rests upon the ground, mourned by angels and men.

A beautiful Nativity in relief decorates the front of the altar. The angles of the chapel contain figures respresenting Charity, a gracious woman tending an orphan child; Justice, bearing sword and scales; Religion, carrying a cross and wearing a glory about the head; The Love of God, a beautiful being, with footsteps guided by the Divine Will, wings for swiftness to perform it, and an upturned face of intense devotion. Opposite the altar are the Angel of Blessing, holding a shell of Holy Water, and the Angel of Resurrection, whose face is bright and calm with trustful hope. More angels float upon the ceiling; in their hands are the signs of the Redeemer's Passion, scourge, thorns, handkerchief of Sta. Veronica, nails, sponge, hyssop and spear.

There is a monument to Count Sommariva by Marchesi. The Angel of Death leads him away, but in departing the father counsels his son to take to his bosom the Arts, which have enriched his own life. The Arts are represented by a fair woman, who holds a sculptor's mallet in her hand.

Re-embarking, we cross to San Giovanni di Bellagio. The Parish Church of San Giovanni is worth a visit for the delicate harmony of its decoration. It bears signs of the opulence and cultured taste of its congregation. It owns a good example of the work of Gaudenzio Ferrari, which was formerly in the first Chapel on the left, but since its exhibition at Como in 1899, has been placed over the first of the two doors that open into the Sacristy. It represents Christ in Glory, to whom S. Paul, S. Stephen, S. John the Baptist, and S. Peter, identified by their conventional symbols, point a kneeling crowd below. The flesh-painting of our Lord and the quaint costumes of some of the kneeling figures arrest attention.

On the steps of the Church you may see the fishermen and their families mending the nets for use on the Lake, forming groups to ravish the soul of an artist.

Immediately on the left of the Church is the entrance to the grounds of the Villa Trotti, most generously thrown open to visitors by the kindness of the Marchese who owns it. Though not extensive, the Gardens are among the most beautiful on the Lake; the part laid out in the Japanese style, with lakelets, toy bridges, a bamboo jungle, dwarf maples, and other delights, is a joy to every beholder.

The Gardens of the Villa Trivulzio, formerly the Villa Poldi Pezzoli, next door to it, are also rich in rare exotic vegetation. In the upper part of these Gardens rises the tower of the Mausoleum, which Cav. Giacomo Poldi Pezzoli built for the sepulture of himself and his family.

There is a picturesque solemnity about the great avenue of cypresses leading up from the water, and the tall Lombard campanile of Sta. Maria Antica, grey against their dark spires, which flank a broad green alley closed by the Villa Giulia at its eastern end. This also is well worth visiting for the beauty of its Gardens, especially in the spring, when the camellias are in bloom.

A short walk brings us to the entrance of the Villa Melzi. Count Melzi d'Eril, who built it, was Vice-President of the Cis-Alpine Republic under Napoleon I., who created him Duke of Lodi. A portrait of the Emperor in his thirty-third year, by Appiani, hangs in one of the rooms. The face is strikingly handsome, and wears a look of deep abstraction. In strange contrast is a bust of Michel Angelo by himself. The strong, stern face of the sculptor makes no attempt to disguise its ugly disfigurement of the nose, early broken by the mallet of a jealous fellow-student. There is a great charm in the frescoed walls of the rooms. In one, groups of children play their various games. In another, we seem to be embowered in the depths of a forest. In a third, the eye is met by every flower that the Gardens of the Villa produce. In a fourth, we are transported to Parnassus and have Muses for company.

In the Chapel is a very unconventional statue of Christ, by Comolli. He is portrayed as a young man in meditation, embracing a cross with his right arm, and recalls the same subject by Michel Angelo in Sta. Maria Sopra Minerva at Rome. A fresco on the right wall has a portrait of Leonardo da Vinci teaching his pupil, Count Francesco Melzi d'Eril, an ancestor of the family, the art of designing, while another shows Leonardo on his death-bed in the act of bequeathing his studio to Francesco. A beautiful friendship bound to-

Photo by T. W. M. Lund

BUST OF JOSEPHINE BEAUHARNAIS AT VILLA MELZI

gether the old Leonardo and the young Francesco. The Melzi family had a lovely Villa at Vaprio, to which the great master often fled from Milan for congenial repose, or to escape the inconvenience of a French occupation. Francesco's fortunes were so linked with Leonardo's that he accompanied him into France when, in 1516, the old artist accepted the invitation of Francis to settle at Amboise. Three years later it was the pupil's sad duty to announce his master's death to the King. Francesco was appointed executor of Leonardo's will, and in writing to the Da Vinci family on the subject he says: "He was to me the best of fathers . . . it is not in the power of nature to reproduce such a man."

The Gardens are crowded with a wealth of rare trees and fragrant flowers. Here are broad lawns set with choice statuary of the Renascence and fantastic modern china dogs; fish-ponds flecked with water-lilies, and quaint conceits of Italian horticulture strange to English eyes and taste. Upon a beautiful terrace, close to the water's edge, is Comolli's group in marble of Dante and Beatrice. It may best be studied from a cool pagoda, of which the doorway so exactly frames in the piece of statuary as to help us to concentrate our thought upon the subject. The artist has contrived to throw into his work the feeling that the genius of Dante was quickened, inspired, and controlled by a lofty and pure ideal of womanhood.

Some people detect in Dante's physiognomy a close resemblance to the late Right Hon. W. E. Gladstone, while others find in it the features popularly given to Mephistopheles, whose prototype is the classic Faun.

Far more interesting are the busts of Letitia, mother of Napoleon I., and Josephine Beauharnais, his wife, attributed to Canova, and placed in the external niches of the front of the Orangery. Both women are strikingly beautiful, and even bear some likeness to each other.

Quitting these lovely grounds, we stroll to Bellagio, beneath a shady avenue of planes, and pass the palatial Hotel Grande Bretagne, unrivalled for its magnificent dining-hall, sumptuously decorated with panels of the Months in Pompeiian style, its luxurious salon and admirable management. Upon the terrace of the Hotel Genazzini is a record worth studying of the inundations of the Lake for a century past.

The old Parish Church, with its sloping floor and Lombard apse, deserves a visit. Its most interesting content is a pulpit of the ninth century, rudely carved with the symbols of the Four Evangelists, and reminiscent of the far nobler work on the Island of San Giulio at Orta.

A short climb by the narrow stairways which serve for streets, brings us to the extensive grounds of the Villa Serbelloni, now a *dépendance* of the Grand Hotel, Bellagio, a lordly fabric which flanks Bellagio on the N. as the Grande Bretagne does on the S.

P. Giovio unhesitatingly assumes that this promontory of Bellagio was the site of that Villa which Pliny called "Tragedy," because it was elevated upon lofty rocks, like the high shoes of a tragic actor. Certainly it is true that this point answers to Pliny's description of an outlook upon the Lake, stretching out on either hand into two wide seas. At a glance we comprehend the derivation of the name Bellagio from its situation, *Bi-lacus*, between two lakes.

In the fourteenth century this headland was not clothed by a wealth of trees, as at present, but was crowned by a fortress, notorious for the shelter which it had long given to the renegades of all the country round. In 1375 Gian Galeazzo Visconti decreed the demolition of this Cave of Adullam once and for ever. The Marquis Stanga, however, a prime favourite of Ludovico Sforza, got permission to build a princely mansion on the southern slope of the hill, but it was burnt down by the pirates of the Lake soon after its completion. These marauders were the Cavargnoni, a clan which got their name from the Val Cavargna in the Val Menaggio, and were distinguished, according to P. Giovio, by a genius for picking quarrels, and a wit chiefly of the sanguinary sort. They were like Burgundy's soldiers—

"Who nothing do but meditate on blood." [1]

G. B. Giovio, in his *Lettere Lariane*, recounts an amusing adventure which befell the natural philosopher, Lazzaro

[1] Hen. V. Act v. sc. ii.

Photo by G. E. Thompson

STREET IN BELLAGIO

Spallanzani, in 1772, when in the company of some friends he made an excursion into the Val Menaggio. Here he fell in with some young girls, who no sooner saw a man surrounded by a group of comrades than they fired off a volley of pistol-shots. The familiar signal brought the Cavargnoni to the scene of action, armed to the teeth. For a moment the poor philosopher thought that the end had come to his researches; but when the gentlemen of the valley discovered the peaceful and scientific equipment of the intruders, not only was a free passage accorded, but every hospitality shown to them. The sortie was due to the impression that the revenue officers were making a descent upon the neighbourhood to claim the salt-tax.

Upon the site of Stanga's mansion an inferior house was built towards the end of the sixteenth century by Ercole Sfondrate, who had commanded the Papal forces in France against Henry of Navarre. It was he who planted the promontory with its groves of trees, retiring to their peaceful shade for the close of his days. His name and the date 1594 appear on a wall washed by the Lake just after rounding the promontory.

It was to gratify Francesco Sfondrate, who owned a lordly property on the Lake of Como, that P. Giovio wrote his *Descriptio Larii Lacus*. To what tune his pen was gilded for the work we have no means of judging, but from the delicate flatteries offered to his patron's wealth, discrimination, and intellect, and our knowledge of the writer's principles, we may feel sure that Paolo was well paid.

Dionysio Somentio tells a pretty story of the publication of this famous pamphlet, in his preface to the first edition, dated 1558.

He had gone to the Lake of Como to investigate a case of murder for his patron, Nicolo Sfondrate, and found himself enchanted by the unimagined beauty of its shores. The promontory of Bellagio, his patron's estate, had particularly fascinated him with its prospect of three Lakes (*tres lacus prospectantis*), its princely mansion big enough for the largest family, its spring of fresh water at the top, its gardens, fruits, wine; most of all, its staircase of eight hundred steps, beautifully made of most durable stone, from the level of the Lake to the crest of the hill. Upon his return, he recounted to his patron the pleasure he had experienced. Nicolo expressed a wish to combine for him a repetition of the enjoyment with immunity from the fatigue of another journey, by conjuring up then and there before his eyes the very scenes he had just left behind; and therewith begged him to fetch from the library P. Giovio's little work, in which he so graphically describes the Lake as to make every feature of it live before the reader. It was Somentio's first introduction to the book, and he at once conceived the idea of publishing it for the delight of mankind and the glory of his patron.

From the Sfondrati the property passed into the famous Milanese family of the Serbelloni, second to none for the soldiers and statesmen whom it has given to its country.

Near the top of the headland is a narrow perch on the edge of precipitous rocks, to which local tradition attaches a grim story. In the castle, which formerly stood close by, a certain Countess di Borgomanero once ruled, who set no bounds to her amours, and had her intrigues with all the gallants of the Lake. But her passions were surpassed by her jealousy, so that even when weary of her lovers, she could brook no transfer of their affections elsewhere. Accordingly she had her whilom favourites dropped from this giddy ledge into the *oubliette* of the Lake below.

Another version of the scandal is, that her victims were welcomed at night and murdered next morning, so that by this simple and ingenious device she was spared the inconvenience of gossip or blackmail.

CHAPTER IV

ISOLA COMACINA

"In seno i sacri
Vasi celando, sugli ignudi scogli
Nuova patria fondava, e dell' antica
Da Varenna scorgea l'ultimo fumo."—FUMEO.

THE steamer bears us along the shore of the bright, luxuriant Tremezzina, or district of Tremezzo, which so well merits its name of "The Garden of Lombardy." Gliding round the point of Balbianello, which terminates the promontory called Dosso d'Avedo, we pass beneath the gleaming Villa Arconati and the blessing hands of its guardian saints, and mark upon the wall within the little port an inscription which runs thus: *Hic Larius lingebat Oct.* 6, 1868 ("Here Larius lapped," &c.).

Larius is the ancient name of the Lake of Como. Cato, in his *Origines*, derives the name from an Etruscan word meaning "chief," or "of first importance," since in the earliest times this Lake ranked first among Italian waters. To this Virgil probably alludes in his apostrophe *Te Lari Maxume*,[1] "as the poet," says P. Giovio, "was a great authority on all antiquarian subjects." Another derivation connects the word with *laurus*, but there are no traces of any exuberance of the laurel on the shores of the Lake to justify this conjecture.

The Lake has long been known only by the name of its chief town, Como, in accordance with a tendency observable in the case of Lakes generally to abandon their old nomenclature and call themselves after their principal places. Thus *Lacus Benacus* has become the Lake of Garda; *Lacus*

[1] Georg. ii. 159.

Ceresius, the Lake of Lugano; *Lacus Lemanus*, the Lake of Geneva.

As to the name Como, Cassiodorus,[1] in a letter to Theodoric, after enumerating the charms of the city, says that it has fitly been called Como, since it rejoices in the adornment (*compta*) of so many natural advantages. *Merito, ergo, Como nomen accepit, quae tantis laetatur compta muneribus.* But philology was not the strong point of the ancients, and the derivation of Como from *compta* is inadmissible.

No doubt B. Giovio is right when he derives the name from the Greek word *κώμη* (Komè), a small town. At a very early period those universal colonisers, the Greeks, settled in every part of Italy, and here, as elsewhere, according to Cornelius Alexander. This original Greek town of Como was destroyed by the Rhætians, after it had been for many years occupied by a Roman colony, a piece of history recorded in the name Coloniola, a suburb of the present city. The depopulated country was recolonised successively by Pompeius Strabo, C. Scipio, and Julius Cæsar, and hence there sprang up on the site of the ruined Como a new city, which received the name of *Novum Comum*, or New Como.

Great facilities are now given for economical travel in Italy. Tickets of various kinds, at large reduction, may be had for the steamers alone, while a considerable saving may be effected on circular tours in combination with the railways. Ample information can always be had from the courteous *hôteliers* of the Lake.

Travellers studious of economy would do well to take second-class tickets on the steamers. They are half the price of first-class fare; the fore part of the boat affords far better views, supplies more air, and avoids the smoke from the funnel. True, one loses the awning which is stretched over the after-deck; but an Italian sunshade, white, green, or red, costing four or five francs, will serve our purpose as well or better. "But the society?" you say. Well, you will find yourself among the peasantry. But have you not come to see Italy and the Italians? You can observe these

[1] B. Giovio's *Hist. Patr. Lib.* i.

picturesque people more closely in the bows of a steamer than elsewhere. The opportunity is brief. There is nothing novel about the people under the awning. Them or their facsimiles you may meet every day at home.

There is much to be learnt on board these steamers about the simple, good-natured, polite Italian folk. Now we meet an *improvisatore*, who twangs his guitar and chants his flowing recitatives. His audience is his subject. His eye is keen and his wit versatile. He pays a compliment here, reddens a cheek there, touches a tender memory in some one else, welcomes the foreigner gracefully, rallies a friend without mercy, provokes in turn the laugh, the sigh, the tear. Then there is the group of acrobats, with music drawn out of a goatskin, and limbs as supple and motions as graceful as those of the wild deer. They breakfast off a crust, and seem to deem it luxury. Or perhaps we have pipers from the Abruzzi, as strange in speech and dress to the North of Italy as the Scotch Highlander is to the South of England. Or we see the bird-seller, with bundles of gay-plumaged denizens of the mountains, ranging in size from the wren to the grouse. In our walks we find scores of snares made of a willow-twig and a noose of string, and baited with a bunch of scarlet berries. These are deadly bird-traps.

A most fatal method of bird-catching is the *roccolo*, which may be seen upon scores of knolls round the Lake. It consists of a circular trellis work about twenty yards in diameter, covered with green creepers, and planted inside with trees so as to form a cool, attractive bower, but open to the sky at the top. Small cages of decoy birds of many sorts are hung among the branches. The circle is enclosed at the sides by an extremely fine silken net, very loosely suspended between two other nets with large diamond-shaped mesh, drawn very tight. Within a few paces is a tall tower, in which a man, armed with a missile called *Il falchetto*, or the hawk, is posted to watch the trap. No sooner does he see a few birds settling upon the trees inside, than with a loud cry he throws the *falchetto* into the air, aimed so as to drop into the midst of the bower. The birds, mistaking it for a hawk, scatter in all directions, and flying low to avoid it, are inextricably caught in the fine net, which is forced through one of the large meshes of the outer net, and closing round its victim like a pocket, holds it faster the more it struggles. As many as two hundred are sometimes taken in a day in one *roccolo*, so that the total destruction must be enormous.

Sometimes a very cruel plan is adopted. A long wire is carried from the tower to the vicinity of the trees. To this several lateral threads are attached, to the ends of which little birds are tied by the leg. The string is then pulled so as to make the wretched captives flutter and attract the passing birds. Sometimes they are left to flutter without this added indignity and irritation. One proprietor estimates the average catch of his *roccoli* at 5000 birds apiece in the season, which lasts from the 15th of August to the 31st of December. He introduced his gardener as "the grand assassin of birds," and the compliment was received with evident pride. The market price varies from 75 centimes to 1½ francs a dozen.

Nature starts with a fair balance of forces, but the equilibrium is disturbed by the excessive destruction of birds. Their thinned ranks are not equal to the task of keeping down the teeming insect life, hostile to the fruits of the earth.

It is amusing to watch the vendor in his efforts to palm off stale goods as "caught this morning," or to inflate prices by keeping out of sight his reserve stock. But, if he can sell well, his compatriots can buy well. The secret of making a good bargain is to be amiable, polite, and complimentary.

Remonstrate with the bird-catcher for the indiscriminate and wholesale slaughter of his prey, and he laughingly replies: "Ah! it is well for you to plead for the birds; you who can furnish your table with many choice and tasty dishes every day. But the poor man has only a piece of bread: it is very dry; he looks up into the tree and sees a bird—'bang!'—and he has a dainty morsel to give a relish to his poor crust."

Or it may be we see a pretty little quarrel, and from the voices and gestures of the disputants anticipate some knifing. But the worst is reached when those hands are rigidly extended, and the knuckles, convulsively shaking, are held defiantly within an inch of one another's nose. The storm subsides as rapidly as it arose.

Then there are cassocked priests, who wear broad-brimmed beavers, and are devoted to snuff. They are mostly of the peasant class, with the advantage of a training at an ecclesiastical college, to which they were sent at an early age. They earn peasants' pay, and are often a bright light in their parishes. It would be hard to find more exemplary clergymen than the peasant priests of some of the parishes on the Lake of Como. If it be one of the Hours of the Church, these good fathers will fall to saying the proper Office, let them be where they may. One of the most impressive sights I ever saw was that of an aged Bishop and his Chaplain, saying antiphonally the Psalms, at the Hour of *Ave Maria*, in a railway carriage. Manzoni's[1] introduction of Don Abbondio to his readers will often come into mind, when we see some Padre repeating his Office on the highway, or deck of the boat, and now and then, between one psalm and another, shutting the Breviary upon the forefinger of his right hand, keeping it there for a mark, and then putting both his hands behind his back, the right (with the closed book) on the palm of the left, and so proceeding with eyes and ears alive to every passing incident, while his lips repeat mechanically the language of his prayers.

Moreover, if it is the time of the Conscription, the poor lads drink too much under the unwonted excitement of quitting home to go out into a new world. They stand in circles with their arms round each other's necks, and bawl out patriotic songs about Italy and war.

One of the novel sights to be seen from the deck of the steamer in the autumn is a large vat full of grapes on the beach, in which are half-a-dozen little boys treading out the juice. They are naked, and as like to Correggio's *Putti* as possible. They shout and laugh and sing, as they dance in the great tub, washing one another's faces with the rich purple liquor, and playing off all kinds of mischievous tricks.

If we wish to see some one "treading the wine-press alone," we must go into the outhouse of a wine-shop ashore, where

[1] *I Promessi Sposi.*

we shall find a strong, patient, bare-legged man, pounding away at the great clusters in a barrel, which he just seems to fit. As he takes the grapes from the crate in which they are packed, and drops them into his tub, his feet catch them, like hands, and crush out the foaming juice in a quite artistic way. People often profess to feel great disgust at this use of feet, but it needs only a little reflection to convince us how much more cleanly they are for the purpose than hands. Until quite recently machinery has been inadmissible, since the crushing of the grape seed must spoil the wine. Now, however, a mechanical process has been devised for pressing the grape, which promises to revolutionise the science of wine-making by the economy it effects.

There is nothing more beautiful on Como than the view, which meets the eye as the boat bears us from the steamer to the beach at Spurano or Isola. Between the shore and the Island of Comacina or San Giovanni stretches away a narrow reach of water, called Zocca dell' Olio, or Bay of Oil, so serenely sheltered as to be almost always a mirror of surrounding glories, and closed in at the farther end by Argegno and the mountains of the Val Intelvi. Zocca in the local dialect means a bay, and this one owes its name to the oily smoothness of its surface, which is rarely ruffled by the wind, thanks to the protecting land around it. We seem to have found a new lake, which compresses into the compass of a glance all the wealth of beauty elsewhere scattered over wider fields. The sheet of water, glowing with reflected colour, is sometimes supposed to be the *Euripus*, of which Pliny the Younger writes in one of his letters. The chief ground for the hypothesis is, that at Lenno, not far away, but on the other side of the promontory of Balbianello or Lavedo, remains of a villa are visible at the bottom of the Lake, when the water is low, which might have been one of Pliny's. The situation answers, to some extent, to the description of his villa, which he humorously called "Comedy," while the promontory of Bellagio would serve well for the site of the sister residence, which he designated "Tragedy."

Let him speak for himself in his letter to Romanus:[1]—

[1] Plin. Ep. ix. 7.

Photo by G. E. Thompson

ISOLA COMACINA

"On the shores of the Lake of Como I have several villas, but two occupy me most, because I like them best. One planted on rocks, after the fashion of Baiæ, overlooks the Lake. The other, no less after the fashion of Baiæ, touches it. So I am in the habit of calling the former Tragedy, the latter Comedy; that, because it is lifted, as you may say, on the tragic shoe, while this rests only on the comic slipper. Each has its charm. This one enjoys a nearer, that a wider prospect of the Lake. This embraces one bay of gentle sweep; that commands two from its perch on a lofty ridge. There, a straight walk stretches above the beach in a long vista; here, a broad terrace gently slopes towards the shore. That one feels no waves; this one breaks them. From that you may look down upon the fishermen below; while from this you may yourself fish, and throw the hook from your bedroom, and almost from your very bed, just as from a little boat."

The passage from which Pliny is supposed by some to allude to the Zocca dell' Olio, is so descriptive of many villas to-day that it may be read with interest. It occurs in a letter to Rufus:[1]—

"How fares Como, our common joy? How is the charming villa, the vernal portico, the shady avenue of planes; the strait, green and jewelled; the Lake stretching below to await your orders; the promenade so soft and firm; the sunny bath; the rooms for the many and for the few; the chambers for mid-day siesta and midnight sleep?"

On our left, about a quarter of a mile from the shore, rises Isola Comacina. Some half a mile in length, three hundred yards wide in its broadest part, and at its highest point 120 feet above the Lake, tenanted but by a hind in the ruins of an ancient chapel at its southern end, and without any complete building, except the little Church of San Giovanni, in which a rough inscription records the year of its desolation, this islet has played a part in history quite out of proportion to its size. As its name implies, it is the one island of the Lake of Como. In early writings of the Christian era the adjective *comacinus* is used to describe what belongs to the city, state, or Lake of Como. Some-

[1] Plin. Ep. i. 8.

times the alternative word *cumanus* is employed. At the present time the island is best known locally by the name of San Giovanni or S. John the Baptist, from the little church dedicated to that saint upon its olive-clad ridge.

S. Giovanni lures back our thoughts to the strange story of the Lombards and their invasion of Italy, so full of startling romance and picturesque incident. We find ourselves midway in the sixth century. The Emperor Justin reigns at Constantinople. His court is honeycombed by intrigue. Narses, a eunuch, has reconquered Italy for the Empire. A general of consummate skill and bravery, he has done what his predecessor Belisarius was recalled for not doing. He has entirely crushed the Goths. Totila is slain. His successor, Teja, is defeated. Their power lies in ruins, but the avarice of Narses has raised up enemies for him. Threats of revolt lead to his recall. The Empress Sophia adds insult to injury. "Arms for men," is her sneering sarcasm; "for women and eunuchs the distaff and spindle. Narses will find them ready for him upon his return."

There is a sting in the taunt, which enters deeply into his soul. Wounded to the quick, he swears that he will spin a thread which all her skill will not avail to unravel. He plans a sweet and ample revenge. Retiring to Naples, he makes overtures to the Lombards, a powerful German nation, to invade and occupy Italy, describing the country in glowing terms likely to excite the cupidity of those northern warriors. They came, those men of enormous stature, long-bearded and loosely clad, with blue eyes looking out from under a yellow shock of hair, fierce, brave, passionate, licentious, striking hard and gripping fast; they came, and the wrongs of Narses were expiated by the loss of Italy to the Empire. The Italians yielded almost without resistance, partly from the panic inspired by the warlike fame of the invaders, partly from the feeling that no change of masters could be for the worse. In five months after leaving his native Pannonia, Alboin was at the gates of Milan. Pavia, which alone defied him, became his capital.

The Lombard monarchy was elective, and after the tragic death of Alboin, devised for him by his wife, Rosamund, in revenge for an act of drunken brutality in compelling her to drink wine out of a cup formed from her father's skull, Clepho became king. But he was speedily assassinated, and the power fell into the hands of thirty dukes, each ruling in his own city. For ten unhappy years this state of things lasted, until Childepert, King of the Franks, took advantage of the inevitable discord to invade Italy. In the face of this danger Autaris was elected king, A.D. 584, in order to unite the Lombard power to meet the forces of Childepert. Autaris was victorious over the invaders, and not only so, but he pushed his conquest of Italy to the South of Calabria, where he rode his horse into the waves of the Mediterranean, and touching the column, which stood upon the shore, with his spear, claimed it as the perpetual boundary of his domain.[1]

But while the greater part of Italy thus lay at the conqueror's feet, one little spot of free soil retained its independence and continued loyal to the ancient Empire.

This was Isola Comacina, nestling under the olive-fringed shores of the Lake of Como, and so sequestered as to be almost forgotten in the din and strife of war. Twenty years before, when Alboin and his army overran Italy, Francioni or Francillioni, an Italian general, probably the Governor of Como, retired to this secluded island, which he strongly fortified and maintained as the one vestige in the North of Italy of that Imperial Power, which had been swept away, at the invitation of Narses, by the flood of barbarian invasion. Many cities, says Deacon Paul, the chronicler of that period, deposited their treasures here to save them from the hands of the conquerors, in the faint hope that before long the tide of affairs might turn.

Refugees flocked to this safe retreat. The years continued to be reckoned by the names of consuls, and the sentiment of allegiance to the inaccessible Emperor at Constantinople was still loyally fostered. The two following inscriptions found at Lenno, of the years 571 and 572 A.D., furnish proof of this statement:—

Hic requiescit in pace fam. XPI. Laurentius V.S. qui

[1] Gibbon's "Hist. of the Decline and Fall of the Roman Empire," vol. v. p. 116.

vixit in hoc saec. ann. LV. dep. s. d. iiii. nonas Julii p. c. dn. Iustini pp. Aug. Ann. vi. ind. iiii.

Here rests in peace Laurence, a servant of Jesus Christ, a venerable priest, who lived in this century fifty-five years, and was buried on the 4th of July, the sixth year after the Consulate of our Lord Justin, perpetual Emperor, ind. 4, *i.e.* 571 A.D.

✠ *Hic requiescit in pace b.m. Cyprianus qui vixit in hoc saeculo annos pm. xxxiii. dep. sub. d. vii. Kal. octob. ind. v. post con. d.n. Iustini pp. Aug. Ann. VI.*

Here rests in peace Cyprian, of blessed memory, who lived in this century thirty-three years, more or less, buried 25*th Sept. ind.* 5, *in the fifth year after the Consulate of our Sovereign Lord Justin, perpetual Emperor, i.e.* 572 A.D.

In such circumstances the island, with its singular fidelity to the old régime, must have been a dangerous nest of disaffection, and a standing menace to the new power. There seems to be some reason for believing, that Francioni erected a stronghold on the site of the Castle of Fuentes to command the Valtelline and protect the many fugitives who sought shelter in its retirement. A corroborative hint is found in the supposed survival of the name of Francioni[1] in the Borgo Francone in that locality, the dyke, which carries off the water that comes down from Monte Legnone. P. Giovi writes:—*Visuntur hodie vestigia dirutae urbis ad Burgum Franconem unde fossa navigabilis ad Delebium usque perducitur. Traces of a ruined city may still be seen at Borgo Francone, from which a navigable dyke is carried as far as Delebbio.*

That as it may, in the process of consolidating his conquests, Autaris was unable to tolerate this perpetual sore in the side of his kingdom, and accordingly took measures to reduce the island. Beset by a numerous fleet of boats, which continually brought reinforcements to the assault from a large army on the shore, this Gibraltar of the Lake held out against the besiegers for six months, and then capitulated through sheer stress of famine. Francioni secured honourable terms, and was allowed to retire to Ravenna, which was still a city of the Empire. The vast

[1] *Cesare Cantù.*

treasures accumulated on the island fell into the hands of the victors.

By far the most important guests to share the hospitality of the island in the time of Francioni were the *Magistri Comacini*, who took refuge here from the indiscriminating sweep of Alboin's sword.

N. Villani says that in those days "male and female, great and small, were either masters or journeymen (*maestri o manovali*)." And because the State of Como supplied artisans of greater skill and in larger numbers than any other district, they were known by the name of *Comacini*. In the extant laws of King Rotharis, who married Theodelinda's daughter, reigned from 636 to 652 A.D., and codified the Lombard customs under the name of "Laws," in the Latin tongue, the term *Magistri Comacini* comprises workers in every branch of the art of Building. They are afterwards described as *Casari* or *Casarii*, house-builders. So these refugees were either architects, or the master workmen of all the trades affiliated to Architecture.

When the first force of the Lombard storm had spent itself, these valuable citizens emerged from their retreat; the importance of their services was duly recognised, special enactments were made for their protection, and freedom and privileges were conferred upon them by their Lombard masters. The Laws of Rotharis constitute their guild under the name of Freemasons, give powers to the *Magistri* or Masters not granted to the assistants, and carefully provide for the safeguarding of their interests. It was not, however, until the country became more settled, under the wise influence of Theodelinda, that building was possible. She gave a new impulse to the art by employing the *Magistri Comacini* to erect her cathedral at Monza, together with other works, of which scarcely any vestige has survived to our time. It is not improbable, that a band of these workmen accompanied S. Augustine on his mission to England. Specimens of their work are supposed to exist in the churches of SS. Fedele, Abbondio and Giacomo at Como, S. Carpoforo at Camerlata, the Baptistery at Lenno, S. Maria del Tiglio at Gravedona, the parish church of S. Fedele in the Val Intelvi, the apse of S. Giacomo at Bellagio, S. Pietro di

Civate in the Brianza, S. Benedetto above the Madonna del Soccorso, and the remains on the Isola Comacina.

The island gains quite a new and reverent interest when we can regard it as the saviour of those men, who alone at that time could keep alive the old traditions of art under the killing blight of barbarism. For such indeed was the case, since whatever specimens of architecture are pointed out to us in Italy as Lombard must be attributed to the preservation of these workmen from death at the hands of the Lombards. As the Lombards gave a name to the Italy which they found, but did not create, just so far are they responsible for the architecture, which existed at the time of their invasion, gradually developed during the two hundred years of their rule, and afterwards became what we see it in some of the splendid churches of North Italy.

Let us glance backwards.

The architecture, which the Goths found in Italy in the fifth century was classical Roman much debased. Among its features were round-headed arches, vaulted roofs, attenuated pilasters, and minute ornamentation. Not for seven centuries after the fall of the Gothic power was that style of mediæval architecture perfectly evolved, which is commonly known by the misnomer of Gothic. It was undoubtedly a development of the old Roman, such as the Goths found and left in Italy, but with the growth of which they had little or nothing to do.

Early in the sixth century, Euclesius, Bishop of Ravenna, paid a visit to Constantinople, and fired by the sight of the splendours of the Church of Sta. Sofia, and the popular enthusiasm in its erection, he returned with a number of Greek workmen in his train to build the Church of S. Vitale, in his own city, after the Byzantine style, A.D. 526. Here, then, for the first time, Byzantine and Roman architecture met face to face, with the result that they gradually became blended, and formed a third great order, which may be called Romanesque, Romano-Byzantine, or Comacine.[1]

Then came the Lombards, fifty years later, uncouth, ignorant, and unlettered. They were an army, not a nation, rather occupying Italy as a subjugated province than settling in it

[1] C. C. Perkins's "Italian Sculptors."

and permanently amalgamating with its native population. Such a people came to rule and not to work. Their conquered subjects would build for them, when building was needed. They could neither read nor write. Their laws were handed down by memory and custom, and when codified, were written in the language of the conquered race. If they made an idol to represent the Deity, they merely rough-hewed the trunk of a tree. It is improbable, that such a people originated a style of architecture.

At the same time, we can readily understand how they influenced the progress of the art, as they found it in the hands of Italian architects and builders. It may be, as Ruskin assumes,[1] that certain features of their wooden churches in Pannonia, for some of the Lombards had embraced Arian Christianity, became petrified, as it were, under Italian influence. What they had done in timber now got itself done in stone. This may be the true account, as Ruskin thinks it is, of the vaulting-shaft as seen in S. Ambrogio at Milan, and of the clustered columns, which are a characteristic of the so-called Lombard architecture.

We can well imagine, too, that some architectural principles, now seen by them for the first time, seized upon their fancy more than others, and that in their capacity as masters they would constantly require to have them reproduced in their buildings. Thus might arise what Fergusson in his "History of Architecture" calls the mania for stone-vaulted roofs, of which, nevertheless, he says, the architects of Lombardy never succeeded in becoming masters.

Still more probable is it, that we owe to the influence of the conquerors "the endless imagery of active life and fantastic superstition," which is seen upon wall, capital, and frieze of Lombard buildings, and in the earliest churches bears a singular resemblance to the figures found upon northern monuments of a remote period.

But with regard to this, too, Ruskin says:[2] "The same leaves, the same animals, the same arrangements, are used by Scandinavians, Ancient Britons, Saxons, Normans, Lombards, Romans, Byzantines, and Arabians, all being

[1] "Stones of Venice."
[2] *Ibid.*, vol. i. App. 8, The Northern Energy.

alike descended through classic Greece from Egypt and Assyria, and some from Phœnicia. The belts, which encompass the Assyrian Bulls in the British Museum are the same as the belts of the ornaments found in Scandinavian tumuli; their method of ornamentation is the same as that of the Gate of Mycenæ, and of the Lombard pulpit of S. Ambrogio at Milan, and of the Church of Theotocos at Constantinople: the essential differences among the great Schools are their differences of temper and treatment, and science of expression; it is absurd to talk of Norman ornaments, and Lombard ornaments, and Byzantine ornaments, as formerly distinguished; but there is irreconcilable separation between Arab temper, and Lombard temper, and Byzantine temper." And then he goes on to say, that the Arab and Lombard are both distinguished from the Byzantine by their energy and love of excitement, but that the Lombard stands alone in his love of jest.

The architecture, which the Lombards found in Italy, and perhaps did something to determine, was the blend of Byzantine and debased Roman. It was a phase in the transitional process from old Roman to the style, which culminated in the so-called Gothic of the thirteenth century. It would save much confusion to remember, that when we speak of Lombard Architecture we do not mean a style of which the Lombards were the authors. "*L'architecture Lombarde,*" says M. de Dartein, "*est celle de cette race mélangée et non pas celle des Longobardes, qui n'en eurent jamais.*" The term is misleading unless we are understood to imply the Italian style prevalent at the time of the Lombard invasion, in vogue with the *Magistri Comacini* when they took refuge from Alboin in the fastness of Comacina, developed in Lombardy in the course of centuries, and forming a branch of that great family of Gothic or mediæval architecture, which sprang from the Roman germ.

It is uncertain whether any complete building of a date earlier than the ninth century still remains. S. Pietro di Civate has strong claims to this antiquity, as also Sta. Maria del Tiglio at Gravedona.

The features which characterise the style of the Lombard occupation are stone vaultings; grouped shafts; added vaulting shafts; round-arched windows; narrow and deep-set cornice arches; ornament of bricks set cornerwise; attenuated pilasters, running from ground to roof outside; an open gallery under the external eaves of the roof, instead of cornice; stone surfaces carved with quaint symbolism; and columns decorated with interlacing circles, forming a close pattern of trellis-work.

The Lombard buildings near the Lake of Como are mostly small and very simple, but conceived in a style of dignity and beauty, which makes them always impressive. In Milan and Pavia they assume magnificent proportions.

At the Southernmost end of the Island of St. John stands the remnant of a small church. It is now turned into a peasant's house and cattle stall. Some fragments of the arcade upon the outside of the apse still remain, together with one or two bases of marble columns, but the wrought stones have been barbarously removed for mending garden walls. Within the cowhouse the courses of black and white marble, which line the apse, are in excellent preservation.

A fragment of marble of irregular shape is built into the outer wall, bearing a rudely-cut Latin inscription, a petrified sob of a forlorn heart, which links the mourners of to-day with those of the Pagan world eighteen centuries ago. The rough tablet is dedicated *Dis Manibus*, "to the Deities of the dead," and commemorates "the wife most dear," *conjugi carissimae*, of some one with an outlandish provincial name.

To the N.E. of the Church of S. John Baptist, a comparatively modern building, are the remains of an apsidal structure, with a noteworthy and beautiful architectural feature. The pilasters consist of courses of stone, alternated at considerable intervals with a thin brick of red terra-cotta. To the S.E. is the base of a cluster of columns. Any one, who will take the trouble to examine the Island carefully, will find traces of walls, buttresses, and arches ample enough to corroborate the tradition of its ancient strength and importance. Some excavations have recently been made, which promise, if extended, a yield of considerable interest.

After the days of Francioni the Island became the asylum of many illustrious fugitives. It acquired the name of Christopolis, or City of Christ, not because of Christians who fled there for protection in times of persecution, of which there is no proof, but because, like the Christ Himself, it became, in the Providence of God, a refuge for all who were otherwise lost and hopeless. Thus, Gaidulfo, Duke of Bergamo, in rebellion against Agilulf, second husband of Theodelinda, for a time found safety here. Cunipert, in the same seclusion, laid plans for the recovery of his throne from the usurper Alachi. Ansprand, the guardian and champion of Liutpert, retired to Comacina after his defeat by the usurper Aribert and the death of his ward, 701 A.D. It may be remembered that Ansprand, after great vicissitudes, won the kingdom for Liutprand, the greatest of the Lombard kings, 712 A.D.

A romantic incident of the tenth century, of great political moment, is linked with the Island. Berengarius, Lord of Ivrea, had made himself master of Italy. He wished to strengthen his cause by the alliance of his own son with Adelaide of Savoy, daughter of one dethroned king and daughter-in-law of another. Upon her refusal, he imprisoned her in a dungeon, the locality of which is variously given by different authorities to Como, Dongo, Mello in the Valtelline, and Garda, on the Lake of that name. She escaped by the aid of one Martin, a priest, her fellow-prisoner, who, after hiding her for some time in a marsh, brought her into the presence of Otho, King of Germany, at Canossa. He married her at Pavia, was saluted King, and so for the first time united the crowns of Germany and Italy, an incident fraught with vast issues to the world. A son of Berengarius took refuge within the walls of Comacina, but the men of the Lake, headed by the Bishop of the diocese, compelled him to surrender, and dismantled the castle.

There is an extant charter of Otho's, granted at Como, 962 A.D., to the islanders (*Isolani*) and Menaggio, which secures to them extensive privileges. Probably the term Isola comprised a considerable district on the mainland.

Before the invention of artillery the rocky shores, strengthened by fortifications, would merit the name of the Gibraltar of the Lake, given to the Island in modern times. Though not impregnable, it was never captured without heavy loss to the assailants. We learn the importance of the place in the Middle Ages from the prominence given to it in the chronicle of the ten years' war between Como and Milan. The islanders threw in their lot with the Milanese, and proved a sad thorn in the side of Como.

But in 1124 A.D. the Island was taken and sacked by the Comasque forces, after a battle, which raged round its shores for several days. Not, however, until forty years after the close of this war did the people of Como wreak their full vengeance upon the islanders for the part they had played in it. In 1169, aided by the Pievesi, they took the Island, after a long and desperate siege, burnt its houses, demolished its defences, and drove out its inhabitants, who went to swell the population of Varenna or to found the village of Isola on the mainland near. In the chapel of S. Giovanni the rude record of this event runs as follows:—

> " M.C. Dant Annos LX. 9 Que notandos
> Insula quādo ruit magna pestilentia fuit
> Divino monitu templi reparata vetustas
> GRADNE (grandine) quassatos servet sacra dona ferētēs
> Lux maii Principiū prima finē ultima dedit
> Operi milleno ano quater centesimoque
> Sex decē atque septē ingaset cuncti DS. Cne "—

of which the chief points are that 1169 A.D. was a notable year, as having seen the destruction of the Island, and that in 1423 the church was rebuilt.

In the Epic poem which describes this war, the bitter hatred of Como towards the Island is expressed in the following lines:—

> " Insula non dormit nec jam tenet illa quietem,
> Cogitat et vigilat, versat furiosa quid agat,
> Namque suos prodit socios, ut Juda magistrum."

> "The island neither sleeps nor gives itself rest;
> It plots and watches, and does madly whatever it undertakes,
> For it betrays its own allies, as Judas betrayed his Master."

It was formerly the custom for the people of the village of Isola to keep alive the memory of their origin by celebrating a Mystery play on the Island upon the Feast of the Nativity of S. John Baptist. In alternate years they represented the birth of the Baptist and his martyrdom in a series of *tableaux vivants*, which were exhibited on the shore, while a gaily caparisoned boat was rapidly rowed backwards and forwards in imitation of the swift galley *Scorrobiessa*, so famous in the ten years' war. This is now superseded by a procession of clergy in a large boat decked with flags and resounding with music, while the Zocca dell' Olio is alive with craft, carrying eager crowds to the festival, the fair, and the fun.

A charge of one lira is now made for admission to the Island, which boasts the doubtful advantages of a landing-pier, an artificial promenade, rustic seats and conveniences for picnicking.

CHAPTER V

ISOLA, MADONNA DEL SOCCORSO, AND LENNO

"The convent's white walls glisten fair on high ;
Rock, forest, lake and mountain all around."

In the Church of Sta. Eufemia at Isola, on the mainland, a marble slab of extraordinary interest is found upon the wall of one of the transepts.

Until recently this slab formed the table of the High Altar in Sta. Eufemia. It is still possible to decipher the following inscription upon its surface :—

"Degere quisquis amat ullo sine crimine vitam
Ante diem semper Lumina mortis habet
Illius adventu suspectus rite dicatus
Agripinus praesul hoc fabricavit opus.

"Hic patria linqvens propriam karosqve parentes
Pro scā stvdvit pereger esse fide
Hic pro dogma patrum tantos tolerare labores
Noscitur vt nvllvs ore referre qveat
Hic hvmilis militare Dō devote cvpivit
Cvm potvit mvndi celsos habere grados
Hic terrenas opes malvit contemnere cvnctas
Vt svmat melivs pracmia digna
Hic semel exosvm saecvlvm decrevit habere
Et solvm diliget mentis amore Dō
Hic qvoqve jvssa seques Dni legemqve Tonantis
Proximvm vt esse gavdet amare svvm.
Hvnc etenim qvem tanta rivvm docvmenta decorant
Ornat et prmae nobilitatis honor.
His Aqvileia dvcem illvm destinavit in oris
Vt geret invictus praelia magna Dei.
His caput est factus summus patriarcha Johannes
Qui praedicta tenet primus in urbe sedem.
Quis laudare valet clerum populumqve comensem
Rectorem tantum qui petiere sibi ?

Hi sinodos cvncti venerantvr quatuor almas
Concilium quintum postposvere malum
Hi bellum ob ipsas multos gessere per annos
Sed semper mansit insuperata fides."

"Whoever loves to spend his life, devoid of blame, always keeps before his eyes the day of death. Mindful of its approach, Bishop Agrippinus built, and duly dedicated this work. He, leaving his fatherland and beloved parents, desired to be a pilgrim for the Holy Faith. He is known to bear so many toils for the doctrine of his fathers that no one can count them. He, humbly and devoutly, desired to fight for God when he could hold the high dignities of the world. He chose to despise all earthly wealth, that he may receive the better lot of worthy rewards. He, once for all, resolved to hold the world in hatred, and will love God only with the affection of his mind. Moreover, following the commands and law of the Lord of Thunder, rejoices to love his neighbour as himself. For this man, whom so many titles grace, is adorned also by the rank of the highest nobility. Aquilea appointed him to be the Captain in these regions to fight, unconquered, great battles for God. Here the supreme patriarch John was made the head, and ranks first in the city just named. Who is equal to praising the clergy and the people of Como, who asked so great a ruler for themselves? These all revere the four venerable Synods. The fifth, false council, they rejected. For many years they waged war for those Synods, but their faith ever remained unconquered."

This precious relic summons before our eyes a whole world of thought and feeling, in which we have no part. It is a record of the bitter ecclesiastical conflicts, which so early raged around metaphysical subtleties, that seemed to their advocates the very marrow of Christianity, but are now as dead as those, who fought for them. Of noble birth, Agrippinus renounced all worldly hopes and resolved to serve God under the humble habit of a Benedictine monk. The clergy and people of Como petitioned John, Patriarch of Aquileia, to appoint him their Bishop in 606 A.D. Agrippinus sided with his patron in the adoption of the dogmatic opinions maintained in the famous "Three Points," which served to divide the Church in that age, and afterwards earned for Agrippinus the title of Schismatic, though he was popularly held to be no less than a Saint.

The case stood thus. Theodore, Bishop of Mopsuestia from 392 to 428 A.D., a man far in advance of his age in his seintificc method of interpreting the Scriptures, was accused after his death of favouring, if not of creating, the heresies of Pelagius and Nestorius, of which the former asserted the freedom of the human will, and the latter the complete distinction of the human and divine natures in Christ.

Theodoret of Antioch, Bishop of Cyrus, who was born in 390 and died 458 A.D., was one of the most illustrious members of the Greek Church, but fell under suspicion of Nestorianism. His "Eranistes," "The Man of Scraps," in which he showed the beggarly patchwork of his opponents' opinions, brought upon him the charge of teaching two Sons in the Godhead.

Ibas, Bishop of Edessa, his contemporary, wrote a letter of scathing severity against Cyril, the champion of orthodoxy, and the Council of Ephesus.

The disputed points in connection with the tenets of these men came to be known as "The Three Heads" (κεφαλάια).

In the year 451 A.D. the fourth General Council was held at Chalcedon, when the orthodoxy of the two living Bishops, Theodoret and Ibas, was acknowledged. A fierce conflict, however, raged between the sympathisers with Nestorius and his opponents. In 544 A.D. the Emperor Justinian published a decree condemning the Three Heads. The Pope Vigilius refused to accept the Emperor's edict, and for a time supported the Three Heads, in return for which he suffered heavy persecution. The fifth Council, which met at Constantinople in 553 A.D., the *Malum Concilium* named in the inscription, formally condemned the Three Heads, together with all who supported them, although it upheld the Council of Chalcedon. After strange vacillation the Pope changed his mind, accepted the sentence of the Council, and anathematised the Three Heads. But the schism was not healed with the surrender of the Pope. The doctrines of the Three Heads were maintained in the Patriarchate of Aquileia by the Bishops, who were subject to the Lombard King, or to the Duke of Friuli, until the Council of Aquileia, in 700 A.D.

Ten years after his appointment to the Bishopric of Como, Agrippinus dedicated a church at Piona, near the north end of the Lake, to Sta. Justina, as was formerly recorded on the wall of its octagonal tower, now unhappily destroyed.

It ran thus :—

AGRIPINUS.
Famulus Xp̄i
Com̄ civitatis
Ep̄s. Hoc orat
orium sc̄tæ Jus
tinæ martyris
anno. X. ordina
tionis suae. a Fon
damentis, Fabri
cavit. et. sepoltu
ras. ibi. ordena
bit. et in omni
explebit. ad. glor.
✠ Dicabit.

"Agrippinus, the servant of Christ and Bishop of Como, built this oratory of the holy martyr, Justina, in the tenth year of his episcopate, and will decree burials there, and will in every point complete it, and to the glory of Christ devote it."

Agrippinus also founded the Church of Sta. Eufemia, on the Isola Comacina, in which he prepared his own tomb, and where he was buried about 620 A.D. Upon the destruction of the Island, in the twelfth century, his body was removed to the Benedictine monastery of Acqua Fredda. Upon the suppression of that house it was transported to Delebbio, near Gravedona. The inscription now at Isola is supposed to refer to the dedication of the original Church of Sta. Eufemia upon the Isola Comacina.

Not far from Isola is the Ospedaletto dei Giovi, or Zobii, as it is locally called, whose old grey tower of graceful, though eccentric, style supplies equal interest to antiquarian and artist. The shaft of the tower, which adjoins a small chapel, is corbelled out to support a belfry broader than itself, pierced on each side by pointed windows, divided in the centre by a light column, and surmounted by a delicate gable. The richly-moulded stucco, fast falling away, discloses the narrow red bricks of which the tower is built. Here and there a lovely cherub's face looks out from a white marble medallion. Contiguous to the chapel is a house of the Giovi, of much later date and with no special features of interest.

Photo by T. W. M. Lund

TORRE DEI ZOBII

Tradition sees in this group of buildings an ancient hospital or resting-place for pilgrims going to and from the Holy Land. Let us hear Paolo Giovio, who may be accepted as an authority on the subject. In his description of the Lake he cruises from the South to the Isola Comacina, which he calls "the corpse of an ancient city" (*cadaver antiquae urbis*), separated from the mainland by the strait, which Pliny named *Euripus*, and "only peopled by a swarm of rabbits" (*solis cuniculis habitanda reliquitur*).

He then records, that his family traced back its origin to the Island, and that in his time substantial proofs of the former opulence of his ancestors were not wanting. As one of these, he quotes the Church of S. Mary Magdalene, in the village of Stabio, opposite the Island, on the strait, and about four hundred yards distant.

This church his ancestors endowed with lands out of their property for the purpose of furnishing food to the needy and wayfaring (*in alimenta egenorum viatorumque*). He then proceeds to recount how for six hundred years his family had retained the unimpaired privilege of electing both prefect and priest; while in proof of their descent, their coat of arms showed a fortress upon an island, which could be none other than Comacina washed by the waters of the Lake. To this Frederick Barbarossa had added the Roman Eagle, while Charles V. had recognised his literary labours by permitting him to use the Pillars of Hercules upon his escutcheon. The little chapel, surmounted by the Torre del Zobio, is the S. Mary Magdalene alluded to, and most likely overshadowed an hospital, where the generous endowments of the Giovi were dispensed in food and shelter.

Benedetto and Paolo, natives of Como, were the two most famous members of the Giovio family. Both the brothers were historians, but the younger, Paolo, attained to the greater distinction. Benedetto was a simple-hearted student, who never travelled beyond Milan, and even there on foot, yet left to the world a mine of valuable and reliable information. His *Historia Patria* is a useful book for those who are interested in Como. "I would have the genius of Paolo, but the heart of Benedetto," says one of his biographers. Nevertheless, he was a man of really vast learning, including in his subjects Greek, Hebrew, Arabic, astronomy, and numismatics, so that he earned the name of the Lombard Varro. He was a poet, too, of no mean quality, and has left a poem of considerable grace, in which he sings the fame of the thirteen fountains of the city of Como.

Upon a visit of Charles V. to Como in 1541 A.D., Benedetto wrote an inscription so epigrammatic in its terseness, yet so pregnant with history, as to make it worth recording:—

> "Orobiorum Graeca colonia hic primum consedit. Eam Galli possiderunt. Rhaeti gens alpina vastarunt. C. Scipio Pompeius et Caius Caesar colonis frequentem reddiderunt. Exorto bello Mediolanenses cremarunt. Fredericus I. restituit. Bellum intestinum bis diruit. Principum dissensio calamitatibus afflixit. Carolus V. in spem felicitatis erexit."

> "A Greek colony of Orobii first settled here. The Gauls took it (the city). The Rhætians, an Alpine nation, destroyed it. C. S. P. and C. C. colonised it. War broke out and the Milanese burnt it. Frederic I. restored it. Civil war twice laid it in ruins. The discord of its chief families harassed it. Charles V. has stirred in it a hope of better times."

Was the chequered tale of fifteen hundred years and more ever so succinctly epitomised?

Born in 1471, Benedetto died in 1544 A.D., and was carried to his grave in the Cathedral on the shoulders of noble youths, who felt themselves honoured by rendering this last service to their revered fellow citizen.

Paolo's position at the Vatican as secretary to Leo X. gave him unrivalled literary opportunities, which he did not fail to use. His masterpiece is the "History of His Own Time," which occupied thirty-seven years of his life. But our admiration decreases when we learn that his contemporary history took its tone from the price that he was paid for it. A biographer naïvely remarks that "in this he was no greater a sinner than the rest of his tribe, but he had the impudence to confess it." A typical saying of his is recorded in reply to a critic, who one day pointed out an error: "*Lascia pur ire, che da qui a tre cent' anni tutto sarà verità*"; "Never mind; it will be all true in three hundred years." He was credited with the use of two pens, one of gold, with which to praise those who paid him well; the other of iron,

Photo by G. E. Thompson

S. FRANCIS AT VILLA ARCONATI

for the contrary purpose. He makes more than one playful allusion to this practice in his own writings. He knew how to use his golden pen in his own interest, and when his patron, Francis I., deserted him, he secured the Bishopric of Nocera for himself from the Mediceau Clement, as an acknowledgment of the praises which he had judiciously lavished upon that Pontiff's family. He was born in 1483 and died in 1552 A.D.

Campo is industrially linked with the family of the Giovi since the Filanda da Seta or Factory for Spinning Silk, now in the hands of Signor Gessner, was the property of Conte Giov. B. Giovio in 1778. But still more interesting is the fact, that Cardinal Tolomeo Gallio built the present Villa in 1596 from designs by Pellegrino Pellegrini, nicknamed Tibaldo. The original founder was the Conte di Balbiano in 1420. Cardinal Durini at one time owned this Villa and Factory, and within the former are several mural inscriptions relative to its history, erected by him. To his munificence and taste we owe the Villa Arconati, which he built under the name of Balbianello, an affectionate diminutive of Balbiano, as a Convalescent Home for sick monks of the Order of S. Francis. This accounts for the prominence given to the figure of that great Saint on the wall of the little port.

In 1810, at Napoleon's dissolution of monasteries, the Home passed by purchase into the hands of Count Porro of Como. He became an exile for his political opinions, and spent the rest of his life in Belgium with his intimate friend the Marchese Arconati Visconti, to whom he bequeathed this Villa, and from whom it took its present name. His widow restored it in 1880 at a cost of 350,000 francs, and as she has only visited it three times since the restoration, each visit has cost her about £4000. The Villa is now for sale, and it would be a graceful act on the part of some millionaire to buy it, and restore it to its pristine use.

To convert it into an hotel, as has been suggested, would be sacrilege, since its gracious charm, sweet tranquillity, and exquisite architecture would inevitably be vulgarised and ruined.

The Villa is associated with such names as those of Silvio

Pellico, Mazzini, and Cristina Trivulzio Belgiojoso, who consorted here with the kindred soul of the owner. Its natural position and the art which has adorned it, have made of it a fairyland. The views of the Lake, stretching in long vistas N. and S., from its graceful Loggia, are held by some travellers of wide experience to be the most beautiful in the world. While it might be invidious to claim for it the first place among the Villas on the Lake, each of which has its own incomparable charm, it is not too much to say, that for daintiness, position, and points of view it is certainly unsurpassed.

It should not be forgotten that the Punto di Balbianello is generally credited with having been the site of Pliny's Villa "Comedy." This whole promontory is called the Dosso d'Avedo.

High above us is perched the shrine of the Madonna del Soccorso, or "Our Lady of Help." We climb towards it, either from Spurano, or Isola, or Campo, or Lenno, by a steep, paved path, which yields entrancing peeps of the Grigna, framed in by the soft, grey fretwork of the olives.

We soon reach a chamber, built on a little grassy platform by the wayside, octagonal, and some twenty feet in diameter. Through gratings, at which there are stones to kneel upon, is seen a representation in terra-cotta of the Annunciation. At intervals in the ascent fourteen similar chambers are reached, containing tableaux depicting the chief historical and traditional scenes in the history of our Lord and His Mother. Some of the terra-cotta figures and painted backgrounds have a rough merit all their own. It is a veritable New Testament for poor people, who cannot read. At last the little church is gained, and the toil is rewarded by the superb outlook from its rocky terrace views.

This church is the shrine of a statue in grey stone, small and uncomely, and called "Our Lady of Help." She is the Genius of the Lake. In any crisis, when human aid seems inadequate, the peasant folk cry to this kind Spirit, or make a pilgrimage to her temple, or offer a gift at her altar, if it be but a candle, sure of her friendliness and sympathy. In a storm on the Lake, in fell sickness, in a time of drought, in the blight of crops, the remedy is sought from Our Lady of Help. Of her cures and rescues and succours the church bears witness in its crowd of votive offerings. Upon the walls rudely drawn pictures portray her miracles of aid. Here is a drowning man saved by a kindly boat in answer to his prayer. There is a child in the act of being rescued from the flames of a burning house. The Helpful Lady is seen above the clouds, pleading with her Divine Son for His compassionate intervention. A pair of crutches and a waxen hand are suggestive trophies of some further grace of healing.

One day I asked the aged priest to tell me the Madonna's story. "Long, long ago," he began, with as much idea of time as an Oriental, whose "forty years" means any period you like; "long, long ago, a little girl, deaf and dumb from her birth, was tending her flock upon the wild mountain side above Isola. There she found a little grotto in the rock, and, upon entering it, saw a rough image of the Madonna with the infant Jesus in her arms. She hurried home to tell the news, and in the excitement of the moment found her speech and cried 'Madonna! Madonna!' Where could the statue have come from in a spot which, perhaps, the foot of man had never trod before? Of course it was plain to everybody, that the Madonna was of heavenly origin and endowed with miraculous power. At first she was placed in a small chapel, built for her near the spot where she was found, but was afterwards carried with great solemnity to the church at Isola. But more than once she returned, in a miraculous manner, to the site of her original chapel, which was such a plain sign of her will, that a fitting temple was built for her in this place of her own choice. This was in 1537 A.D., and she has been a great blessing to the country ever since."

Upon the wall of the church, near the entrance to the Madonna's chapel, is a curious picture, which is designed to illustrate the mystery of the Trinity. From one point of view is seen the venerable head which stands for the Father, from another the pathetic Christ, and from a third the symbolic dove.

An annual pilgrimage takes place on the 8th of September, when thousands of peasants flock from the whole country round, filling the night with their songs, and polishing with feet and knees the round stones, which pave the ascent to the church, until they are as bright and slippery as glass.

Above the church a rocky staircase leads rapidly up into meadows enamelled with sweet cyclamen and shaded by broad chestnut-trees. The beautiful ravine in front is the Valle Perlana or Val di S. Benedetto. For the botanist it is a mine of wealth. For the archæologist the Benedictine Monastery at the head of the valley is full of interest. The eleventh-century church, 2700 feet above sea-level, with three apses, and round arches, of typical Lombard character, is in good repair. What remains of the monastic buildings is used for farm purposes. A little higher up the valley is a bridge, by which we can cross the stream and return by the Northern side of the ravine. Before doing so, good walkers would do well to make the summit of Monte Galbiga, 5000 feet above sea-level, about four hours up from Campo, which affords the finest view on the Western side of the Lake, not even excepting the superb panorama from Monte Generoso. The route may be continued over the crest which links Galbiga with Crocione. Resuming our walk down the south side of the Val Perlana, we should remember, that this road is carried along steep limestone cliffs, and has been polished by innumerable feet into an inconvenient slipperiness. These conditions, while devoid of danger, add considerably to the fatigue.

When we have reached a point below the level of the Madonna's Church, on the Northern side of the valley, we strike off to the left towards a white building, sentried by a row of stupendous cypresses, which are said to have no rivals for size in Lombardy. They stand in a mournful line upon a grassy terrace, in what was once the courtyard of the Cistercian Convent of Acqua Fredda, together with which they date back to 1142 A.D. The house got its name from a spring of delicious water, which gushes out of the rock close by, and renders good service to the silk mills lower down the valley. These mills are all alive with bright-eyed girls, engaged in winding the silk from the cocoons, and putting it through the various processes preparatory to weaving. This silk industry is the livelihood of thousands

Photo by T. W. M. Lund

OBSOLETE HEAD-DRESS OF COMASQUE WOMEN

of people in the neighbourhood of the Lake. The mulberry vies with the olive and the vine in every garden. Tree after tree is stripped to supply the voracious little worms with food, which will enable them to spin their silken coffins. The culture of the worms furnishes occupation to great numbers of people. Large buildings are erected for the reception of the chrysalides during the period of hibernation. Then follow the processes of winding, dyeing, and weaving, which employ no small proportion of the female population. It is almost incredible to reflect, that the seeds of this great industry were those few eggs, which two Nestorian pilgrim monks of Persia filched from under the eye of the rigid protectionism of China, and carried in the hollow stems of their sticks, in the year of our Lord 530, across a continent to the Emperor Justinian at Constantinople, where they were hatched in the heat of a dunghill.

In the narrow street we meet a little party of gaily dressed girls. One of them carries a cushion. Upon it lies a tiny swaddled baby, which they seem proud to exhibit. They are taking it to its baptism, they say. "And which of you is its mother?" innocently ask we; at which inquiry they laugh until the baby is nearly rolled off its cushion. "Why, its mother is in bed," is the reply; "it was only born last night." When the weather is inclement these babies of a few hours old are often carried to church in a glass case.

The plaiting of the hair upon silver pins or *spille*, arranged at the back of the head so as to resemble the aureole of sainthood, was formerly the holiday custom of the whole province. It was an operation of many hours, and when completed precluded the possibility of lying down, except in one position, as long as the head remained dressed. This head-dress is now a very rare sight, though twenty years ago it was the universal custom. "My husband wants me to give up wearing my silver pins," said an old friend, a handsome middle-aged woman, who sells fruit at the Menaggio Railway Station; "he would like me to look more modern. But I tell him I prefer to stick to my old-fashioned ways—'*tengo la mia antichità.*'"

In the little Piazza at Lenno, through which we pass to reach the steamboat, are two features of special interest.

On the left hand is an octagonal Baptistery of the Lombard period of architecture. Possibly the octagonal form owed its adoption to the idea expressed by S. Ambrose, that eight was the mystical number. Each side is divided by a light central shaft into two arched panels, which are alternately pierced by small, deep, narrow windows, with very curious effect.

On the right of the Piazza, beneath the Eastern end of the church, are two Crypts, assigned by antiquarians to no later a date than 357 A.D. In one of these the two Easternmost columns are of cippolino marble, the rest of stone. The lightness of the pillars and the form and carving of the capitals seem to belong to an early period in the Christian era. The variety of material and design implies, that they are part of the wreck of other edifices, possibly Pagan temples, so that their style affords but little clue to the date of the chapel itself. Terra-cotta pipes have been found, from which some infer, that we are here on the track of a Roman hot-air bath, while others conclude that we have struck the channels of oracular responses, and that at least part of the present building belonged originally to a heathen temple. Some colour is given to the theory of the site of an oracle from the discovery in this locality of a slab, on which is sculptured the face of a horned deity, with holes for eyes, nostrils, and mouth, and which may possibly have been let into a wall and served as the outlet for the oracular voice. But it is more likely, by analogy with the Bocca della Verità, and a splendid slab in the Palazzo Colonna, carved with a Gorgon's Head, in Rome, to have been a grid let into the ground for purposes of drainage. It was recently to be seen at No. 7 Rue Muralli, Como.

A Roman inscription is built into the walls of the church above.

Both this Crypt and the Baptistery are under the protection of the Italian Government as historical monuments.

When the Lake is very low the ruins of a Roman villa may be distinctly seen beneath the water, not far from the shore, and this, as has been already said, is conjecturally one of those, which Pliny describes as of his own building. P. Giovio writes: "*Ad Lennum procul dubio villam Plinii*

Photo by T. W. M. Lund

THE BAPTISTERY AT LENNO

fuisse indicamus quam comaediam appellare solebat"; "Without a doubt we fix at Lenno the site of the villa which Pliny used to call Comedy." But Paolo hazards no guess as to its position.

The road from Lenno to Tremezzo or Cadenabbia leads through a populous and highly cultivated district, and has many beauties to reveal.

CHAPTER VI

CADENABBIA

"Who hath seen thee, O, never in his breast
The heart grows wholly old!"—ANON.

CADENABBIA is a resting-place second to none on the Lake of Como. The derivation of the name has been a source of solicitude to many philologists. G. B. Giovio and C. Cantù think beyond doubt that it is a corruption of *ca-di-naulo*, "the home of sailors," since *naulon* in Greek and *naulum* in Latin mean "passage-money by ship."

There is, however, a Greek word *nabla*, a Latin word *nablia*, and a Hebrew word *nabel* or *nevel*, which signify a stringed instrument of music. Whether in old times Cadenabbia was so famous for its harmony as to merit the distinction of being called "the home of the lyre," there is no corroborative testimony; but may not the name be regarded as prophetic of the distinguished musical circle, who long colonised the locality, headed by the brilliant violoncellist, the Cavaliere Piatti? The prophecy is at least as plain as some others, which rest upon a philological guess, and form the basis of superstructures of far-reaching importance.

P. Giovio, however, proposes another solution, by no means so complimentary to the good folk of Cadenabbia in his time. Having Latinised the name into *Cathenae Apiae*, in which we can only surmise that he alludes to the parsley wreaths used in the carousals of classical times, he derives it from the bibulousness of the boatmen (*nautarum temulentia*), who made Cadenabbia the half-way house in their voyages up and down the Lake (*veluti expleto mediae navigationis cursu*), since they found the tavern-keepers (*caupones*) all too ready to supply them with wine more copious in quantity and stronger in quality than at any other place (*quum nullibi liberalius aut meracius caupones praeter navigantibus propinent*).

But derivations as they may, the perfect environment of Cadenabbia, its outlook, its accessibility either by carriage or boat, its pretty English chapel, its famous avenue of planes, and its choice of excellent hotels make it at least the rival of Bellagio and Menaggio.

The Hotel Belle Vue is unsurpassed in Italy for situation, management, and society, nor are its charges excessive when we consider what it gives. The Britannia is admirable at considerably cheaper rates. The Belle Ile is a comfortable pension for those who wish to study economy. Cadenabbia has a little colony of English residents, located in a group of pretty villas, which line the shore of the Lake. One of these was once the home of Signor Piatti. In another, well known to Englishmen by its hospitality, now the Villa Margherita, once the property of the great Milanese music publishers, the Riccordi, Verdi, the musical composer, was a frequent guest in bygone years, and is said to have written his masterpiece. The octagon of glass is perfect in its acoustic properties.

A speaking portrait of Cadenabbia hangs in the Bureau of the Hotel Belle Vue, in the form of a MS. poem by Longfellow, written on the spot, and entitled "Cadenabbia." It is published in "Poems of Places," but is so little known that no apology need be offered for reproducing it here :—

"No sound of wheels or hoof-beat breaks
   The silence of the summer day,
As by the loveliest of all lakes
   I while the idle hours away.

I pace the leafy colonnade,
   Where level branches of the plane
Above me weave a roof of shade,
   Impervious to the sun or rain.

At times a sudden rush of air
   Flutters the lazy leaves o'erhead,
And gleams of sunshine toss and flare,
   Like torches down the path I tread.

By Sommariva's garden gate,
  I make the marble stairs my seat,
And hear the water as I wait,
  Lapping the steps beneath my feet.

The undulation sinks and swells
  Along the stony parapets,
And far away the floating bells
  Tinkle upon the fishers' nets.

Silent and slow, by tower and town
  The freighted barges come and go,
Their pendent shadows gliding down
  By town and tower submerged below.

The hills sweep upward from the shore,
  With villas scattered one by one
Upon their wooded spurs, and lower,
  Bellagio blazing in the sun.

And dimly seen, a tangled mass
  Of walls and woods, of light and shade,
Stands beckoning up the Stelvio Pass
  Varenna, with its white cascade.

I ask myself, 'Is this a dream?
  Will it all vanish into air?
Is there a land of such supreme
  And perfect beauty anywhere?'

Sweet vision! Do not fade away;
  Linger until my heart shall take
Into itself the summer day
  And all the beauty of the lake:

Linger until upon my brain
  Is stamped an image of the scene,
Then fade into the air again,
  And be as if thou hadst not been."

As has already been said, the wide extent of valley, rock, and hill which lies in the rear of Cadenabbia, between the Lake and Monte Crocione, is a field of infinite interest, variety, and charm. Fine views and fresh air can be reached with small fatigue, and an hour's walk lands the rambler among Nature's solitudes.

In the afternoon of the first Sunday in September there is a pretty festival to be seen at the Parish Church of Griante, ten minutes' walk from Cadenabbia, where the green Piazza commands one of the typical views of the Lake. It is called *La Festa dei canestri*, deriving its name from the baskets in which the people bring their offerings. These are tastefully arranged in every available part of the church, and contain, among other things, live rabbits and doves, roast geese, ducks and fowls, sausages and pork, pasties and puddings, cakes and confectionery, pomegranates, apples, pears, grapes, vegetables, butter, hares, partridges, boughs hung with little birds, and other varieties of game; fish, sugar-loaf, olive oil, and wine. After the gifts have been duly offered, a procession is formed to walk through the village. The banners are hoisted, the lanterns are lit with much gesticulation and noise; the men wear coarse surplices and red capes, the women white or black veils. Both sexes are members of religious guilds. All sing lustily as they wind up and down the steep, narrow ways, through quaint old archways or under low arcades, now in sunshine, now in shadow, with their candles and lanterns, and banners, and crucifixes. The old men have amazing voices, and the earnestness of their weather-beaten faces is a study. The chant which all seem to know so well, proves to be a Litany, in which the aid of every saint in the calendar is invoked in their behalf.

The whole scene calls to mind the Ambarvalia of ancient days, when at harvest-time priest and people traversed cornfield and vineyard to propitiate the bountiful Ceres and Bacchus, and the mysterious Dea Dia, with praises, prayers, and gifts. We are but assisting at rites familiar to Latin and Sabine before the birth of Rome, only clothed in a Christian dress. The instinct of humanity to court the grace of Powers beyond its control is the same in all ages, by whatever name it approaches them.

This ceremony over, an auction of the offerings is held outside the church, and the proceeds of the sale are devoted to the maintenance of the fabric and worship. Great rivalry characterises the bidding, and some of the articles are knocked down at fancy prices. The spirited competition of the English and American visitors makes the fun fast and furious, and adds largely to the contents of the parish purse. Similar festivals are held during the autumn at all the parish churches, those of Bellagio, S. Giovanni, Bolvedro, and Lenno counting among the most attractive.

At this point one word may not be inopportune on the subject of "the Continental Sunday," of which English people so often speak with pious horror. The term is ambiguous, for the use of Sunday on the Continent of Europe differs widely according to race and religion. In Italy, however, Sunday is kept with no less ecclesiastical observance than in England. English travellers fail to see this, because they are generally in bed on Sunday morning long after the people of the country have been to church. The Italian is generally at Mass by eight o'clock at the latest, whereas, if the average Englishman contrives to attend a service at all, it is rarely until eleven o'clock at the earliest. At this hour he sees the natives, in gala dress, sitting in groups under the trees, or going to visit their friends, or promenading to the music of a military band, and he promptly moralises upon the frightfully irreligious state of the country. The Italian calls Saturday by its old Hebrew title, *Sabbato*, or the Sabbath. To Sunday, the first day of the week, consecrated to the triumphant Christ, he gives its rightful name, *Domenica*, or the Lord's Day. There are religious and irreligious in Italy, as there are in England. But the way in which the religious keep their Lord's Day is so reasonable in its early devotion, its social brightness, and its restful enjoyment, that we might do well to reconsider our own method, and ask which is more in harmony with the spirit of the Gospel itself.

Every one knows the way through the quaint street of Griante to the white church of S. Martino, 2500 feet above sea-level, upon its colossal limestone bastion. This short pilgrimage may be judiciously supplemented by a walk of little extra fatigue, but of infinite beauty and delight. As we descend again from S. Martino, just before reaching the shrine dedicated to *Maria, stella Maris*, "Mary, Star of the Sea," we strike up a footpath leading to two sheds, then cross the little gorge and still pursue the winding path. Presently we turn the flank of a huge pyramidal crag, which rears itself in the centre of the ravine and divides the landscape into two exquisite vignettes. A little farther on we arrive at a breezy meadow, which, half a century ago, hospitably received the fugitive population of Griante, who encamped here for some weeks during an invasion of their district by cholera. The manœuvre resulted in the complete discomfiture of the invader. Not a life was lost, and the old inhabitants looked back to the long picnic as one of the most delightful experiences of their lives. In a shoemaker's shop at Menaggio is a fresco of S. Roch, beneath which is inscribed: "*Ora pro nobis, Sanctus Rochus, et serva nos de morbus cholerae.* 1836." Of the Latin we must not be critical!

Crossing the meadow to the right, and leaving the precipices and cone of Crocione to the left, we pass a small cowhouse, traverse a narrow cleft, and emerge upon one of those ravishing surprises with which these hills abound. We survey at a glance the whole scene from the Stelvio Gap on the right to the peaks over Lugano on the left, the little blue Lake of Piano lying at our feet, and the mysterious ravine of Sanagra, capped by a coronal of feudal towers, winding in among the opposite mountains, and beckoning us to explore its secret.

To the right of this Col, a hundred feet above us, rises the Dòsso di Griante, which no one should fail to ascend, for the sake of its still wider outlook upon mountain, valley, and Lake.

Bearing to the left, through woods brilliant with autumnal berries of many kinds — the coral berberis, the crimson spindlewood, or "priest's cap," as the people picturesquely term it, from its likeness to the *berretta*, the scarlet butcher's broom, the vermilion sheath of the cape gooseberry, the purple juniper, the velvet arbutus, the brilliant holly—we descend to verdant swards and the shadow of great chestnut-trees. Here we trend to the right along a grassy terrace, instead of going down to the village of Croce on the Porlezza road. In five minutes we reach a point that juts out over Menaggio, and is marked by a wooden cross, locally known as Al Piz or La Crocetta. All that we saw at S. Martino is here, and much more besides. The view of the Lecco arm of the Lake is delicious in its perfect perspective and calm. The broken lines of its hills and shores stretch away to the scene of Manzoni's *I Promessi Sposi*. Legnone and the Grigna tower in proud rivalry. The jagged teeth of Resegone vindicate its name of "the Saw." The outline of Napoleon's face, upturned in the repose of death, is cut against the sky. The Corni di Canzo rise like a dromedary's back. It is such a picture, and of such hues, as the great Lombard artists loved to paint.

If, instead of descending through the copse named above, we take the path to the left and follow the road along the side of Crocione, a splendid walk takes us as far as the village of Piano.

We may spend a perfect day in the Val Menaggio as follows. After passing the Parish Church and Cemetery of Loveno, the long, peaceful meadow of Pianura is traversed, and we reach the bridge which spans the stream. We go up to Cardeno, whence we make for the main road to Porlezza, and descend on Piano. We may loiter a pleasant hour or two on the little Lake, so exquisitely set among the surrounding mountains, woods, and villages. Then we return by Bene Lario and keep straight on up the valley through beautifully wooded pastures till we reach the ideal Golf Links, unrivalled for their superb situation. The park-like scenery between the Golf House and La Crocetta, with its splendid timber, rocks, flowers, cattle, and peasant folk, as we traverse these pastures before descending to the main road, makes a charming finish to the day.

The pedestrian wishing to reach Menaggio from La Crocetta should descend by the zigzag path to the main road, and then take the successive short cuts, which save considerable distance. On the side of a peasant's house, a little above the tunnel between Menaggio and Cadenabbia, is a small fresco, interesting, first, because after more than a century of exposure it remains in perfect preservation; and next, as being a copy of a miraculous picture at Hiezing, near Vienna, 1730 A.D., a fact set forth in the annexed inscription. The shape of the flowered dress of the Virgin makes her appear like a large extinguisher, of which the child in her arms is a smaller edition.

Those who take the carriage-road to Cadenabbia will find

Photo by T. W. M. Lund

LAKE OF PIANO

a small marble tablet, let into the wall at the wayside after a familiar Italian custom, upon which an inscription asks repose for the soul of a Syndic of Griante, drowned near the spot while bathing alone from his boat in July 1881. A week's search for the body proved fruitless, but on the 25th of October 1883 it was accidentally caught in a fisherman's net, and was still recognisable as that of the unfortunate Syndic. Of the many, who are drowned in this Lake, the bodies are rarely recovered. They are supposed to sink into the cavities formed by the slanting strata of rock at the bottom of the Lake, and so to pass beyond the reach of drag or current.

CHAPTER VII

MENAGGIO

" How sweet and solemn at the close of day,
After a long and lonely pilgrimage
Among the mountains, where our spirits held
With wildering fancy and her kindred powers
High converse, to descend as from the clouds
Into a quiet valley."—WILSON.

MENAGGIO is a busy little town, the terminus of the miniature Railway from Porlezza. It has two fine hotels—the Menaggio, close to the railway station, and the Victoria, one of the best in the world for situation and management, planted upon an airy promontory near the town pier; while the Corona is an excellent Italian inn for those, who wish to be entertained at more moderate cost. The position of Hotel Victoria is without rival. Removed from the vicinity of rising ground, it is fanned by every breath of air that moves, while there is not a window from which a superb view of Lake and mountain is not seen. The neighbourhood of Menaggio is second to none in the grandeur and variety of its scenery.

In the Contrada di Sta. Marta, the main street of Menaggio, not far from the quay, the following Latin inscription of the first century of the Christian era is built into the wall in front of the Church of Sta. Marta. It was found near Rezzonico, and is supposed to have formed part of the tomb of Lucius, who was evidently a man of considerable importance.

LMINICIVSLFOVF . EXORATUS.

N DIVITITIAVGVESPASIANICONSENSUDECVRIONTRMILIIIIVIR

APIIVIRIDPRAEFFAB.

ISETCOSPONTIF SIBIETGEMINIAE QFPRISCAE

VXORI . ET MINICIAELFB ISIAEV.

Photo by G. E. Thompson

MENAGGIO

"L. M. E., son of Lucius of the tribe of Ofentina, flamen of the deified Titus Vespasian, by the consent of the decurions military tribune, quattumvir edile, duumvir of justice, prefect of the artisans of Cæsar and of the Consul, pontifex; to himself and his consort, Geminia Prisca, daughter of Quintus, and to Minicia Bisia, daughter of Lucius, he made this in his lifetime."

In the upper part of Menaggio, called Castello, from the fortress, which once stood on the site of the Church of S. Celso, are many scattered relics of antiquity; old doorways built up into the walls of houses, quaint bits of sculpture, scraps of terra-cotta peeping out in unexpected places; and in the Piazza, before the church, a porphyry heart, worn with time, let into a side wall. The *castello*, or fortress, of which the outer wall may still be seen towards the Largo Fossato, is said to have been founded by the Gauls, nor is it likely that any dominant power would fail to fortify such a commanding position. In the ten years' war between Como and Milan, 1121, it was stormed and burnt by the men of Como for its sympathy with their antagonists. In 1296 its interference with the civil broils of Como exposed it to another siege, which ended in its falling into the hands of Matteo Visconti. Early in the sixteenth century it was the object of unsuccessful attacks by French and Swiss, but the latter were so exasperated by the obstinacy of its resistance, that in revenge they burned the whole country round.

A quarter of an hour from the Castello brings us to Loveno, a village full of country houses and picturesque studies. As we pass the Villa Bolza, occupied by Count Bolza, who was head of police in Milan during the Austrian rule, a fresco of the Madonna and S. Anthony, dated 1482, restored 1741, and almost hidden by an immense vine laden with superb clusters of grapes, peeps out from the corner of the house nearest the road.

A little farther stands the Villa Wachs Mylius, with beautiful garden and glorious views. Still higher is the Villa Vigone, noted in the guide-books for its little gallery of sculpture: *e.g.* Eve by Baruzzi, Ruth by Imoff, David by Manfredini, Moses by Gandolfide; but if the truth be told, far more worthy of renown for the charm of its lovely grounds and enchanting vistas.

In a little temple in these grounds there is a bas-relief by Marchesi, representing a youth at the point of death recumbent upon a couch, and a young girl in profound grief hanging over him, while his father and mother also take their last farewell.

Above is the dedication *Alla Memoria di Giulio Mylius.* Beneath are the lines :—

> "Sul fior degli anni in stranio lido li muore
> Fra gli amplessi e le lagrime de suoi.
> Al bacio vola dell' eterno amore
> E acerbo duolo è cio che resta a noi."

"In the flower of life, on a foreign shore, he died amid the embraces and tears of his friends. To the kiss of the Eternal Love he flies, and bitter pain is all that is left to us."

Of the many visitors who pass by this monument, few know the romance which it records. Giulio loved an Austrian lady of noble birth, who reciprocated his affection; but a difference in their religious education formed a bar to their marriage in the eyes of the lady's parents, who, having made home intolerable for her, disowned her when she fled to the house of a sympathetic uncle. Meantime her lover lay dying at Trieste, of a broken heart it is said. Thither she went and became his wife upon his death-bed, in order to give his parents the right to assume her protection after his decease. This was in 1830. The young widow afterwards married a Vigone of Milan, and was endowed by the father of her first husband with this charming Villa and a large share of his property. A picture in the Villa commemorates an odd adventure, which befell this Giulio Mylius. A passenger in the first steamer on the Lago Maggiore, he had climbed into the small boat hanging at the stern, and contrived to fall into the Lake without the accident being observed by any one on board. Happily for him, he was able to keep afloat until rescued by two boats, which chanced to be near.

Opposite to Marchesi's sculpture, in the little temple, is a bas-relief by Thorwaldsen. The Genius of Life stands in the car of Nemesis or Retribution, whose wheel revolves with alternations of Fortune, Good and Bad, Plenty and

Want. The charioteer drives two horses, Loyalty and Self-will, the one docile and quiet, the other wayward and restive. The dog of Faith leads the way. Behind follow winged youths, bearing the sword of Punishment, or wreaths and fruits for Reward. Time is signified by the over-arching Zodiac, in which the scales of Justice are uppermost.

Thorwaldsen's *motif* was probably inspired by the poetic myth, which Plato puts into the mouth of Socrates in the Dialogue of Phaedrus,[1] where the soul is compared to a chariot with a winged pair of horses, one of which alone, in the human soul, is good, the other being violent and rebellious, and often disobedient to the charioteer. The unruly horse in the team may win nothing but moral ruin for the soul, which may nevertheless attain to virtue as its reward, should the better-natured steed prove the stronger of the pair.

A climb up to the Swiss House, enclosed in the domain of the Villa Vigone, repays the slight effort with fine air and expansive views. From this point there is a delightful ramble to the village of Barna, across a breezy alp disclosing a glimpse of the five peaks of Monte Rosa.

A few yards below this Villa is the Parish Church of Loveno, which contains a picture of interest, whether by B. Luini or another. The Mother of Sorrows is supported on either hand by S. Lorenzo and S. Agnes, who present two kneeling donors, two citizens of Cremona. A Lamb lies on the steps of her throne, and above are circular pictures of the Seven Sorrows of the Virgin, the Circumcision, the Flight into Egypt, Christ Lost in the Temple, the Via Dolorosa, Crucifixion, Pietà, and Entombment.

Loveno ought to be but the first stage in a day's walk to Breglia, at the foot of the rocky cone of the Monte Grona. The little Church known as La Madonna della Breglia is one of the beacons in this part of the Lake, high above La Madonna della Pace near to Nobiallo. We come down the romantic valley on the other side of the Col to Acqua Seria on the Lake itself.

One of the best expeditions from Menaggio is that into

[1] Plato's *Phaedrus*, c. 52 and foll.

the Val Sanagra, *Sanatch*, as the peasants call it. The most convenient way of reaching it is to use the train as far as Grandola, and then descend into the valley by way of Codogno. At the second mill we cross the stream and make straight for the narrowest part of the gorge, where we climb some rocky steps to what was formerly a *cheminée*, known as the Sass Corbé. A narrow pathway steeply skirts the ravine for a short distance, when it merges in the broader road that comes down from Barna, and continues up the Val Sanagra by a uniformly gentle ascent, at first across green pastures, then through rocky gorges among shady boskage, and always by the tumbling stream, unfordable in times of heavy rain. The chief tenants of this lonely valley are the noble eagles, which wheel curiously overhead, foxes, badgers, and mountain hares. Some three hours of steady walking from Grandola bring us to a spring, which gushes out of a crevice in the limestone, so icily cold, that it is impossible to drink a copious draught of it. It is credited with wholesome properties, which account for the etymology of the name Sanagra, *sanat aegros*, a cure for the sick. In returning, it is better to hold on by the broader road to Barna, since there is not a point or turn devoid of surpassing interest; and when in the evening light Barna and Bellagio burst into view, the one against the sky, the other glowing upon the Lake, there is a *coup d'œil* as perfect as Nature can create. Barna from a distance is a fair feature in the landscape, but its little irregular Piazza, with church and fountain, and flight of steps, and balustrades, and children at play, and women at work, is a fertile subject for the sketch-book. Then we descend a broad staircase through cool chestnut woods, cross the green Pianura of Loveno, astir with cattle that chime their bells like a vesper peal, as the long shadows fall across the vivid green of the velvety meadow, and so, very quickly to Menaggio. Those who cannot make the longer expedition, should at least walk up to Barna from Loveno, and return the same way for the sake of the views. Or from Barna the mouth of the Val Sanagra may be crossed, and the steep path on the other side scaled as far as Naggio upon its high perch.

The Val Cavargna is another of the fine expeditions that can be made out of the Val Menaggio. Up to Sta. Lucia and down to Lugano is a long day's work, but one which well repays our enterprise. The valley is redolent with memories of S. Carlo's famous visitation of his diocese. He fearlessly traversed even these wild and lawless tracts of country, and one place is pointed out where he slept on the ground, that his servant might enjoy the luxury of the straw which formed the only bed. It is still the smugglers' high-road from Switzerland. An army of guards, armed to the teeth, is kept on the frontier, and the peasant caught with a pound of contraband tobacco upon him is sure of two years' imprisonment besides a ruinous fine; but the temptation is too strong for the risk and the penalty. One knapsack full of tobacco, cigars, or salt, safely landed, yields a small fortune, so heavy are the Italian taxes upon these articles. The customs officials cannot guard every point at once, and their movements are closely watched and reported by the people, who are all in league against them. They are often put on the wrong scent by misleading rumours, and then a dozen sturdy fellows by as many pathless ways steal over into Italy under cover of the night and the wildness of the country. Sometimes disaster overtakes them, when the bale is sacrificed and the smuggler flies. The law allows the official to shoot him, if he refuses to halt, and such a barbarity occasionally occurs; but carbine practice in the dark and in such country is apt to be somewhat uncertain. The electric searchlight, worked from a gunboat all night long, testifies to the zeal of the Fiscal authorities and the profits of the smugglers.

Menaggio was the cradle of one of the distinguished sons of the Lake, Leone Leoni, commonly called *Il cavaliere Aretino*. Morigia in his *La Nobiltà di Milano* states that Menaggio was his birthplace, though in his *Storia di Milano*, 1555, he calls him a Milanese citizen. Gianbattista Giovio in his *Lettere Lariane* accounts for this by the Lombard custom of expressing a country by the name of its chief city.

A goldsmith by trade, Leoni first won notice as a diesinker, in which capacity he produced a number of portrait-medals of considerable excellence. The Emperor Charles V., struck by his ability, took him into his service, and commissioned him to execute a bronze statue of himself, which the artist did with a skill so ingenious and a flattery so overwhelming, that his fortune was ensured. Vasari,[1] who was a contemporary of the sculptor, thus describes the work:—

"This figure, which was somewhat larger than life, Leoni invested with a splendid suit of armour, by means of two very thin plates of metal, which could easily be put on or taken off; the effect is most graceful, and the artist has managed his work so perfectly, that whoever sees the figure clothed, could never suppose it to be sometimes nude; and whoever sees the nude statue, would find it difficult to believe that it could ever be armed. The Emperor, resting on the left foot, places his right on a chained figure lying beneath him, and representing Rage or Fury, with a torch, and various arms. On the pedestal of the statue, which is now in Madrid, are the words, '*Caesaris virtute furor domitus*,' 'Rage fanned by the valour of Cæsar.' Having completed that figure, Leoni then made a large die, for the purpose of striking medals, of the Emperor, with Jupiter launching his thunderbolts at the Titans, on the reverse."

Charles V. marked his appreciation of these works by ennobling Leoni; pensioning him with one hundred and fifty ducats a year, secured on the Mint of Milan; giving him a house in the Contrada de' Morone in Milan; and treating him with the most familiar intimacy. To enumerate the statues and busts, which he made for the Imperial family and Court would be too tedious. What concerns us most are the five bronze pieces on the tomb of Gian Giacomo de' Medici in the Cathedral of Milan, which he made by command of Pope Pius IV., brother of Gian Giacomo, for the modest sum of seven thousand eight hundred crowns. Of this worthy and his monument we shall hear more presently.

Leoni employed part of his wealth in building his house in the Via Morone in Milan, known as Casa Degli Omenoni, in the Milanese dialect "big men," from the Caryatides, resting on stone pilasters, which adorn the façade. He

[1] "Lives of the Artists," vol. v. p. 430.

named the house Casa Aureliana, from a plaster copy of the equestrian statue of Marcus Aurelius on the Roman Capitol, which he placed in the courtyard. His house was not only famous for the fanciful designs with which he embellished the exterior, but for the wealth of Art, which he gathered within its walls. It is near the Palazzo Belgiojoso and the Poldi Pezzoli Museum.

Leoni was a man of fierce and vindictive nature, which early threatened to clip the wings of his ambition and destroy his career. Having seriously maltreated the Pope's jeweller in revenge for an alleged insult to his wife, he was arrested and condemned to the galleys. At Genoa, however, he was released by order of Andrea Doria, Prince of Melfi. Writing to his friend Pietro Aretino on this escape, Leoni says: "I pass my time in snapping my fingers at the priests, and praying God will cause the bad among them to burst, and the good to prosper." On another occasion his temper was seen in his employment of a bravo to assassinate his pupil Martino for refusing to return with him from Venice to Milan. He added to this fault of vindictiveness a sordid and dishonest spirit; for it is recorded that on one occasion he attacked the son of Titian in his own house, and inflicted severe wounds upon him, in the attempt to possess himself of a large sum of money, which his unhappy victim carried with him. Leoni was born towards the end of the fifteenth century, and lived beyond the middle of the sixteenth.

CHAPTER VIII

NORTHERN PART OF THE STRADA REGINA

"So extraordinary were the social circumstances of Renaissance Italy, that almost at every turn, on her seaboard, in her cities, from her hill-tops, we are compelled to blend our admiration for the loveliest and purest works of art amid the choicest scenes of nature, with memories of execrable crimes and lawless character."

—J. A. Symonds.

The most beautiful part of the Strada Regina, the road on the Western side of the Lake, lies between Menaggio and Gravedona. The construction of this *cornice* of the Lake of Como is traditionally attributed to Theodelinda, the Lombard Queen, who is said to have been carried along it in her litter to visit the Baths in the Val Masino off the Valtelline. Although this mule track has now been superseded by a fine carriage-road along the margin of the Lake, it is by far the more interesting and picturesque, and will be followed in this chapter. In the popular mind Theodelinda is the fairy godmother of the Lake, to whom every good thing is assigned, for which no other origin can be found. She was to the Lombards what Bertha was to the Anglo-Saxons and Clotilda to the Franks. Her story is a romantic one, and contains enough of authentic record to make it worth recital on the Lake of Como.

In the sixth century, Autaris, "the long-haired," King of the Lombards, who took the Imperial name of Flavius, sent an embassy to Theodelinda's father, Garibald, King of Bavaria, to ask her hand in marriage. Impatient of delay and eager to see his bride, Autaris accompanied his ambassador to the Court of Bavaria, but in the strictest incognito. Admitted to the King's audience, he advanced to Garibald and stated that though he had no official authority in the matter, he was the intimate friend of Autaris, who had sent

Photo by T. W. M. Lund

A BREEZE AT MENAGGIO

him for the express purpose of carrying back a description of the charms of his future wife. Accordingly, Theodelinda was summoned to undergo this trying ordeal of inspection. Her great beauty and womanly grace won the heart of Autaris. He hailed her Queen of Italy, and begged that, according to national usage, she would present a cup of wine to the first of her new subjects. When the turn of Autaris came to receive the goblet, he contrived to touch the princess's hand significantly, and at the same time to signal her to silence. Theodelinda was already in love with this bold and handsome messenger, whose advances she disclosed at night to her nurse, who divined that he was no other than the Lombard King himself. As the embassy returned home, they no sooner reached the Italian frontier than Autaris, poising himself in his stirrups, hurled his battle-axe at a tree with singular force and skill, exclaiming to the astounded Bavarians, "So strikes the Lombard King!"

Political troubles having driven Garibald and his daughter from their home, they fled to Verona, where Theodelinda became Queen of Lombardy. Autaris only survived his marriage a brief year, but meantime Theodelinda had so endeared herself to the people, that they pledged themselves to accept for King the man whom she might choose for her second husband. Her choice fell upon Agilulf, Duke of Turin, and such was her influence, that she won him over from the worship of his ancestral idols to the adoption of the Orthodox Christian Faith. He gave practical proof of his sincerity by abandoning, at his wife's entreaty, a project for the siege of Rome. His tomb is to be seen in the Church of S. Lorenzo at Milan.

It was out of gratitude for this generous protection, that Gregory the Great, who then filled the Holy See, presented Theodelinda with the most precious gift he could bestow. This was a fine circlet of iron, large enough to fit the head, and believed to have been beaten out of one of the nails of the Crucifixion, discovered by S. Helena on Calvary, and given by her to her son, the Emperor Constantine. This is the famous Iron Crown, or *Il Sacro Chiodo* (the Sacred Nail), of the Lombard Kings, which is still kept and shown at the

Cathedral of Monza, between Como and Milan. The nail is splendidly set in a Byzantine coronet of gold, decorated by twenty-two magnificent precious stones, and made in six pieces, so as to be capable of expansion and contraction to suit the size of any head, that may have to wear it. The crown is said to have been in existence two hundred years before the sacred nail was inserted, to have been brought from the East by S. Helena, and to have been used at forty coronations. It is kept in an iron safe behind an altar on the South side of the choir, and is shown upon payment of a fee of five francs. An exact model of it, however, is exhibited without charge.

Monza is redolent of the saintly Theodelinda. She built the cathedral to commemorate Agilulf's conversion. Her portrait is still to be seen in the ancient bas-relief over the West door, as those of Justinian and Theodora are preserved in the mosaics of Ravenna. She is represented, above the Baptism of Christ, as presenting at once the Cross of the Christian Faith and the Crown of Lombardy to Agilulf. Her simple tomb, which originally stood in a chapel to the north of the choir, but was ejected by S. Carlo Borromeo, because she had not been canonised, in accordance with a decree of the Council of Trent directed against an unseemly rivalry among great families in the erection of sumptuous tombs within the churches, is now found near the door of the sacristy. Too heavy to be removed in its entirety, it was opened, and the contents left no doubt of its identity.

In the sacristy are preserved some curious relics of the great queen, such as her fan, her comb, her sapphire cup, the cover of her missal, and her crystal cross, the gift of S. Gregory. Her symbol of the hen with seven chickens, significant of the seven provinces of the Lombard kingdom, which appears also in the bas-relief above the Western entrance, was formerly kept here in pure gold. The First Napoleon appropriated this precious material, and left behind, as sufficiently good for the purpose, a copy in silver gilt.

There is a tradition, that after her patriotic labours, her church-building, her road-making, and her defence of orthodoxy in concert with such great names as those of Gregory and Columban of Bobbio, Theodelinda sought rest, and at last

Photo by T. W. M. Lund.

AT NOBIALLO

ended her days in the old castle of Vezio, which crowns the hill behind Varenna. The story of Autaris and Theodelinda cannot but remind us of Lancelot and Guinevere, or Paolo and Francesca; only in this case the future husband was his own messenger, and so no heart-tragedy throws its fatal shadow across the grace and joy of the romance.

Heading round the serene little bay to the N. of Menaggio, and passing by the church tower of Nobiallo, shaken perilously out of the perpendicular by the earthquake of 1868, we reach the Chapel of Sta. Maria della Pace, "Saint Mary of Peace," guarded by immemorial cypresses like those of Acqua Fredda. Then follows a short climb by a steep staircase up the Sasso Rancio, or yellow rock, with its *coup d'œil* of the Lake that transcends all fancy.

An Austro-Russian alliance succeeded in expelling the French from Lombardy in 1799. Part of Suwarrow's army, under General Bellegarde, approached Milan by way of the Lake of Como. While most of the troops were conveyed from Colico by water, a detachment took the perilous route of the Strada Regina. The pathway over the Sasso Rancio is described by Paolo Giovio as unfit to be traversed by any horseman in his senses, and under the name of *Saxa rancida* he depicts the frightful precipices, which it would turn a man dizzy to look down. The road is now several feet wide and flanked by a parapet, but at the time of the Russian invasion it was still narrow and unprotected. At this point the horses became restive, and in several instances plunged with their riders over the yellow cliff into the Lake below. There is a tradition, that one officer fell over with his horse, and that both escaped unhurt. Signor Piatti, in digging up a cyclamen bulb at this spot, unearthed a small Russian eagle of bronze.

Near the foot of the descent of the Sasso Rancio, on the northern side, a path leads through a gate on the right, in five minutes, to the pleasant Garden of Gaeta, a choice resort for picnicking or sketching, where visitors are free to enter, and will find excellent wine, made from the grapes grown on the grounds.

Through the thriving little town of Acqua Seria and the hamlet of S. Abbondio—or still better, by boat, since this is the least interesting part of the road—Rezzonico is reached, where a stately fortress of three hundred years ago, with forked battlements, seems to challenge that of Corenno, on the opposite shore.

The name is said to be a corruption of *Rhaetionicum*. In the Roman period, this Lake was comprised in Gallia Cisalpina, or Gaul South of the Alps, and a people called the Rhaeti occupied the country, which corresponds roughly with the present Swiss Grisons. They were warlike and aggressive, frequently dashing down from their mountain fastnesses and harassing the Roman power, until their final conquest and settlement as a Roman province, in the reign of Augustus. Rezzonico, therefore, is most likely a relic of some Rhaetian colony, which crossed the Alpine barrier and established itself on the softer shores of Como.

The great family, which took its name from Rezzonico, gave a Pope to the Church in Carlo Rezzonico of Como, who, as Clement XIII., ascended the Papal throne in 1758. He was a man of undoubted piety, but his championship of the Jesuits in defiance of all the secular powers of Europe, and in disregard of the policy of his predecessor, brought him disappointments, which broke his heart. He died in 1769. His monument in S. Peter's at Rome is Canova's masterpiece, and one of the best works of sculpture to be found in that church. Humble devotion is finely portrayed in the figure of the kneeling pontiff. On one side a winged youth with inverted torch, as the genius of Death, lies limp and spiritless, but gazes across at the majestic form of Faith, as though to gather hope from her calm strength and unshaken confidence.

There are many names of places upon the Lake full of interest for the antiquarian. On the other shore is the Val di Varrone, leading from Dervio to Val Sassina, which is said to take its name from the Consul Varus, who, early in the Christian era, perished with a fine army in an attempt to bring Germany more completely under the Roman power. Varus is supposed to have advanced from Lecco, possibly *Forum Licini*, up the Val Sassina, and to have encamped a part of his men in the valley, which bears his name. He would then descend to Bellano, embark his troops for Colico, and thence follow the Roman road across the Splügen into the Upper Rhine valley, and so approach the scene of his disastrous campaign. It was upon hearing the fate of this expedition, that the aged Augustus abandoned himself to a passion of childish grief, and continued to utter the futile cry, which has become famous, "Give me back my legions."

Then there are names like Nesso, Asso, Dorio, Dervio, Lenno, Corenno, Colonno, Lemna, Gaeta, Piona, Lecco, Palanzo, Lierna, and Pigra, which are forcibly suggestive of a Greek origin. Pliny the Elder records a tradition that this region was very early colonised by emigrants from Greece. It is, however, a matter of history, that when the population had been all but exterminated in the fierce raids of the Rhaetians, the country was repeopled by successive batches of colonists, of which not the least noteworthy was an imposing band of Greeks, introduced by Julius Cæsar, who was quite alive to the advantages likely to accrue from their commercial instincts and love of enterprise. It is probable that the settlers brought to their new homes the names of Grecian cities, which they had left.

Beyond Rezzonico is Cremia, remarkable not only for the beauty of its position, but for the possession of two noble pictures. To the left of the Strada Regina stands the Church of S. Michele, in the hamlet of Vignola, which contains an altar-piece by Paolo Veronese, in his best style. The subject is the Archangel S. Michael, triumphant over an impersonation of evil. The conflict is over; the two combatants hang upon the edge of a precipice, up the sides of which flames are ascending. The Archangel is unarmed, except with the scales of judgment, which he holds aloft in his right hand, while with the left he grasps his foe. The personification of Evil is a coarse, dog-faced monster, with the horns of a chamois, and a grey moustache. In his left hand he clutches an ugly instrument, armed with hooks for catching souls; with his right he grips the arm of his conqueror, though his long talons can inflict no injury upon the angelic form. The colouring is rich and warm. The tight-fitting blue tunic of S. Michael is particularly beautiful. But the Archangel bears no marks of battle, and the power of Evil wears no features to mark him out as the tempter of any but the brutalised.

Count Giovio, in his *Lettere Lariane*, relates how Count di Fermian offered a handsome price, his favour to the Commune, and an exact copy of the original, in return for this picture. At a Communal meeting, an aged member arose and said: "Friends, our ancestors have bequeathed us two legacies—this picture and a heavy public debt; let the Count take both." The picture remained where it was. The same writer tells us how Cremia came into possession of so rich an inheritance of art. He says, that it was the gift of one of the Pizzetti family, a native of Cremia. At the time when he wrote, 1827, the Pizzetti were a prosperous patrician house at Vicenza. Pier Tara and Georgio Fontana gave the frame in 1586. Another picture of interest, Christ Delivering the Keys to S. Peter, is attributed to one of the Campi of Cremia.

On the North wall of the same church is another interesting picture, painted on wood, in six compartments, by an unknown artist, though sometimes quite falsely attributed to Ambrogio da Fossano, called Borgognone. Its subjects are a Pietà and Angels, SS. Jerome and Dominic, the Madonna and Child, SS. Sebastian and Roch. Nevertheless, Cremia can boast a most lovely picture of the Madonna and Child by this great artist. It is one of the most refined examples of the Master's manner—his restraint of colour, beauty of expression, and general harmony. It is found in the Church of S. Vito, conspicuous by its two towers, close to the shore, ten minutes below S. Michele. It is seen to the best advantage in the afternoon light. The mother's face is of a noble type of womanly beauty. The book in her right hand suggests devotion. A curious touch of symbolism is noteworthy in the cincture of the Virgin, tied in a knot in front so as to bear a close resemblance to a cross. Against her left arm, the wistful, winsome Child leans in an easy posture, an apple in His hands, bracelets of crimson coral, prophetic of His martyrdom, on His wrists, and a pretty amber robe enwrapping His body. A Seraph stands in adoration on each side of the Madonna's throne. The seraphic nature is symbolised by the golden forks of flame, embroidered upon

Photo by T. W. M. Lund

S. VITO AT CREMIA

the necks of their white robes. The picture was restored in 1873 by Brissone of Milan, at the expense of the Marchetti family of Cremia.

Little seems to be known of the life of Ambrogio da Fossano, commonly called Borgognone, beyond the fact that he was a native of Milan, flourished about the year 1500, combined, like so many of his time, other kindred arts with that of painting, as the façade and stall-work of the Certosa of Pavia bear witness, and left behind him ample proofs of his industry and skill. In the peculiar softness of his manner, he is allied to the older Lombard School. His drawing is sometimes faulty, and there is some want of strength in his design; but these defects are atoned for by an individual charm of style. Few painters have left such sweet and gentle faces on their canvases, or delineated devoutness of feeling so truly, or illustrated with such accuracy of detail the life, manners, and dress of the period in which they lived. We shall often meet with this Milanese painter's work, but none will appeal to us more tenderly than this Virgin Mother and her Child at S. Vito.

From Cremia to Musso is a short walk of enchanting beauty. High above Musso stands a ruined castle, which now forms an additional charm to the landscape; but three and a half centuries ago it was a grim terror to the whole country round. It is built upon a rock, which rises abruptly out of the Lake to the height of five hundred feet. Apparently impregnable from the land, it was practically accessible only from its fortified port, some of the defences of which still remain. At great expense a good road has lately been cut round the face of the rock, winding among garden terraces, planted with rare shrubs and flowers, belonging to the Manzi family. On the edge of the precipice rises the little white chapel of Sta. Eufemia. A line of four bastions, connected by a wall, climbs up the ridge of rock, to a height several hundred feet above the level of the church, where the fortifications begin. It would be difficult to imagine a more perfect robbers' nest. Such is the outlook to Onno, on the Lake of Lecco, and to the Lake of Riva on the North, that not a boat could approach but it would be descried from this lofty, commanding eyrie, long before the most favourable wind or the swiftest oarsmen brought it near. On the opposite promontory of Piona we can see a large, lonely building with handsome, open *loggia*, a small port and three ruined arches. It is the Dazio or Toll-house, from which the master of this fortress levied tax upon every vessel that passed on that side of the Lake.

A romantic history clings about the rock and walls of the Castle of Musso. Frenchman, Spaniard, Sforza, and Swiss were all playing their own game for sovereignty in this part of Italy. A clever, resolute man, unimpeded by scruples, who could come in between these rival powers, might have a chance of securing for himself some pickings worth the having. Such a personage was Gian Giacomo de' Medici, commonly known by the sobriquet *Il Medeghino*. It is one of the diminutives in which the Italian tongue is so rich, and suggests that the owner of the nickname was either small in stature, or an object of popular idolatry. His mother was of the Serbelloni family. On his father's side he claimed cousinship with the great Florentine clan of Medici, and emblazoned on his flag the golden pills of their coat of arms, which betokened descent from ancestors of the medical profession. Having laid the Duke of Milan under obligation to him for his dukedom, Il Medeghino asked for the Castle of Musso as his reward. The Sforza promised it, if the assassination of a dangerous Visconti were thrown into the bargain. Il Medeghino promptly fulfilled the condition imposed, and took possession of the stronghold. The Duke had given him a sealed letter to the Governor, which he judiciously opened, and, finding that it gave orders for cutting his throat upon arrival, suppressed. He contented himself with presenting the Duke's cordial letter of commendation, requesting the surrender of the castle to his friend, Il Medeghino, but he did not forget the contents of the secret packet, and shaped his course accordingly. He now became the corsair of the Lake of Como. Desperadoes and adventurers soon flocked to this hawk's nest. They strained every nerve to make the fortress impregnable. Even the pirate's sisters, one of whom afterwards became the mother of Carlo Borromeo, Archbishop and Saint of Milan, are said to have used their hands in the work. Il

Medeghino largely contributed to the defeat of Francis I. at Pavia in 1525, by his spirited invasion of the Grisons, when he captured Chiavenna and harried the Val Bregaglia. This diversion drew off the Swiss allies of the French King, and left him to downfall and captivity.

Then came the Spaniard's turn to supersede Duke and King at Milan. Il Medeghino maintained a large navy on the Lake, was at the head of several thousand men, and lorded it over a wide and rich province. The Spaniard thought it more prudent to make an ally of him and establish him in his piratical power. But Gian Giacomo's run of luck was almost over. In 1529 Francesco Sforza was again Duke of Milan, and Il Medeghino imprudently defied him. At this point Fortune seemed to desert him. Heroic efforts by land and water proved fruitless against overwhelming forces of Swiss and Milanese. Although he rallied for a time from a disastrous defeat by the Duke's navy in the Bay of Menaggio, he was unable to maintain the conflict, and at last sought to make terms, and very good terms were granted him. He exchanged his old titles of Marquis of Musso and Count of Lecco for that of Marquis of Marignano, receiving large gifts of money and land, free pardon for his forces, and all the honours of war. No sooner had he left the Lake than the Swiss dismantled the fortifications at Musso, sparing only the little chapel of Sta. Eufemia, which still stands a white landmark among the ruins.

For some years Il Medeghino continued to pursue a successful career as a *condottiero* or soldier of fortune, hiring himself out to conduct the wars and massacres of Kings and Leagues, and conspicuously accomplishing that hideous extermination, which has ever since left the fertile Maremma a fever-stricken wilderness. When he died, in 1555, his corpse was followed to its grave in Milan Cathedral by the entire population of the city, who worshipped him as the very soul of manly virtue. The historian, Cesare Cantù, sums up his character in the following notable language:—

"Pirate, king, brigand, liar, rebel, assassin, hero, he furnishes us with a picture of some adventurers of our own time."

A splendid monument was erected to his memory, in the South transept of Milan Cathedral, by his brother, Pope Pius IV. Menaggio furnished the artist for the figures upon his tomb in the person of Leone Leoni, though the general design of the work is by some attributed to Michel Angelo himself.

In the neighbourhood of the Castle of Musso is a quarry of fine white marble, used in the building of the Cathedral of Como. At Dongo there is a small museum of arms and relics, found in making the new road and gardens.

CHAPTER IX

GRAVEDONA

"Far from the madding crowd's ignoble strife."—GRAY.

EVERY one who passes Gravedona by steamer will notice the great square building rising upon large buttresses out of the Lake, with an imposing tower at each corner, half fortress, half palace, and surrounded by a grove of solemn cypresses. It is the Palazzo del Pero. It was built by Cardinal Tolomeo Gallio in 1586, after designs by Pellegrino Pellegrini, nicknamed Tibaldo, of the Val Solda. The Cardinal was born at Cernobbio in 1527, and died in 1607 A.D. Although but the son of a fisherman, he rose to be successively Bishop of Martirano, Archbishop of Siponto, Prefect of various Congregations, and finally Cardinal Secretary of State to the Holy See. He became the possessor of vast estates and enormous wealth, holding in feud the Tre Pievi, and purchasing the Neapolitan Duchy of Alvito, and the Marquisate of Scaldasole, near Pavia. It is said of him, that though seven days' journey from Rome, yet, in travelling there, he never slept out of his own house. The fact was, he had a villa at every stage of the journey. Besides his splendid palace at Gravedona, he had two other residences on the Lake of Como—one, the Villa Balbiano, at Campo, and the other at Cernobbio, now known as the Villa d'Este. The palace at Gravedona was rifled of its treasures in the seventeenth century, and the boat bearing them away is said to have foundered in the Lake. The Cardinal used his wealth for the amelioration of that poverty, with which he had been so familiar in his youth. He established a college at Como, and endowed it munificently for the education of poor boys, wisely providing that those who had no aptitude for the pursuit of literary studies should be taught some mechanical trade. Nor did he forget the girls, for whom he left a large sum of money to be bestowed in marriage dowers, thirty at the same time, while whatever surplus there might be was to be spent in relieving the needs of the poor.

As a tribute to his beneficence a statue was erected to him in the Cathedral of Como in 1860, in the inscription upon which he is beautifully described as *Angelo di luce, Apostolo di carità del povero*, "Angel of light, Apostle of charity for the poor."

A local tradition is cherished, that it was once in contemplation to transfer the Session of the Roman Council from Trent to Cardinal Gallio's palace at Gravedona, in consequence of the outbreak of pestilence in the former city. The supposition has probably no further foundation than a set of chairs in the great hall of the palace, which were originally brought from Alvito, and bear the names of various members of the College of Cardinals.

Gravedona, Dongo, and Serico bear the name of *Le Tre Pievi*, "the three parishes," and these in the Middle Ages constituted a small republic, making its own laws, war, and peace. An eulogy upon the great Cardinal, inscribed in gold letters upon a marble slab in the Palazzo Gallio, thus alludes to the three parishes:—

Ptolemous Gallius Cardinalis comensis Trium Ploebium Gravedonae, Surici, Dungi, Comes et Dominus, Aeris, temperiem Loci amoenitatem sequutus oppidum nobile Gravedonam amplissimis oedibus, hortis, fontibus exornavit et nobilius reddidit.

Cardinal Ptolemy Gallio of Como, Count and Lord of the Three Parishes of Gravedona, Serico, and Dongo, aided by the mildness of the climate and charm of the place, adorned the noble town of Gravedona with buildings, gardens, and fountains, and made it still more noble than before.

The Pievesi espoused the cause of Milan in its ten years' war with Como in the twelfth century, though during the truce between those two cities they aided Como in wreaking her vengeance upon the allies of the Milanese in the vicinity of the Lake. But this alliance was a mere parenthesis, and we find them entering with great zest into the final sack and ruin of Como. Their relations with the Emperor Frederick Barbarossa show a similar fickleness of character. His partisans upon his first descent into Italy, they changed sides before the battle of Legnano, where they were found in the ranks of the Lombard League. They revenged themselves for their exclusion from the treaty concluded by the Emperor at Venice, by plundering his convoys as they passed into Germany. These acts of defiance so embittered Barbarossa, that when the Peace of Constance, which recognised the independence of the Italian States, was concluded, in 1183 A.D., he is said to have exclaimed:[1] "Pardon to all but the perfidious people of Gravedona." In 1185 A.D., however, they were admitted to the same privileges as the rest of the Lombard cities.

In the middle of the next century the ill-omened name of the Holy Office of the Inquisition overshadows the Three Parishes. Peter of Verona became a Dominican friar at an early age. While cloistered at Como, he confided to a Brother, that he had been favoured with a vision of the three saints, Agnes, Cecilia, and Catherine. Thereupon the Brother, with what reason does not appear, charged him with admitting women into the monastery. It would seem, that the saintly ladies were properly impressed with their obligation to extricate their protégé from his difficulty, for miraculous interference was promptly exerted to dispel the scandal, and vindicate Peter. He at once developed into an enthusiastic champion of the Church. In Florence he distinguished himself by his zeal in establishing the Inquisition, and by the eloquence with which he stirred religious passion against the heretics of the day. Returning in triumph to Como as Inquisitor-General under Pope Honorius III., he used his power with pitiless energy. The sects of the Poor Men of Lyons, the Believers of Milan, the Brethren, the Band of Love, the Followers of Purity, gave him ample scope. Their blameless lives were no set-off against tenets which menaced the Holy See. They held the dangerous belief, that Christ had not left to S. Peter and his successors the vicariate claimed for them. Added to this was the damning fact, that these heretics were patronised by the Ghibelline faction, which

[1] Mur. Ant. A.D. 48.

was the sworn foe of the Pope. Peter's relentless hostility stretched to Gravedona, where he held an Inquisitorial Court, and burnt a number of persons for the crime of heresy, or for affording shelter to fugitive heretics. For nineteen years he scourged the country, until at length a plot was formed for his assassination, which was effected upon one of his journeys between Milan and Como, on the 28th of April 1252 A.D. This constitutes his claim to the title of Martyr, by which he is distinguished. He was canonised by Innocent IV. a year after his death. One of Titian's greatest pictures portrayed his murder, but it was burnt in the Chapel of the Rosary, at Venice, in 1867. In the Dominican Church of S. Eustorgio at Milan, where he had so often denounced the heretical sects, a splendid shrine, the masterpiece of Balduccio da Pisa, was raised over his body in 1339 A.D. The head of the Saint, gashed by the blow which killed him, is exhibited upon the altar of the Chapel, which contains his shrine.

After this period the Pievesi felt the yoke of many masters, the inevitable penalty of the disunion, which they had fostered. Dukes of Milan, Counts of Chiavenna, unscrupulous adventurers like Il Medeghino, Spanish Vicars, an Italian Cardinal and his heirs, the French, the Austrians, the Kings of Italy, have given them laws and taken their tribute. Perhaps they never had a better lord than Cardinal Gallio, who bought them from Philip II., in 1580 A.D.

But the glory of Gravedona is the small church of Sta. Maria del Tiglio, "S. Mary of the Linden Tree," a few minutes' walk to the South of the town, standing side by side with S. Vincenzo, on the margin of the Lake, against a lovely background of water and mountain. It is commonly called a Baptistery, but the large font in the centre is comparatively modern, and in the record of an Episcopal Visitation in 1593 it is called the Church of Sta. Maria del Telio. The theory of the Baptistery, however, is supported by the tradition, that the building was originally dedicated to S. John the Baptist, whose life is portrayed on the wall of the principal apse in frescoes, which may be assigned to the fifteenth century. In the earlier centuries of the Christian era one font sufficed for the whole town, and was placed in a building of adequate dignity, with provision for the immersion of grown-up people, who might be converted to Christianity from the heathenism around; and if this church was indeed the Baptistery of Gravedona, we have one before us unique in style, and not unworthy to rank with the splendid examples at Ravenna, Florence, and Pisa. Its foundation is popularly assigned to the piety of Queen Theodelinda, but the greatest uncertainty prevails as to the origin and history of the curious little church, and archæologists suggest widely different solutions of the problem, some referring the building to a remote antiquity, others assigning it to the tenth or eleventh century; others, again, explaining it upon the hypothesis of a gradual development from the seventh to the twelfth century.

An old French chronicler, Aimoinus, records a miracle, which was reported as having happened in the Church of S. John the Baptist at Gravedona, in the year 823 A.D.[1] He says that a picture of S. Mary with the Infant Jesus in her lap, and with the Magi in the act of presenting their gifts, painted in the apse of the same church, but almost ruined by reason of its great age, shone with such brightness for two days in succession, that to the beholders it seemed to surpass the beauty of a new picture in all its freshness. This brightness did not, however, illuminate the figures of the Magi, but only their offerings. The news of this portent, says the chronicler, caused great alarm to Louis the Pious of France, a weak man, more fitted for a cloister than a throne.

On the authority of Aimoinus and the French Chronicles, which corroborate the story, Sigonius,[2] Baronius,[3] and others recount it. These authorities are enumerated upon a wooden tablet in the Church of Sta. Maria del Tiglio, beneath the remains of a fresco, preserved under glass, and reputed to be the miraculous Madonna; but it is not in the apse, as the Chronicle states, but on the wall to the right of the High Altar, though it agrees with the description given of it in the passage cited above.

[1] *Gesta Franc.*, lib. ix. cap. 3.
[2] *Histor. de Regno Italico*, lib. iv. fol. 109.
[3] Tom. ix. p. 6.

If we could show this picture to be the original referred to by Aimoinus, we should have made a great step towards proving the church to have belonged to the sixth or seventh century, since in 823 A.D. the fresco was already faded, by reason of its great age. Such a picture would be preserved with the greatest care, and by continual repainting might be kept on the wall for many centuries. But even if an earlier church was replaced by the present building, which in some of its details seems to belong to the tenth or eleventh century, a picture so sacred would at least be copied with the utmost accuracy, supposing the art of transferring fresco was unknown.

On the wall to the right of the High Altar three layers of fresco have been laid bare, which experts assign to the ninth, eleventh, and seventeenth centuries respectively.

The church is rectangular, and built of the black marble of Olcio, inlaid on the outside with courses of the white marble of Musso. The North, South, and East sides have each a projecting apse; on the West side the symmetry is maintained by a square tower, supporting an octagonal campanile of elaborate and elegant design. The tower is evidently contemporaneous with the church, the octagon of later date. The small deep windows are beautifully moulded. Small cornice arches and stones set corner-wise enrich the exterior. In the lowest storey, on the West side of the tower, a rudely sculptured tiger or panther climbs one of the columns. It cannot be seen from the outside; only by going up the tower. Over the principal entrance some slabs of marble are inserted, sculptured with figures in low relief, after a fashion often seen in churches of the early Lombard period. We find a Centaur in pursuit of a wounded stag, a writhing snake, an arabesque, a Byzantine device, two breasts and a human head. If the present church is a successor of an earlier one, these figures may have formed the decoration of a primitive pulpit, such as we may see at Orta, and been built into the wall when the first edifice was demolished. Similarly, in the great Lombard church of S. Michele at Pavia, the curious sculptures which adorn its façade are believed to be fragments of decoration from an earlier church.

The Centaur[1] is supposed to stand for an embodiment of evil. In early times it is the power, that persecutes the Church, represented by a hare or a deer. When the days of persecution are past, it is chiselled over the portal of the church to warn the Christian worshipper, that life is a conflict with temptation, and that he must arm himself with the shield of faith to quench the fiery darts of the wicked one. Giotto, in his roof-painting of Obedience at Assisi, makes the Centaur the emblem of self-will. Dante, who makes every sin its own punishment, uses it in the *Inferno*[2] to represent deeds of violence. In the Cathedral of Siena Hercules and the Centaur are placed side by side with David and the Lion. In an allegorical picture in the Louvre, Mantegna employs Centaurs and Satyrs to portray various vices.

What the other figures may mean it is difficult to conjecture. Is the head an allusion to the martyrdom of S. John the Baptist?

The church has two doors—one in the middle of the tower, and a second on the south side. A third on the same side has been walled up. Inside there is a lofty open roof of wood. A high gallery, approached by stair turrets in the wall on each side of the tower, runs round the building, with arcades, each of seven arches, on the North and South sides. The lower columns have capitals, decorated with simple acanthus leaves or birds, supporting imposts, also moulded in front, and giving the appearance of double capitals, as we see them at Ravenna and Venice. The capitals in the columns of the arcades are plain, except in two instances.

The general effect of the interior is of height and space far out of proportion to the actual size of the building, which, exclusive of the apses, is only about forty feet long and thirty-five feet wide. This is probably due to the broken character produced by numerous recesses, galleries, and arcades. The Eastern side is curiously divided into five semicircular recesses. The chancel and all the apsidal alcoves are roofed by semi-domes. The triple apsing of the

[1] Piper, *Mythologie des Christlichen Kunst.*
[2] *Inf.* xii. 45.

chancel is a peculiar feature, found also in S. Fedele at Como, the Benedictine Church in Val Perlana, and the Crypts of S. Carpoforo at Camerlata and the Parish Church of Lenno.

On the left wall and the reverse of the façade are various saints with allegorical figures, representing the principal Christian virtues and their opposed vices, *e.g.* Patience and Avarice, beneath which are written respectively:—

"Grande patientia hio portava per fa che l'arma (l'anima) sia salvada."

"Great patience I exercised to save my soul."

"Per l'avarixia che a abiuda l'anima mia or son perduda."

"By the avarice which destroyed my soul I am now lost."

Higher above the door is a Last Judgment, with the Redeemer enthroned in the midst, and a quotation from S. Matthew, beginning, "I was hungry and ye gave me meat." These are all of the same period as the frescoes of S. John in the apse. To an earlier date belong the Virgin and Child, and SS. Bernard and Christopher near the basin of holy water. Some remains are visible of a fresco of S. Calocero of Civate, known to have been there in 1018 A.D. On the left of the High Altar is a great Byzantine Crucifix, carved out of one piece of wood, and said to have been brought from Spain. Its great antiquity is proved by the robe, which drapes the figure of Christ from waist to knees. Of late years some barbarian has covered it with a coat of white paint.

The Church of S. Vincenzo, or Vincent, adjacent to the Baptistery, is sometimes described as a Basilica; but whatever may have been its earlier form, at the present time it wants at least one important feature of the normal Basilican Church. We shall, however, meet so often with the term in our Italian travels, that it may be worth while to pause here and briefly review the probable origin and sense of the expression, about which, as about all antiquities, the widest discrepancies of judgment divide the critics.

To begin with the name, which means literally "Royal," it may have been descriptive of the comparative magnificence and splendour of the kind of building to which it was applied. But it is more likely that it was borrowed from the Court (στοὰ βασίλειος) of the Archon Basileus (Ἄρχων βασίλευς), or King Archon at Athens, one of the chief magistrates of that city, whose duty it was to hear the indictments for religious offences, and before whom, it will be remembered,[1] Socrates was impeached for Atheism and corruption, and Euthyphron proposed to prosecute his own father on the charge of murdering a slave. The suggestion gains strength from the fact, that Cato the Censor,[2] a Roman who affected Greek taste and style, was the first to build in 184 B.C. a Basilica—the Basilica Portia, in Rome.

The term was primarily applied to a building with colonnades and flat roof, which enclosed a portion of a Forum, and was used as an Exchange, a Law Court, and generally as a sheltered place of assembly for all who found any cause to congregate. We also find it employed to describe the large halls in private mansions, warehouses, and riding-schools, as well as Herod's triple colonnades on the South of the Temple at Jerusalem.

One distinctive architectural trait characterised all these various buildings, and brought them within the range of the name Basilica, and that was the elevation of the central hall above the side avenues, which were divided from it by colonnades.

The form of the normal Basilica is only known, and that imperfectly, by the descriptions of ancient writers, and the ground plans unearthed in Rome, Pompeii, and elsewhere. It consisted broadly of an oblong chamber, divided by rows of colonnades into a central space, and two or more side aisles. Above the colonnades, which surrounded the entire hall, ends as well as sides, were galleries protected by balustrades, from which spectators might view the scene below. Above these galleries was the clerestory or wall, amply pierced for the admission of light. The flat roof would probably be decorated with the square *casettes* common in classical ceilings. The end of the chamber was sometimes rectangular, as at Pompeii, and in the Basilica Julia in the Roman Forum; sometimes apsidal, as in the Basilica Ulpia in the Forum of Trajan, though in this case, as we learn

[1] Plato's Euthyphron. [2] Plutarch's Lives.

from the Capitoline plan, the apse was practically cut off from the main building by a triple colonnade. The apse, therefore, *was no essential part of the Classical basilica*, since in some instances it had no existence, and in others was isolated by the intervention of columns. It might, however, when present, furnish a convenient Court for the Prætor, who, supported by assessors, occupied an elevated platform called Tribunal, a name suggestive of the time when the judicial office was in the hands of the Tribunes. That the apse was put to this use in the Basilica Portia we conjecture from Plutarch,[1] who relates how the Tribune of the people wished to remove a column, which interfered with access to the Tribunal. This might well refer to the colonnade, which cut off the apse from the main body of the hall.

We thus see how the distinctive features of the Basilica seem to have been *its division into nave and aisles* and the *admission of light from a clerestory* or free wall above the colonnades and galleries. Nor should we forget, that this identical type of construction is found in the colossal hall at Karnak, in the Nile valley, a coincidence which links our Christian churches, as far as they owe anything to the classical Basilica, with the dim antiquity of ancient Egypt.

Here, then, the parallel ends between the Pagan Basilica and the Christian Church; yet it is commonly assumed that, since the Christian Church borrowed the name of Basilica, it was also a copy of the basilican model in every detail. But *the apse*, which was not essential to the classical Basilica, *was of the very essence of the Christian Church* in the fourth century. At an early period it was the alcove of the chapel erected over the martyr's tomb in the Christian cemetery. This touching use of the apsidal form no doubt consecrated it to Christian sentiment, as an architectural feature of the Church. Men of fervent imagination forgot that in turn it was copied from the Pagan *cellae* or memorial chapels of the dead, just as the feasts at Christian tombs were the continuity of birthday commemorations in these same Pagan mortuary chapels.

And not only so, but when the old custom of going

[1] Cato Minor, 5.

out to worship at the chapels built over martyrs' remains in extra-mural graveyards changed, those remains were brought to the churches within the city walls, and buried beneath the altar in the apse, in an excavated chamber communicating with the church, and known as the *Confessio*, because it contained the relics of those, who had sealed by blood a confession of the Christian Faith.

In the modern Roman Church Mass may not be celebrated upon an altar, which is not hallowed by the relics of a Saint, and this rule is but a memorial of those early times, when a catacomb was the church, the tomb of a martyr the altar, and the words of S. John lived fresh in mind: "I saw beneath the altar the souls of those, who were slain for the Word of God and for the testimony which they gave."

Considerably before the fourth century, when the term Basilica first began to be used of the Christian meeting-place, the *Scholae* or guild-rooms of religious brotherhoods in the Pagan world, oblong in form and apsidal in termination, furnished a suitable pattern for the Christian Church. There, like the elders in the Jewish synagogue, which was certainly apsidal sometimes, the presidents of the Guild sat round the semicircle of the apse, with the small altar for libations or incense in front. If the *Schola* formed the model for early Christian meeting-halls, and there are Christian mosaics and Pagan ground-plans extant which strengthen the supposition, then these seats would be taken by the clergy, the Bishop sitting in the centre, and the Christian Lord's Table would be substituted for the Pagan altar.

At any rate, it is clear, that we must look elsewhere than to the Classical Basilica for the apse, so essential a feature in the Christian Church, and we find it in the Jewish synagogue, the Pagan *Schola* or guild-room, the memorial *cella* or chapel in ancient cemeteries.

The *Atrium*, or open court, enclosed by colonnades, through which the Christian Basilica was entered, and which we find in S. Vincenzo at Gravedona, and conspicuously in S. Ambrogio at Milan, is often considered to be a repetition of the forum, from which the Pagan Basilica was approached. More probably it is a reminiscence of the peristyle or court of the private house, such as we see at Pompeii, through which the large hall was entered, where we know, that Christian meetings were often held.

The fountain in the centre of this court, placed under a *cantharus* or canopy, and used for washing before entering the assembly, survives in the use of holy water at the doors of the church.

The separation of the sexes in public worship is sometimes traced to the hypothetical Roman plan of assigning different parts of the Basilica to male and female litigants. But as early as the time of underground meetings in the cemeteries or catacombs this division had to be provided for, since, as S. Chrysostom pointed out, some purity of heart was soon lost, and it was found needful to place barriers in the churches to keep the sexes apart. The galleries, such as we see in Sta. Agnese at Rome and in the little Basilica of S. Giulio at Orta, are supposed to have been used for the convenience and isolation of women, under the name of *Matroneum*. It is possible, that we retain a trace of them in the Triforium of our Northern Cathedrals.

But the reproduction of the galleries of the Pagan Basilica was by no means universal in the Christian Basilica, a fact which seems to favour the hypothesis that the Christian Basilica was the *Schola* enlarged rather than the Pagan Basilica simplified. When the galleries were omitted in the Christian Basilica, large bare wall spaces were left above the colonnades, which were relieved by glowing mosaics, such as we find in S. Appollinare Nuovo at Ravenna.

The *Narthex* or Vestibule at the entrance is probably of Byzantine origin, and may have formed the limit beyond which Catechumens and Penitents might not pass. The Narthex often served as the only representative of the Atrium.

As the Clergy developed into a caste, and Ceremonial, growing in importance with more prosperous times, demanded larger space for its display, changes arose in what we may call the furniture of the Christian Church, or the internal arrangements independent of structure. The raised daïs in front of the apse, on which stood the Table of Christ, and behind which the presbyters sat, was soon separated, under the name of *Bema* or Presbytery, from the rest of the building, for the sole use of the Clergy, by low pillars or rails, called *Cancelli*, which is the origin of our word chancel. Presently the Choir, a space enclosed by walls and gates, encroaching largely upon the area of the nave, was added to the Presbytery. Round three sides of the Choir the congregation of the Laity gathered to hear the Gospel and Epistle read from the *Ambones* or pulpits built into the enclosure, one on either side, and to join in the other Offices of the Church.[1]

In weighing this question of the relation of the Classical and Christian Basilicas we must not forget how heavily we have to discount the literary hearsay, which continually repeats the legend of the Donation of Constantine, or his supposed gift of Basilicas to the Christian Church by the Edict of Milan. That Edict was one of Toleration merely, not of Establishment, and it would indeed have been an event so unprecedented, that every Christian writer of the period must have noticed it as nothing short of portentous, had a lately tolerated and previously persecuted sect been forthwith installed in the finest buildings of the Empire, to the exclusion of all the commerce and business, which had been housed within their walls so long.

But further, an examination of the passages upon which this gift of Constantine relies, shows at once the need to verify quotations, and the absence of any solid ground whatever for this contention. Even in the most fulsome panegyrics of Constantine by Christian writers there is no mention of this donation of Basilicas to the Church, which would have been a deed without parallel, and would have afforded the amplest scope for praise and flattery. When Ausonius, for instance, in a high-flown letter of thanks to Gratian for the Consulship, says that the Basilica, "formerly full of business, is now full of vows undertaken for the Emperor's welfare"—a passage quoted to prove that Basilicas had by this time passed from uses of commerce to those of Christian worship—he links with it the palace, the forum, and the senate house in such a way that we must con-

[1] *Cf.* Fergusson's "History of Architecture."

clude all, or none, to have been converted into Christian churches.

Fausta, the wife of Constantine, gave a Basilica to the Christians, but it was the private hall attached to her own palace, which was once the sumptuous mansion of Lateranus, beheaded by Nero, who has thus given his name unwittingly to the Mother Church of Rome.

Another writer[1] is adduced to support the theory of the conversion of Pagan Basilicas to Christian uses, who speaks of "the Basilica of Sicininus, where there is a conventicle of Christian worship."

Socrates,[2] writing on the same point, describes that conventicle as "in an out-of-the-way corner of the Sicininian Basilica." A meeting of Christians in an out-of-the-way corner of a huge public building used for many purposes is as unlike as can be to a surrender of the entire Basilica to the Christian Church.

This brief sketch may best be closed by quoting a passage from that exhaustive and fascinating study, "From Schola to Cathedral."[3]

"The whole question of the origin of the Christian Church may be summed up as follows:—

"The Christians met first in private halls, and when they erected buildings for themselves, these took the form of unpretending lodge-rooms or *Scholae;* they also assembled on occasions in or before the *cellae* of the cemeteries. At the end of the third and in the fourth century larger buildings were needed, and side aisles were added to the simple halls, which were now lighted in the basilican fashion. Partly as a reminiscence of the *exedrae* of the cemeteries, but chiefly as a natural consequence of the uses to which these buildings were put, they received universally an imposing apsidal termination, which gave them a marked architectural character. Accordingly, there is produced from a union of all these elements the Church of the fourth century, with its forecourt and fountain, reminiscent of the private house; its oblong plan and tribunal, or seat for the presidents,

[1] Amm. Marcell. xxvii. 3.

[2] Hist. Eccles. iv. 29.

[3] G. Baldwin Brown, Esq., Professor of Fine Art in the University of Edinburgh.

Photo by G. E. Thompson

CRYPT OF S. VINCENZO, GRAVEDONA

derived from the primitive *schola;* its apse and *confessio*, recalling the memorial *cella* of the cemeteries; but in its size and grandeur, its interior colonnades, its roof and its system of lighting, a copy of the Pagan Basilica of the Roman cities."

The Basilica of S. Vincenzo probably dates back to the fifth century, though the crypt seems to be the only portion left of the original structure. The outer walls of the church show the features of the Lombard style, but the building has been practically rebuilt in recent times.

Two Christian inscriptions, of the years 502 A.D. and 508 A.D. respectively, are preserved in the church. They are as follows:—

"B. M.
Hic requiescat in pac . . . .
Famula Xri Agnela que . .
Xit in hoc seculo an pl. m
xxx Deposeta sub die iii Kal A
prilis Avieno vcc ind x."

"In blessed memory. Here rest in peace Agnela, a servant of Christ, who lived in this century more than thirty years, and was buried 30th March 502, in the vice-consulate of Avienus."

"B. M.
Hic requiescat in pac . . . .
Famula Xri Honoria qu . .
vixit in seculo an plm xx
Deposta sub die viii Kal iv . . .
As Venantio vcc ind. v."

"In blessed memory. Here rest in peace Honoria, a servant of Christ, who lived in this century more than twenty years, and was buried 24th June 508, in the vice-consulship of Venantius."

The Sacristy contains several very precious treasures. The principal one is a splendid processional cross of the fifteenth century, nearly two feet across the arms, by three feet in height from the top of the staff, bearing the inscription—

"Haec crux fabricata fuit per Franciscan de S. Gregorio de Gravedona."

"This cross was made by Francis of S. Gregory of Gravedona."

S. Gregorio is a hamlet of Gravedona.

The metal work of the cross is silver gilt; the extremities are of lapis lazuli. In the elaborate niches of an arcaded tabernacle, surrounding the lower part, are figures of SS. Christopher, Victor, Sebastian, George, Michael, and the Christ, Whose suffering form is in significant contrast to the robust vigour of the rest. At the foot of the crucifix above is S. Mary Magdalene, with her cruse of ointment. On either hand are S. John the Evangelist and the Virgin Mother. Above is S. Vincent, carrying in his hands the millstone, which plays so conspicuous a part in his legend. Surmounting the whole is a small effigy of S. John the Baptist, introduced as the Herald of these mysteries. On the reverse side is the glorified Christ in benediction, surrounded by the symbolic forms of the Four Evangelists, and medallions of the Doctors of the Western Church. Note the fine work of the golden hair of Christ.

Scarcely less beautiful is a chalice of the same century. Round the base are six medallions, in finest Limoges enamel, of the Crucifixion, the Madonna and Child, SS. Michael, Anthony of Padua, Vincent, and Martin. In niches above are three rows of small medallions of the same material, also inlaid with saintly figures, the topmost rank consisting entirely of virgins.

A silver Pax of the fourteenth century completes the list of precious objects. In the Mass the priest holds it by the wooden handle, and presents it to the worshippers with the words, *Pax Vobiscum*, "Peace be with you." It bears a figure of the Redeemer.

The legend of S. Vincent runs thus. At twenty years of age he was a deacon of the Christian Church at Saragossa. Falling upon the evil days of the reign of Diocletian, and having boldly defied the cruel pro-consul Dacian, he was subjected to tortures of the most ingenious refinement. When these proved ineffectual to shake the faith of the invincible youth, Dacian tried to subdue him by the insidious seductions of comfort and luxury; but the angels came and bore away his spirit from further trial. His furious persecutor then ordered his dead body to be thrown to the wild beasts; but a wonderful Providence frustrated his purpose by the championship of a raven, which mounted guard over the corpse. Still further enraged, the pro-consul commanded the body to be sewn up in an ox-hide, as in the case of parricides, and thrown into the sea, with a millstone fastened to it. His servants carried the corpse far out to sea, and threw it overboard, but when they arrived at shore again the martyr's body was lying there upon the sand. Horror-stricken, they fled, and then the waves dug a grave and buried him out of sight and knowledge, until after many years his burial-place was revealed to certain pious Christians. After strange vicissitudes, in which a flock of crows befriended the holy relics, the body of the martyr rests in the Cathedral of Lisbon. The hymn of Prudentius, a famous Latin composition of 403 A.D., tells the tale of S. Vincent with horrible minuteness. The millstone is the ordinary symbol of this martyr, but he is sometimes typified by the sign of a raven or crow, since at various crises in his history his remains were guarded by one or other of these birds. At Lisbon they have a special endowment for their maintenance.

Gravedona, like so many of the little towns on the Lake of Como, can boast at least one distinguished son. This is Giuseppe Maria Stampa, brother of the unfortunate prisoner of Fuentes, who aided Muratori in his literary researches, and is especially famous for his share in the publication of the anonymous epic upon the war between Como and Milan, first brought to light in the 5th Book of *Scriptores Rerum Italicarum*.

The Church of S. Giacomo, built upon a cool terrace, in a chestnut grove, at Peglio, an hour and a half above Gravedona, is reported to possess pictures by Luini. The climb is steep and hot, the views are far and dreamy and delicious, but there are no traces of Luini. The seventeenth-century paintings which the church contains will not repay the pain of reaching them. The most important is a Last Judgment by Gian Maria Fiamminghino.

Some of the women in these remote mountain hamlets still wear a unique costume. It consists of a brown monastic frock without sleeves, reaching to the calf of the leg, and girt round with a leathern strap fastened by a large silver buckle. A bodice with white or red sleeves is worn underneath, and a red petticoat appears below the dress. On gala days they add red stockings and white shoes, and trick themselves out with gay ribbons, red coral, gold or pearl necklets, and a great display of silver hair-pins. The costume of the Pievesi women is said to be due to a vow, made in the time of the great pestilence in 1450 A.D. The favour of Sta. Rosalia of Palermo was solicited, and the price to be paid was the assumption of the monastic dress. Those who follow this fashion are called *Moncucche* or *Mondonghe*, which is probably a corruption of *Monaca* or "nun." Visitors to the villages of San Germano, Garzeno, or Stazzona, will be sure to meet with some of these picturesque historical dresses. But the old costumes are fast dying out. The younger women deem them old-fashioned, and prefer a newer style, little thinking how much they lose by the change. An aged peasant at the Gravedona Fair was asked to sell her silver buckle. For some time no argument would move her, until at last it was pointed out that her daughter would never wear it, but sell it as quickly as she could, to buy some ephemeral finery. "So, *carissima*, you might as well have the spending of the money yourself in your lifetime." She saw the humour, as well as the practical force of the reasoning, and lost no time in turning her buckle into cash.

A rare surprise awaits those who have the enterprise to visit the little Church and Cloister of Piona. From Gravedona we make for the promontory of Piona, on the Eastern shore of the Lake, which holds one of the most interesting and beautiful treasures of ecclesiastical Art in the Diocese of Como, little known to any but antiquarians. We land at the foot of a sloping garden, at the other side of which rises the white tower of the Church of S. Nicholas, planted among the luxuriance of a scientifically cultured farm. Behind S. Nicholas is the ruined apse of the Oratory of Sta. Justina the Martyr, which was built here between 586 and 607 by Bishop Agrippinus of Como. Its one low, deep-set, clumsy window, with full-sized Gothic tufa arch, and the small arches beneath the eaves, two salient features of Lombard and pre-Lombard architecture, mark its antiquity.

Photo by T. W. M. Lund

CLOISTER AT PIONA

Recent restoration, intelligently carried out, has not only removed the overgrowths of centuries, but thrown light on the history of the Monastery. It would seem that the original Oratory fell into disuse and ruin, and in the eleventh century Benedictine monks of Cluny built the Priory, of which the Church of S. Nicholas and the Cloister alone remain. The discovery of the arms of Cluny carved to the W. of the first window, in the N. side of the Church, supports this conjecture. An inscription, disclosed during the restoration, tells that the Church was originally dedicated to S. Mary the Virgin, and later to S. Nicholas, Bishop of Mira, whose cult was awakened in Italy in the eleventh century by some merchants of Bari, who were bringing home his relics. The Church shows in its architecture every feature of the Lombard period. Two beautiful lions in white marble, now placed at the sides of the principal entrance, retain traces of the columns for which they formerly served as pedestals, on which rested a wooden cross. The lioness holds a calf between her paws, and resembles one in the Baptistery of Parma, from the chisel of the sculptor Benedetto Antelamo, in 1196. The Apse is decorated with frescoes of the Twelve Apostles, life size, which preserve the Byzantine stiffness, though the names of the Saints are written in pure Gothic lettering. On the roof, surrounded with the symbols of the Four Evangelists, and holding in His hand a book of the Gospels, is a heroic figure of the Redeemer. The legend on its page is also in fine Gothic characters. These frescoes are attributed to the fourteenth century.

At present the charm of Piona is its fourteenth-century Cloister. That it is of later date than the Church seems probable from the fact, that while it is built up against the S. wall, that wall is pierced with windows, and its eaves are decorated with small arches, an extravagance which would have been avoided had there been no use for these details. As we enter the Cloister by the door alongside the main entrance of the Church, its beauty of form and colour breaks upon the eye as a rare surprise. It is built in an irregular quadrangle, the sides having eight, ten, eleven, and twelve columns respectively. On two sides the arcades are of brick, marble, and granite, while on the other two they are of black, white, and rose-tinted marble. An old well in the centre, and a quaint, irregular, upper storey, add to its picturesqueness. From the variety and character of the marbles employed, together with the introduction of Roman brick, we should infer that the material for the structure was quarried by the monks from more ancient buildings in this locality. The capitals and cushions are singularly varied, and present a rich harvest of sculpture. Here we find heads human and grotesque; birds and serpents; foliage, flowers, fruits, shields, and stars. The approximation of this beautiful work to French Gothic has given rise to rival claims of origin. Is this Cloister the work of the great Guild of Comasque craftsmen, or is it due to French artists employed by the Cluniac Brothers? Another alternative suggests that the Cloister is due to the Magistri Comacini, but that they had become imbued with the style of French Gothic by contact with the Cluniac School, which had made its way into N. Italy, or, still more, by their own journeys into Germany, where French Gothic had already established itself.

As we approach the Cloister, on the wall opposite the ogival door the restoration has disclosed a fresco representing the Magdalen before the Redeemer, who carries in His hand a ribbon with the legend: "Lux et Vita sum. Noli me tangere," "Light and Life am I. Touch me not."

From Colico to Piona by boat takes three-quarters of an hour, but a boat from the Railway Station at Piona only takes a few minutes.

The little town of Corenno, grandly compared by G. B. Giovio,[1] with patriotic pride, to the Acropolis of Corinth, from which it probably derives its name, furnishes the artist with one of the most attractive studies of the Lake. It is particularly beautiful from Dervio, seen through a framework of grey olives, that are enriched with every kind of parasitic growth.

[1] *Lett. Lar.*, p. 23.

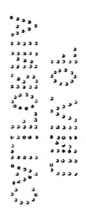

Photo by T. W. M. Lund

FROM THE CASTLE OF VEZIO

CHAPTER X

THE CAINALLO PASS

"Oh, I have passed a miserable night."—SHAKSPEARE.

A VERY typical expedition takes us up the Val Esino, over the Cainallo Pass, and into the Val Sassina. There is a path on both sides of the valley, but the Southern side is preferable, as being less fatiguing and enjoying the shade to a much later hour. We take the road which leads up to the Torre di Vezio, crowning the hill above Varenna, where the people love to believe that their heroine, Theodelinda, spent her latest days. The picturesque ruin of this reminiscent stronghold, in a garden of grapes and peaches, makes it worth while to pause for a few minutes under the shadow of its walls, but the real repayment for a slight digression from our path is found in the superb view gained from this coign of vantage. We quickly clear the handful of cottages, taking care not to cross to Perledo on the other side of the valley, and follow a rough and rapidly ascending track. The stream murmurs in a deep gorge far below; the sides of the narrow valley are richly clothed by forest. Here and there our way winds near the top of the ridge that divides us from the Lecco arm of the Lake, and a divergence of a few yards gives us magnificent views of far-stretching water and broken masses of mountain. As we rise, the range of peaks at the head of Como assumes its true proportions. It is dwarfed when seen from the level of the Lake. The higher we climb, the higher the summits seem to soar. It is a parable of Life. Great minds and souls are only appreciated as we approach the height at which they live. If we are down in a hole intellectually or morally, we cannot see how near to heaven some of our neigbours rise. True culture is the cure for all scorn of others.

The valley opens out in front of us. The white spire of Esino gleams on a wooded promontory in the midst. We pass the charcoal burners, a dell full of shield and holly ferns, a stony torrent bed, a picturesque water-mill, where the miller's wife serves us rich milk in wooden bowls, and then comes a tough little climb to the hamlet of Esino Inferiore, whose apologies for streets are dignified by such names as Via Bernardino Luini, Via Galileo Galilei. Tolerable walkers should reach this lower village in something over two hours. The Hotel Codeno, standing apart on an eminence, furnishes plain food, good wine, and clean beds for those who wish to make an early start for the ascent of Moncodine, otherwise known as the Grigna.

I once spent a night here. When I was shown to my sleeping-cell by the landlord I left several people below. Presently all took their departure, I heard the key turned in the door from the outside, footsteps and voices died away, and I realised that I was locked up for the night in solitary confinement. This caused me no regret or inconvenience, but the cream-jug and sugar-basin provided for my toilet did. A bath had been promised for the morning, but, though I heard my gaoler arrive early, no bath appeared. So I dressed and descended, when he expressed the deepest disappointment at seeing me, for with infinite pains he was just getting the water to boil! A hot bath at 5.30 A.M., the ground thick with frost, was a novel notion. But things are changed now, and in the season the Albergo offers *pension*, and sports a full-fledged waiter from Milan. It is a fitting spot to which to fly for tonic air from the close Lake below.

An hour of park-like country, studded with splendid chestnut and walnut trees, brings us to the top of the Cainallo Pass. For escort, *en route*, I once had the landlord of the inn and an intelligent Italian doctor, who were laying their plans for a day's shooting. They invited me to join them, and pointed out a glade where any ladies of my party might sit to witness the sport. "The hares will be driven," said the doctor, "and in that position the ladies will see every one of them tumble over." Our conversation led to inquiries about English sport, such as, for example, "When you hunt the fox, do you shoot him?" followed by "When you have killed the fox, do you eat him?" Politely subdued pity greeted my negative reply to the latter question.

An English gentleman, resident in Italy in an official capacity, once gave me an account of a day's sport got up in his honour. Fourteen gentlemen, in top-boots and green coats, with a pack of dogs of various breed, and a host of serving-men, set out, marching in an extended line, under strict orders from the chief of the party. For hours they advanced, without catching sight of the smallest bird, until at last they reached the top of a high hill, and were confronted by a precipice.

"To proceed is impossible," cried the rank and file. "Then, halt!" shouted the general in command. Just then the dogs, which had been sent round below, gave tongue, and up scrambled a very little hare, right in front of the line of guns. Every one screamed at the top of his voice, every one fired his piece, but no one hit the game, the sensation produced by its appearance being too profound. But the poor little hare was so terrified by the unwonted scene, that it lay still and let the dogs seize it. Then the Master of Ceremonies came forward, amid intense excitement, and, with much emotion, congratulated the Englishman upon having killed the quarry and being the hero of the day. Our countryman, however, entirely repudiated the flattering honour, which he generously accorded to the dogs. The fact was, he was a sly fellow, who knew the custom of the country, and that, had he accepted the compliment, he must have given a supper to the whole party. So they all marched back, carrying aloft the poor little worried hare, and then, amid the blowing of horns, enthusiastic cheers, and a popular demonstration, entered the town and closed the day by supping together, each at his own expense. Perhaps we English are singular in our ideas of sport and game. At any rate, it was here that I met with the American lad, who asked me, "Is there any game in these parts—squir'ls or anything?"

There is, however, ample work for the sportsman upon these wide uplands. He will find the pheasant, grouse, partridge, mountain-cock, quail, hare, marmot, badger, occasionally a wolf, and, still more rarely, a bear. Nearer to the Lake are the otter and a variety of water-birds. But one noble kind of game, the steinbock, can no longer be numbered in this list, though P. Giovio [1] tells us that, three hundred years ago, it was hunted among the mountains at the upper end of the Lake. If his account be reliable, it had methods of eluding pursuit, which added the charm of uncertainty to the chase, even when the prize seemed to be within the hunter's grasp. He describes it as an animal in colour and size like an ass, with long horns curving back upon its shoulders, serving by an admirable provision of nature to save its life, when pushed by the hunter to the edge of a precipice. For then, drawing its legs together and bending its neck down upon its chest, so that its horns form a buffer for its back, it rolls itself down the rocks like a ball, makes the perilous descent in perfect safety, and leaves its baffled pursuers to seek another quarry. The steinbock is still to be found in one of the lateral valleys of the Val d'Aosta, which was the special preserve of the late King Victor Emmanuel.

Our friend the Italian doctor, an advanced Socialist and Freethinker, unlike his compatriots, declined to smoke. His philosophy catalogued the habit among the chief causes of bodily decay. In return for pleasant company he made us a present of what he said was his best prescription, expressed in this neat couplet—

> "Bacco, Tabacco e Venere
> Riducon' uomo a cenere,"

which we may almost literally render—

> "Wine, tobacco and lust,
> Turn a man into dust."

But we are standing in the gap of the Cainallo, four thousand feet above the sea. To Westward, behind us, lie the soft overlapping outlines of many mountain ranges, with glimpses of blue water deep among them, and, towering over all, the five glistening peaks of Monte Rosa, flanked

[1] *Descr. Lar. Lac.*

Photo by G. E. Thompson

NEAR LIMONTA

by long barriers of eternal snow and ice. To Eastward, in front of us, are the grey pinnacles, buttresses, and awful precipices of Moncodine, almost within a stone's throw; and then, four thousand feet above, rises its jagged dolomite ridge. Of all the mountains in the neighbourhood of Como, the Grigna, or Moncodine, best repays the ascent. It can be approached either from Varenna, on the Lake of Como; Mandello, on the Lake of Lecco; or Ballabio, in the Val Sassina. On this last route the Edelweiss, Stellina delle Alpi, is still found in quantity, its habitat not having yet been despoiled by wanton visitors. The Italian Alpine Club has erected a hut at the summit, capable of housing about a score of people, with a resident attendant during the climbing season, while with lavish generosity it has provided shelters on the route from Varenna in the Capanna Monza, and on the route from Mandello in the Capanna di Releggio, at about six thousand feet above sea-level, for those who have failed to reach the top in daylight. The hut is indispensable, as the ascent occupies eight hours. The view on a clear day in October, the best month for long vision, extends from the Ortler Spitz to Mont Blanc. Upon Monte Croce, one of the spurs of Moncodine or the Grigna, is a curious fissure, into which the snow drifts and solidifies throughout the winter, and from which a plentiful supply of ice is cut during the summer, and carried down upon a man's back thrice a week for use upon the Lake of Como. On the opposite side of the Val Sassina, into which we are looking, looms the mountain called the Tre Signori. It gets its name, not from any fancied resemblance of its three peaks to Italian gentlemen, but from the fact that the confines of the three States of Venice, Milan, and the Grisons anciently met upon its flanks.

We plunge down the very steep and rough path, which descends in an hour to the Val Sassina. Through this valley a good road has for centuries connected Lecco and Bellano. We take our way to the left, through Corte Nuova, an obscure village. My wife and I once arrived here in the late evening, and sought a lodging at the little Albergo. We were led into a vast, dark and cheerless room, scantily furnished, with a dirty brick floor, and a huge door, like that of a church, leading into the street, outside of which a little crowd gathered to peep at the foreigners through the wide chinks. No food was to be had, except sour bread, black coffee, and very thin wine. At bed-time we were conducted to a room upstairs, the fac-simile of the one below for size, dinginess, and discomfort. But what was our dismay, upon advancing with a rushlight, to find the bed occupied by what seemed to be a very stout tenant. When we appealed to our hostess for an explanation of this seeming outrage, she assured us, with conciliatory gestures, that it was "only the priest." The poor woman, seeing a brewing storm of indignation plainly betokened in our manner, hastened to turn down the bed-clothes, when the priest proved to be nothing but a species of warming-pan, which is sometimes called "the monk." It is a wooden frame, in which is placed the *scaldino* or pot of charcoal embers for airing the bed. This arrangement serves the double purpose of keeping the clothes off the glowing coals, and making room for the warm air to circulate and do its work.

But our trials were not at an end. The constant chiming of a double church clock, the arrival of a lumbering vehicle, which seemed to take hours to discharge its cargo, and the strident voices of a streetful of men and women, were a successful antidote to sleep. We had forgotten to acquaint ourselves with the name of the village before going to bed, and there was a weird sense of desolation in passing this wakeful night in a nameless place. At 3 A.M. the air became more restful, and was full of hope. But the promise was rudely dashed by a sprightly cobbler, who thought it never too early to mend, and hammered and sang, and sang and hammered, just across the way beneath our window, until the reiterated refrain burnt into one's brain and became a refined torture of ingenious cruelty. When the bells clanged for early Mass, we hailed their sound as a sign of salvation, arose, dressed, and fled upon our way.

In an enchanting walk of three hours Bellano is reached. Manzoni gives a harrowing description of the march of foreign armies, century after century, through this portal of Italy. Like locusts, they devoured all before them, leaving the rich country a lean wilderness. Neither life, nor honour, nor property was respected. Their filthy habits left pestilence in their wake, and their foul persons carried it with them where they went. Sigismondo Boldoni, historian and poet, born at Bellano in 1597, recounts the advent of a German army to his native town in 1629, coming by boat from Colico to enter Italy through the Val Sassina. The people fled, carrying off all their portable goods. The troops, dirty and fetid, proved an army of thieves, and swept everything valuable before them. An outbreak of pestilence followed their arrival, and a year later poor Boldoni[1] himself fell a victim, having caught the infection through wearing a coat sent home by a plague-stricken tailor. If Bayard, the cavalier "without fear and without reproach," was unable to restrain his troops from lust and rapine when they entered Como in 1505, what must have been the suffering when less scrupulous men were in command of invading and irresponsible armies? There are ferruginous waters at Tartavalle, near Taceno, in the Val Sassina, where there are several hotels. An automobile service connects Taceno with Lecco.

At Bellano the stream that drains the Val Sassina enters the Lake by one of those deep, narrow, gloomy chasms in the rock which the Italians call an *orrido*, but it is spoilt by the water-pipes, that convey a portion of the stream to the cotton factory below, which employs about two thousand hands. The word *orrido* is derived from the Latin *horridus*, and means, literally, a place to make one shudder, to try one's nerves, to set one's hair standing on end. So, Ovid writes:—

> *Si premerem ventosas horridus Alpes,*
> *Were shuddering I to step the wind-swept Alps;*

and Virgil, *Horresco referens*, "I shudder to tell it." A short time ago you were sure of a pure article, if you bought a silk dress near the Lake of Como. Now the raw material is in such demand for France, that it is exported in large quantities; and to supply the deficiency, cotton is being woven with the Italian silk in the Comasque factories.

[1] G. B. Giovio, *Lett. Lar.*

A few yards from the quay is a little piazza, at one end of which rises the pretty campanile of the Church of S. John, and at the other the handsome façade of the Parish Church of S. George. It was built in 1348, and is particularly interesting as the work of three members of the Guild of Magistri Comacini, to whom reference has already been made—Giovanni da Campione, Antonio da Castellazzo, and Cornelio da Osteno. The upper courses of masonry are of white and red marble, the lower of black and white. There is a fine rose window of dark green and purple majolica. S. George stands in benediction above the door. But perhaps the most interesting feature is the relic of a dead feud in the arms of the Torriani and Visconti, which are carved on the right and left sides of the façade respectively. The former consists of a tower (*torre*), encircled by a laurel wreath, and on each side the letters NA.TR.; the latter, of the well-known serpent swallowing a man, accompanied by the letters I.O.

P. Giovio[1] ascribes the construction of the capacious port to Azzone Visconti, born 1302, died 1339, and the building of this church to his uncle, Giovanni Visconti, Archbishop and Lord of Milan, born 1290, died 1354. The church was built in 1348, so that the letters IO stand for Iohannes, the Latin of Giovanni, or John, Visconti.

There is more difficulty in accounting for the other letters NA.TR., which are almost certainly the initials of Napoleon Turrianus, Napoleone della Torre. But he died in 1278, many years before this church was built. It is conjectured, that this marble was a victorious trophy of Napoleone's successful campaign in the Valtelline, and was built into this façade under the rule of the Visconti, side by side with their own arms, as a double emblem, first, of their authority in the Valtelline, derived through their predecessors, the Torriani, and then of their triumph over the Torriani themselves. The Visconti originally had their name from the rank of Viscount, or deputy, conferred by the Archbishops of Milan, when they held the sovereignty of the province. Their arms are attributed to Ottone, who is said to have killed a giant in the first crusade, upon whose

[1] *Descr. Lar. Lac.*

shield was a dragon, with a child or man in its mouth. Tasso has immortalised Ottone and his deed in two lines of his great poem—

> "O'l forte Otton, che conquistò lo scudo,
> In cui da l'angue esce il fanciullo ignudo."[1]

> "Or the brave Otto, who won the shield,
> On which from the snake issues the naked child."

In accordance with the use of the times the arms of his vanquished foe became his own, and were afterwards adopted by his family, the city of Milan, and Lombardy. When the Visconti supplanted the Torriani, it was said that the snake (*biscia*) had made its nest in the tower (*torre*). The Torriani claim relationship with the kings of France, in whose escutcheon the red tower alludes to their traditional descent from the heroes of Troy.

Inside the church are two *ambones*, and in a chapel several pictures of no merit.

In the Church of S. John are scenes from the Passion, in terra-cotta.

On the quay is a statue of Tommaso Grossi, the author of *Marco Visconti*, born here in 1790. The last time the writer saw it, a wasps' nest was built in a fold of his robe. Referring to Manzoni's tribute, inscribed on the pedestal—"Tenero e poderoso poeta, a chi ispiro il cuore"—he said to an Italian standing by, that it was a pity the author could not hear the praise. "At any rate," was the smart reply, "he cannot feel the wasps' stings." This seemed a consolatory criticism of life and death.

Above the town is a pretty Cemetery with a charming outlook upon belfries, roofs, Lake, and mountains. Leaving it on the left, we can make a beautiful excursion, of about one and a half hours, high above the Lake to Regoledo, about 1300 feet above sea-level. Formerly a Milk Cure, this establishment is now admirably equipped with all modern electrical therapeutic appliances, which, in conjunction with an excellent supply of water, furnish the means of treatment for every variety of nervous affection. The

[1] *Gerusalemme Liberata*, canto i. st. 55.

Hotel is large and commodious, commanding superb views, and planted in the vicinity of romantic scenery. It can also be reached by a carriage road, and by a very steep funicular railway from the level of the Lake. Steamers during the summer stop at Riva di Gittana Station several times a day, and trains at Regoledo.

Regoledo is mainly frequented by the Milanese.

There is a motor-car service from Varenna Station and Varenna Pier to Regoledo, and this may possibly supersede the train-stop at Regoledo.

Photo by G. E. Thompson

ARCADE AT VARENNA

CHAPTER XI

PIAN DI TIVANO AND VAL ASSINA

"There is a deep melancholy in the highest order of beauty, and a holiness."—T. ERSKINE.

THE early steamer lands us at Nesso, an ideal village on the Eastern shore of the Lake. The water of a deep ravine behind it forces its way into the Lake through a narrow gate of rock, taking its final step in a plunging cascade. The houses, with warm brown roof-tiles and cool walls coloured white, or azure, or lemon, hang over the sides of the chasm and cling to each projecting ledge. From the narrow landing step the village street rises at once in a steep zigzag, across a slanting bridge, under a vaulted passage, past the garden of an *osteria*, until it sets us on the wide arch that spans the Orrido di Nesso, where we can peer into the gloom of the abyss, or command a soft vision of sunny water and rich-toned hill. Here we have ample choice of routes: northwards we may follow the coast line to Lezzeno, or southwards to Torno, to find lavish luxuriance of beauty flung around on every side.

The walk to Lezzeno is one of the most charming on the shores of Como, and is specially attractive to sketchers. The hamlets of Lezzeno are set so deep under the wooded shoulder of S. Primo, rising steep and high behind them, that they never feel the sun during the winter months. This misfortune is recorded in a proverb, which says—

> "Lezzeno dalla mala fortuna
> D'inverno senza sole, d'estate senza luna."

"Ill-starred Lezzeno has neither sun in winter nor moon in summer."

Perhaps the melancholy climate of Lezzeno was in part responsible for the notoriety, which it gained in the fifteenth and sixteenth centuries as a hotbed of witchcraft.

At this time the whole province of Como, in common with the rest of Italy, was seized by an infatuation, which the Inquisition fostered, to hunt down and break up the witches' ring, which was supposed to exist for purposes hostile to humanity.[1] The indictments against them included the infliction upon men, vegetation and animals, of the direst diseases, outwitting the skill of the cleverest physicians; the inspiration of hatred and love; the blight of marriage; conversation with Diana and Herodias; and the power of changing themselves and others into inhuman shapes.

They were reputed to ride to their trysts on the devil's shoulders, and then to renounce the faith, baptism and the Blessed Virgin; to trample on the cross, swear loyalty to the powers of evil and join in obscene revelries; in return for which they received fruits, powders, ointments, counterfeit coins, rings, and other charms, with which to work their enchantments. Among these, not the least convenient was the power of converting a piece of wood into a horse, ass, or goat, as occasion required.

Confessions of these absurdities were wrung from the suspected by tortures, hideous beyond human fancy. Sometimes the victim was raised from the floor by a rope, and then shaken so violently that the shoulder-blade was dislocated; or mounted upon a red-hot horse of bronze; or the most sensitive parts of the body were roasted at a slow fire; or bits of resinous wood were fixed under the nails and then lighted. Is it wonderful that all sorts of wild admissions were made to escape these horrors? Some were brave enough to endure, and then before execution they were stripped of their clothes, their bodies were shaved, and purgatives administered to dispel the sorcery lurking in the skin and bowels. Confession only meant more agonies, for then their hands were cut off, their bones broken, their shattered limbs interlaced for hours in the spokes of a wheel.

[1] Fra Bernardo Rateguo, De Strigiis, Inquisitor at Como, 1505 A.D.

At last they were burnt, often[1] penitently commending their souls and bodies to God, uttering the most holy name of Jesus amid the crackling of the faggots, in response to the fervent ejaculations of the vast crowd of pitiful spectators, and as a pledge of safety, wearing the rosary round their necks.

The depositions are still before us, the very questions asked and answers given, with details of the torture employed and the punishment inflicted. Year after year the average number of cases tried was a thousand; the Inquisitor had ten or more assistants always at work, and in 1416 and 1514 A.D. three hundred persons were actually executed. The people rejoiced when the fires were many, "for," said they, "things will go better when the witches are burnt." Locarno, Lugano, the Valtelline, every village in the province, seems to have given its victims to the horrible holocaust. In many places the witch-houses are still shown, and in Lezzeno among others. Its sacrifice to the popular superstition was quite out of proportion to its size and number, and one quits the melancholy strand of this isolated Commune with a sense of oppression at the heart for the follies and sufferings of humanity. But we feel no repining for the "good old times," and the *Laudator temporis acti* finds an antidote in the thoughts awakened about Lezzeno.[2]

The thin wine of the district at one time acquired a great reputation for usefulness in cases of gout and kindred complaints (*aestuosis visceribus calidisque podagris*), through the patronage of Ludovico Sforza, Duke of Milan, who drank it by the advice of his physicians, and found it very beneficial. P. Giovio,[3] however, preferred it when mixed with a moiety of the wine of Griante or Varenna, and one almost hears the smack of his epicurean lips as he dwells upon the delicate bouquet and brilliant colour of this favourite blend (*quae delicatas vires spirant, et nitido caesio colore salienti in poculis sitientibus arrident*).

Our way from Nesso lies upwards through vineyards at

[1] Letter of Oltrecchi to San Carlo.
[2] *Cf.* "Life of S. Carlo," by J. P. Guissano, vol. ii. pp. 193–202.
[3] *Descr. Lar. Lac.*

first, then into the shady forest, alive with the songs and laughter of families gathering in the countless wealth of walnut or chestnut trees. The men beat the branches, the children gather up the nuts, the patient women bear them home in huge panniers on their back, the baby croons in the cradle, guarded by the dog.

At Zelbio we are not yet clear of the shady woods. But the *Pteris cretica* no longer follows us, filling the niches in the limestone with its tall sheaves. The path begins to be fringed with the waving spikes of the great blue gentian. The scent of the sweet cyclamen rises among rock and boskage. Then we emerge upon the surprise of a wide meadow, set in an amphitheatre of soft green hills. We hear the drowsy chime of the cow-bells from the pasturing herd. Shaggy men tend the wilful kine, and as there are no fences the herdsmen's hands are full. This restful pasture is the Pian di Tivano, about three thousand feet above the sea. Here and there a sparse copse, gorgeous in crimson and gold, relieves the sweet monotony. The cone of Monte S. Primo towers on our left.

Old chroniclers [1] assert, that on this Pian di Tivano, Andefleda, wife of the great Theodoric, King of the Ostro-goths, and sovereign conqueror of the West, built for herself a summer residence. What authority there may be for this supposition, beyond some vague tradition, it is hard to find. A more serene seclusion into which to withdraw for repose from the anxiety of government and the turmoil of a court could not be imagined. The conjecture derives an air of likelihood from the certainty, that Theodoric took a warm interest in Como. Not only is he credited with frequent sojourns upon the shores of its Lake, but we have an extant letter of his secretary, Cassiodorus, the last writer who did justice to the Latin tongue, from which it appears that an antique bronze statue having been stolen from the city of Como, the Emperor promised to the culprit a munificent reward and pardon for his crime if he restored the work of art; but threatened him with death should he fail to confess his guilt and then be discovered by other information.

When the meadows are crossed, an obvious path leads up

[1] Cantù's *Storia di Coma*, vol. i. 76.

to a dip in the Eastern wall of the amphitheatre. But before reaching the Col we pause to see Monte Rosa once again, half hidden by the peaks and precipices of Monte Generoso. Then advancing, we turn a sharp corner of cropping rock, and the glory of the Brianza, or tongue of land, which lies between the Como and Lecco arms of the Lake, lies at our feet. It is the Val Assina, sunny, smiling, and luxuriant in its setting of bare, grey, craggy peaks, stretching down from Asso to Erba, out and away into the breadth of the Lombard plain. The Lambro makes this valley rich and busy, turning the wheels of the silk mills in its deep and rapid channel. These mills are built down in the narrow cleft of the gorge, which the river has eaten out for itself. Nothing of them is visible except their brown roofs glinting in the sunshine. We see the girls coming out from their work at midday, out into pure air and sunlight upon green sward and under spreading trees, giving vent to their bright spirits in song and frolic. As they seize one another's hands and spin in the whirling dance to a merry roundelay, it seems that Fra Angelico must have watched the youths and maidens play such gambols before he painted them among the joys of Paradise. It was a profound soul that set those childish pleasures there. In his Last Judgment, in the Academy at Florence, the Paradise is a flowery garden full of souls, that have reverted for their pleasure to the innocent romps and sports of childhood. As I stood before it one day a country clergyman and his wife came up. "No. 41," said he, and then read solemnly from his catalogue, "Last Judgment, by Fra Angelico da Fiesole." "Nonsense," interposed the lady; "why, they are dancing in a ring, just as our children play 'Here we go round the mulberry bush' at the school feast. That's no Last Judgment."

As we watch those silk winders and weavers dancing in their mulberry groves, we cannot but sadly think of the "hands" in the northern towns of "Merrie England," dwelling in wildernesses of brick and dirt and ugliness, breathing a poisonous air under a sky from which the smoke blots out the sun; where for green fields stretch unsightly wastes of verdureless brown, and trees are but dwarfed and leafless skeletons; where the face of Nature never smiles into those wan and sickly faces, and healthy play rarely cheers their toiling lives.

From the Col the descent is rapid to Asso, through which one road goes southward to Canzo and Erba and the Lombard plain; another, eastward to Onno on the Lecco arm of the Lake, a very beautiful route; and a third, northwards, up the Val Assina to Civenna and Bellagio. Bellagio being our goal, we take a *sentiere* or path, on the left, at the bottom of the zigzag, to Barni and Magreglio, without touching Asso, and so gaining both in time and scenery. As the path is unlikely to be found without inquiry, a hint about the dialect of the Brianza may be opportune. There is a tendency to abbreviate words by dropping the last syllable, so that should you ask the way to Magreglio, Onno, Bellagio, you may be met by a hopeless shake of the head and the fatal words, *So ming* ("I don't know"). Ask for "Magregl," "Bellagg," "Onn," and you will receive a courteous explanation. Indeed, people will not hesitate to go half a mile out of their own way to set you securely on yours. The following comparison between the shape of the Lake of Como and the body of a man, written in the dialect of the district, illustrates the need for judicious excision of terminal syllables :—

"El noster Lagh' e come on omm
G'ha on pee a Lech e l'olter a Comm,
El coo a Domas," &c.

"Our Lake is like a man who has one foot at Lecco, the other at Como, his head at Domaso," &c.

The footpath lies along the slopes of the valley, high among terraces and gardens and meadows and woods, until the highroad is struck. We pass by women washing at a fountain, in water that gushes out of a rocky grotto, green with the luxuriance of the *Capilli di Venere*, or maidenhair fern. Others again, wrinkled, and shrivelled, and lean, and yellow, are busy with distaff and spindle, and appear to be the very counterparts of Michel Angelo's famous picture of the Fates.

In these country rambles the lower forms of life afford a special interest. We catch sight of the large green lizard, the most royal of his numerous race in Italy. Nearly a foot in length, and clad in a coat of mail, that shines with all the lustre of emerald and gold, he is so timid, alert, and agile, that a good view is rarely possible. A great contrast to the life and grace of this little animal is found in another acquaintance that we make. Our attention is attracted by a newt-like creature, about seven inches long, fat and flabby, slow in movement, and handsomely marked with yellow and black, looking out from a hole in a loosely built wall on the roadside. It proves to be the common salamander. It grips the stone convulsively with its fore-feet, and stretching its head forward to the utmost limit of safety, peers down into the path below with an intelligent eagerness and pain in its bright eye, which no one can mistake. Directed by its conduct, we look in the grass at the foot of the wall, and find that its mate, which has fallen from the hole, is severely hurt, and cannot get upstairs again to the house door. Upon being restored to its companion, it is received with touching solicitude.

A small specimen of the praying mantis affords us much amusement. A thin insect, about three inches long, and of irregular bulk, it resembles a very little woman in a light green gown. In fact, it is like nothing so much as the wives of Noah and his sons, which we knew in the arks of our childhood. It gets its name from the devotional attitude, which it assumes when interfered with. Raising itself on end, it crosses its arms upon its breast, looks appealingly into its persecutor's face, and waits for the mercy which it seems to ask. An artist friend, who had carried a mantis home for the amusement of his family, was so conscience-stricken by the almost human pathos in its eye and gestures, that the next day he retraced his steps three miles before breakfast to restore his captive to the spot from which he had taken it. Naturalists try to rob us of this pleasant shred of sentiment by showing, that the attitude of prayer assumed by the mantis is really one of defiance and assault, and that it is a creature of violent temper and quarrelsome habits.

Dark nooks and crannies, especially in old wood and under rocks and stones, are frequently haunted by tenants, which it is undesirable for naked hands to encounter. These are scorpions, which resemble a very juvenile crayfish, and though small, are sufficiently venomous to inflict serious inconvenience. The first that I ever saw was in a large hotel; it jumped out of my towel as I was about to use it, and took refuge under the bed. Upon my ringing the bell and pointing out the intruder, which was an unusually large specimen, the entire staff of servants assembled, armed with sticks, brushes, dust-pans and brooms, with which they strategically attacked and destroyed the hapless interloper. During the onslaught the assailants loudly vociferated, that the animal was a scorpion, that they had never seen such a thing before, that it would ruin the house, and that it must have come in my luggage. Experience has taught, that a large amount of luggage would be necessary to furnish a tithe of the scorpions, which haunt snug corners in old floors and roofs and walls.

Now and then a beautiful snake glides rapidly across our path, though more often it lies crushed upon it. These reptiles are not only for the most part harmless, but, like the little birds, invaluable in keeping down minute insect life, destructive of the fruits of the earth. But the rustics indiscriminately beat them to death when they meet them. They have forgotten that the serpent was once their ancestors' symbol of wisdom and health. Gay butterflies float around us, and the ground is alive with grasshoppers, green, and red, and golden. Beetles and flies in rich costumes march hither and thither, or whirl past with a dreamy thrum. Large ants hurry upon their errands. The hot air is full of the shrill vibrations of a million insect wings.

The only carriage available in these primitive valleys is a *Legno*, or wooden cart, drawn by a pair of grey oxen, plodding dreamily along the road. This the driver politely places at our disposal, and in spite of the want of springs, the slow pace of the cattle, and the swing imparted to the vehicle by their clumsy action, we are grateful for this help over a couple of miles of the hot road. There is a classical character in the experience, and when a hasty garland of wayside flowers is woven and flung about the necks of the oxen, there seems little in outward form to divide us from the days of Horace and Catullus.

The richness of the lower part of the Val Assina is exchanged soon after Magreglio for a calm and grassy vale, restful to both eye and spirit. The purling Lambro meanders through it. A copse of golden larches, or a knoll of dark pines, breaks the monotone of green. Then, after a rapid rise, followed by a descent in zigzags, with a short cut for pedestrians, our road becomes a broad ledge, from which we look down over the billowy chestnut foliage of the mountain side into the Lake of Lecco, stretching out two thousand feet below us. Nowhere else can we gaze so directly into the rugged face of the colossal Grigna as here. The twin campaniles of Civenna loom against the sky. An ever-changing panorama of splendour accompanies our advance along a green terrace, enamelled by a wealth of autumnal flowers and shaded by glorious trees. At one time the whole length of the upper arm of Como comes in sight; at another the Tremezzina, crowned by Crocione, reveals its bays and villas. Now the entire scene is hidden from sight, and again it bursts upon the eye in new blends of form and colour. Civenna is an easy journey of two hours, on foot, from Bellagio; but few, save the peasants of the locality, ever see the beauties which it guards.

To cross the Lake at the close of such a day's experience is a fitting sequel to its glories. The stars hang lustrous in the sky, and answering stars burn in the mirror of the Lake. And as our boat pushes its way through their thick-sown ranks, and hustles them with its ripples, they grow into broad suns of glory, that illuminate the night with their splendour.

It should not be forgotten, that there is a fine carriage road from Bellagio to Como by Civenna and the Val Assina, and the magnificent drive of five or six hours is strongly recommended to all who are wanting in pedestrian energy. Those interested in archæology should inquire at Civenna for *La Pietra della Luna*, a stone which will claim a little attention in the next chapter, in connection with others of a kindred sort.

For those whose energies do not rise to the walk over the Pian di Tivano from Nesso, a good alternative is the drive from Lecco to Bellagio, which includes the magnificent piece of road from Barni, already described, and adds to it the pretty scenery along the chain of little Lakes between Lecco and Canzo, the lower part of the Lambro Valley, and in particular, the exceedingly picturesque pilgrimage Church at Lasnigo. A carriage and pair costs about 40 francs, and by making a long day of the trip, S. Pietro di Civate can be visited *en route*, as the road passes close to the village of Civate.

Photo by T. W. M. Lund

PILGRIMAGE CHURCH AT LASNIGO

CHAPTER XII

VILLA PLINIANA AND TORNO

"A woman's soul, most soft, yet strong."

By far the most delightful approach to the Villa Pliniana, for good walkers, is made by the coast road from Nesso, though it is less fatiguing to be set down by the steamer at Palanzo, almost at the gates of the gloomy old palace.[1]

Close to the shore by Carate on the opposite side a grey pyramid can be descried, one hundred and twenty feet in height, bearing upon its front a medallion portrait, with the name inscribed underneath, in colossal letters, "Joseph Frank, 1851." This personage had such a shabby imagination and so poor a hope of immortality, that he left his fortune of about four thousand pounds for the erection of this memorial of himself.

There was a nobler philosophy of immortality in the advice which Pliny[2] gave to Rufus:—

"Leave mean and sordid cares to others, and devote yourself to culture in your profound and rich seclusion. Make this your business, your leisure, your work and rest, your thought in wakeful hours, and the motive of your dreams. Mould and forge something, which may be for ever your own. The rest of your property will pass from master to master, when you are gone; but this, when once it is yours, will be yours for ever."

In the following letter to Caninius, Pliny describes the natural scenery of the Lake in his day, and will touch a chord of sympathy in the hearts of those busy men whose

[1] It will save disappointment and some energy to remember, that the Villa can be entered only from the water side. The door in the rear of the grounds is closed.

[2] Epist. i 3.

very holiday is haunted by the tyranny of a successful career :—

"Do you study, or fish, or hunt, or all together? For all can be done together on our Como, since the Lake supplies fish, the forests which gird the Lake provide wild animals, and that profound seclusion in which you dwell is favourable to study. But whether you do all or any of these things I will not say I am envious. Yet it vexes me to be denied those pursuits, which I crave for as sick men crave for wine, or the bath, or the cool spring of water. But, if I may not untie these tight and irksome bonds, shall I never snap them? Never, I think. For to old business new is continually being added, before the arrears are wiped off. And so, entangling me and riveting, as it were, innumerable fetters upon my life, a daily increasing train of work arrays itself before my eyes."

The Villa Pliniana stands close to the shore, at the foot of a high cliff swept by a fine cascade. The gardens rise in cool, luxuriant terraces. Many cypresses and its sunless aspect give a touch of melancholy to the scene. The Villa gets its name from the intermittent spring, of which the younger Pliny [1] has left an account in a letter to Licinius Surra, descriptive of its phenomena, for which he suggests explanations quite as ingenious as some, which have been offered in later times :—

"I have brought you a little gift from my native place in the shape of a problem quite worthy of your profound knowledge. A spring rises in the mountain, runs down among the rocks, and is received in an artificial chamber where one can lunch. After a short stay there it falls into the Lake of Como. Its character is extraordinary. Three times a day it waxes and wanes with regular rise and fall. That is plain to be seen, and is very interesting to watch. You lie near to it and eat your food, while you drink from the spring itself, which is intensely cold. Meantime, it either ebbs or flows with sure and measured movements. Suppose you place a ring or anything else you like upon a dry spot. The water reaches, and at last covers it; again it slowly retires, and leaves the object dry. If you watch longer,

[1] Epist. v. 7.

you may see this double process repeated a second and a third time.

"Can it be that some subtle wind alternately opens and shuts the mouth and jaws of the spring, as it rushes in or is driven out again? For that is a phenomenon, which we see happening in the case of bottles and the like, in which the vessel is neither wide nor voided in a moment. Articles of that kind, even when turned upside down, discharge their contents with what we may describe as a volley of gulps, owing to some resistance of the air.

"Or is the nature of the ocean the nature of this spring as well? On the same principle, that the former ebbs and flows, does this modest stream experience its alternate tides?

"Or, as rivers which run into the sea are hurled back by counter winds and incoming tides, so is there something, which checks the flow of this spring?

"Or, in subterranean arteries is there some reservoir, whose periods of filling and emptying affect the activity and volume of this stream?

"Or is there some sort of mysterious law of compensation, which gives a fillip to the spring when it is low, and throttles it when it is full?

"Investigate, for you can, the causes of so wonderful a phenomenon. For me it is enough to have given you an adequate account of it."

A deep-seated reservoir, fed by perennial springs and connected with the outer air by a syphon-like channel in the rock, would fulfil all the conditions requisite to account for such a well as this at the Villa Pliniana. Intermittent wells are found in the limestone districts of Derbyshire and Yorkshire, but in no case do they ebb and flow with such regularity as we see here.

The spring flows out of a cleft in a rock into the courtyard of the Villa, beneath which it falls into the Lake. The cave, into which it first issues, might well be Pliny's *coenatiuncula manu facta*, or artificial dining-room. The water is slightly magnesian, and is highly prized in the neighbourhood for its medicinal qualities. In the warm summer days many parties picnic here in a fashion after Pliny's own heart.

There is a tragic gloom about the Villa Pliniana, which befits its history. It was built in 1570 by Count Giovanni Anguissola. For a moment we must carry our thoughts to a distant part of Italy. Pope Paul III., with unblushing effrontery, had made his natural son, Pier Luigi Farnese, Duke of Parma and Piacenza. Ugly in person and morally deformed, the Duke had lived a life of nameless vice. He soon succeeded in drawing upon himself the bitter hatred of the nobility, and even contrived to throw Gonzaga, the Spanish Governor of Milan, into the ranks of his enemies. At length, Giralmo and Camillo Pallavicini, Agostino Landi, Gian Anguissola, and Gian Luigi Gonfaloniere, men of the highest rank in Piacenza, resolved to rid the world of the loathsome tyrant. A good omen was found, according to the superstition[1] of the day, in their initials forming the word PLAC, an abbreviation of the Latin *Placentia*, found on the Duke's coinage. Adriani and Gofellini both assert that Gonzaga was an accomplice, nor is Charles V. himself left above suspicion.

On the 10th of September 1547, the five conspirators and some thirty-seven confederates gained access to the citadel. Anguissola and two others entered the Duke's room, and at once despatched him with their poniards. His vicious habits rendered him incapable of resistance, and indeed he had long been unable to feed himself. Meantime the other conspirators had made themselves masters of the citadel and the Duke's armoury, and seized his family as hostages. When the populace, whom the Duke had pleased by his oppression of the nobility, made some show of resistance, Landi let down the corpse by a rope from the wall into the ditch below, so as to leave no doubt of the Duke's death. At the same time he shouted for Liberty and the Empire, and proclaimed the speedy advent of the troops of Gonzaga, a course which summarily allayed the popular ardour. Anguissola was made Governor of Como, in acknowledgment of his services to the Empire, and built for himself the Villa Pliniana, as we have said, in 1570 A.D.

[1] The superstition survives still. Such a coincidence would be quite enough to induce many an Italian to risk his entire savings in the public lottery.

But his conduct had raised up for him many political foes, especially on the part of France, whose sympathies went with the Papal nominee. Repeated plots were made for his assassination, and this, together with the unrest of his own conscience, robbed his life of that peace essential to happiness, which even the seclusion of his Villa failed to give. He is said to have died at last a victim of remorse and apprehension.

The Villa Pliniana is connected, in our own times, with the name of another revolutionary, described by one [1] of her own countrymen as "conspirator, wit, and heroine, whom Europe admired and Austria dreaded." Princess Cristina Trivulzio Belgiojoso, born at Milan in 1808, was a woman of remarkable beauty, powerful intellect, and high spirit; the darling of her family, and beloved by all who knew her. At the age of twenty-three, having taken refuge from an unhappy marriage in the distracting excitement of political life, she had so identified herself with principles and movements hostile to the existing régime, that she found it necessary to leave her country, took up her residence in Paris, and devoted herself to Liberal journalism. In 1846 she returned to Italy, where, in 1848, she enlisted, equipped and commanded a volunteer battalion, which shared the disasters of Charles Albert's campaign against Austria. She was sentenced to banishment, and her property was confiscated; but she nevertheless contrived to join the Garibaldians in their defence of Rome against the French in the following year.

In 1856 an act of amnesty on the part of Austria enabled her to return to Lombardy and to recover her property. In 1859 she advocated the cause of Italian Unity in all parts of the country, under the inspiration of Cavour.

Her travels and residence in the East, after the fall of Rome in 1849, enabled her to make some valuable contributions to literature in *Ermina*, *Récits Turco Asiatiques*, *Souvenir d'Exil*, and *L'Asie Mineure et la Syrie*, all published in Paris. After the peace of Villafranca she edited in Milan the journal *Italia*, where she also published *Osservazioni sullo stato attuale dell' Italia e sul suo avvenire.*

[1] A. Gallenga's "Italy Revisited."

She died in 1871, leaving behind her a name as brilliant and heroic as any in the annals of patriotism. She was probably the type upon which the author of "Lothair" modelled the best features of his heroine, Theodora. For further details we refer our readers to a Life called "A Revolutionary Princess," by J. H. Whitehouse.

Within the Villa there is little of interest except portraits of the unfortunate Giovanni Sforza and his beautiful young wife, Isabella of Arragon.

In the last century the property came into the possession of Scipione Visconti, and his is the crest of the child issuing from the serpent's mouth, which appears on the entrance steps. It is often pointed out as the canting emblem of Anguissola, but *Anguis Sola* would be represented by the "Serpent Alone."

Shelley in his "Letters from Italy," written in April 1818, has the following passage: "The finest scenery (on the Lake of Como) is that of the Villa Pliniana; so called from a fountain, which ebbs and flows every three hours, described by the younger Pliny, which is in the courtyard. This house, which was once a magnificent palace, and is now half in ruins, we are endeavouring to procure. It is built upon terraces *raised from* the bottom of the Lake, together with its garden, at the foot of a semicircular precipice, overshadowed by profound forests of chestnut. The scene from the colonnade is the most extraordinary, at once, and the most lovely, that eye ever beheld. On one side is the mountain, and immediately over you are clusters of cypress trees of an astonishing height, which seem to pierce the sky. Above you, from among the clouds, as it were, descends a waterfall of immense size, broken by the woody rocks into a thousand channels to the Lake. On the other side is seen the blue extent of the Lake and mountains, speckled with sails and spires. The apartments of the Pliniana are immensely large, but ill-furnished and antique. The terraces which overlook the Lake, and conduct under the shade of such immense laurel-trees as deserve the epithet of Pythian, are most delightful."

A short walk brings us to Torno, haunted by some dismal memories of the sixteenth century. Ludovico Sforza had called the French into Italy to aid his ambitious schemes. Francesco II., his son, was glad of the Spaniard's help to drive them out again. In 1521 the Marquis of Pescara besieged Como with an army of fourteen thousand men. The city speedily surrendered on favourable terms, but these perfidious sons of the most Catholic country in Christendom treated this Catholic town as their brothers in arms treated America. Lust, rapine, and atrocity were rampant for a day and a night. Convents were outraged and churches pillaged. In all her disasters Como suffered nothing so bad as the Spanish sack.

The French interest remained dominant over a considerable part of the Lake, and especially at Torno, a town of four thousand people, with thriving industries and commerce. The people of Como having complained to the Duke, that the French ascendency on the Lake was imperilling their supplies, he sent urgent orders to the Commandant to abandon his defensive attitude, and at all costs to make headway against the French. Accordingly, the capture of Torno was resolved upon; but the first attempt proved a failure, owing to the unexpected rising of the Tivano, the north wind, which usually blows until noon, and then gives place to the Breva from the south. This *contretemps* frustrated the co-operation of the naval and land forces, and the attack was vigorously repulsed. A second assault, however, ended in the capture of Torno, which was given over to pillage, sword, and fire. Even the church bells, plate, and votive offerings were carried off as spoil. The men, who were unable to escape by water were butchered. The people still cherish the memory of a young girl, who leaped from her chamber window into the Lake on that fearful day, preferring death to dishonour. The fugitives, bereft of home and livelihood, filled with despair, and burning for revenge, betook themselves to piracy, which they practised with unparalleled atrocity.

Torno, however, is distinguished by less ghastly associations. It ranks with Rome, Monza, Milan and Trèves in possessing one of the nails of the Cross. The story goes, that a German Bishop returning from the Holy Land in the time of the Crusades, with a leg-bone of one of the Innocents and a nail of the Cross, rested at Torno. But when he would have proceeded on his journey, he was prevented by the obstinate opposition of the elements, until, divining the purport of the sign, he deposited his treasures in the Church of S. John, where they remain to this day. This Church of S. John the Baptist is of the twelfth century, and has an elaborate doorway of marble sculptured with subjects from the life of its patron saint. Within, the points of interest are a basin for holy water near the South-West door, and several pieces of tapestry made at Torno in the time of its prosperity.

At the Church of Sta. Thekla, on the quay, there is a beautiful rose window, and in a Chapel to the left of the entrance a small fresco, dated 1402 A.D.

Ten minutes from the port, on the Como road, are the extensive and beautiful Gardens of the Villa Taverna, which, by the courtesy of the owner, are always open to visitors.

But the neighbourhood of Torno has special geological and archæological interests secluded among rare beauties of natural scenery. We will take the road to Mompiatto, which is simple enough to follow, when we have escaped from the entanglement of paths, which beset the first quarter of a mile. Then the way lies up through cool woods of chestnut and walnut, with feasts of blaeberries and blackberries, and wide beds of the vermilion-sheathed Cape gooseberry, and carpets of sweet cyclamen, and long spikes of the tall gentian. Here and there, hot glimpses of Torno far down at our feet, ablaze in the full sunlight, make our shade the cooler. An hour brings us to the high-perched Chapel of Mompiatto, attached to an inn, which is all that remains of the convent suppressed by S. Carlo, though the spot retains sanctity enough in the popular mind to make it the scene of a gay pilgrimage in the month of July. Five minutes higher up, in the midst of a bit of green pasture, is a great, erratic block of granite, balanced upon the apex of a conical piece of limestone, and only prevented from oscillating by the chestnut-tree which overshadows it. In appearance it resembles a gigantic mushroom, measuring fifteen feet in diameter and six feet in height. This phenomenon is locally known as *Pietra Pendola*, or "the Rocking

Photo by T. W. M. Lund

PREHISTORIC TOMB NEAR TORNO

Stone." A good deal of physical history is wrapped up in that voiceless block, and if it could speak it would set many questions at rest. It has indeed an eloquence of its own. It is a stranger in a strange land, for no granite is quarried within many miles of this spot. And yet it is not alone, for scattered among the hills between Como and Lecco are many similar blocks of vagrant stone. How did they travel here so far from home? Most likely they were borne from the Val Bregaglia or the Splügen upon a colossal glacier, until it was arrested by the relaxing hand of climatic change, and, as it wasted away in summer streams, dropped its burden on this mountain side. Signs are not wanting that a great moraine was once deposited along this shore of the Lake.

There are other blocks so characteristic as to be also distinguished by descriptive names.

Above Sorto, a hamlet of Blevio, is a huge monolith, called *Nariœla*, containing sixty cubic yards of granite. It is seven yards long, four wide, and two and a half high, and so curiously placed on the hillside, horizontally, touching the ground lightly at one end, and supported in the middle by a piece of limestone, that, from some points of view, it presents the appearance of a block hanging in the air.

Above Geno is *La Praja*, a dialectic corruption of *La Pietra*, an immense irregular block planted on a steep slope and jutting out at the end towards the Lake sixteen feet, so as to furnish a roof for a cottage, which has been built on the hillside beneath its shelter.

The *Pietra della Luna*, above Civenna, is perhaps the most remarkable of these blocks. A cube of four yards, it is perched on the edge of a precipice, and kept from rolling down by three supports of granite, one of which is so adroitly adapted to the larger block as to give the impression of having been placed there by the hand of man. Moreover, on one side may be traced the figure of an inverted half moon, which can scarcely be the result of accident. The Gauls, who occupied this country six centuries before the Christian era, worshipped shapeless blocks of stone, on which they offered sacrifices, and from which they drew their auguries. They also affected a moon-cult, which survived the ruder stone-worship, as is corroborated by the articles of bronze, pottery, and stone, made in the shape of a crescent moon, which have been found in the sepulchres of Cis-Alpine Gaul. This hint may prove valuable in estimating the era to which some other granite monuments belong, upon which human skill has been obviously expended, and to which we will now proceed.

From Mompiatto, a rough path, which a boy from the inn will show, leads down through beautiful woods, in a quarter of an hour, to Negrenza, the name given to a few farm buildings. It is best to ask to be conducted to the *Avelli*, or tombs. Descending to the edge of a deep gorge, with precipitous walls luxuriantly overgrown by creepers, we follow the road to the right, and then, crossing a bridge to the left, find an irregular mass of granite, embedded in the soil, in a patch of green grass, among thick wood, close to a stone shed. Part of the upper surface of this block has been hollowed out with straight sides and rounded ends to the length of about five feet seven inches, the width of two feet six inches, and the depth of one foot eight inches. This excavation is surrounded by a rim about three inches thick, which is cut square at the ends. The tomb, if such it be, has the peculiarity that, where the block of granite rises above the level of the rim, a channel has been made outside the rim deep enough to carry off the rain water and prevent it from penetrating into the excavated part.

A few yards further, among the trees, by the side of the footpath, is another block, of which the surface is almost level with the ground, and treated in precisely the same way, though the dimensions are rather smaller.

Two hundred yards further, in the direction of Molina, we find another block, six yards long, and rising to a height of two yards out of the ground. The excavation here is of the largest size, and is made upon the only level surface at the top, in the corner nearest to us, as we look down upon it from the rising ground above.

Three minutes more bring us to a gigantic piece of granite, measuring eight yards on its longest side, and three yards in height. It is perched on the edge of the hill, and touching the ground with only a small part of its base, has all the appearance of a *pietra pendente.* The excavation is distinguished by being quadrangular in shape, and having at one end a sort of stone cushion to raise the head of the corpse, as it would seem. It is also more roughly cut than the others, and has one side crooked.

Above Lemna is one, which has been partially destroyed in the construction of the road, and is singular in being shaped like an inverted funnel, wider at the bottom than the top.

At Palanzo there is one of which the rim does not follow the curve of the excavation at the two ends, but forms an almost perfect quadrilateral, leaving a triangular elevation at the four angles.

Somewhere on the road from Torno to Mompiatto is a triangular block, known as *Al Maas* (dialect for *Masso*), in which is a tomb with no special feature. Within living memory there was yet another, a few steps from the *Pietra Pendola* on Mompiatto.

Crossing the Lake, we find in the Val Intelvi, on the road which leads from Scaria to the Parish Church of S. Lazzaro, and a few steps from a building decorated with a fresco of Sta. Lucia, a granite block, nearly covered by the débris of a kiln and the road constructed above. An old resident states, that he saw it prior to the making of the kiln or the road, when it was as big as the church itself. In this stone there were three excavations parallel to one another; now but two remain, and these partly hidden by the wall that supports the road. Rather nearer to the church is another block, buried in the ground, but with an excavation exposed to view, which is better worked than the others, and without the usual rim. All have semicircular ends.

Thus it appears, that if in less than half a century several of these excavated blocks have been destroyed, we cannot tell how many may have perished in the course of centuries. More destruction is stayed by the intervention of the State, which stamps each stone with the letters P.P. (*Proprietà Provinciale*—the property of the Province), and saves them from being broken up for walls and hovels. One general plan governs all, though there are such slight variations as have been noticed. A block seems to have been chosen with a suitable surface, and in this a hollow is cut, large enough to hold a human body. It is rounded at the ends, and enclosed by a rim, which might serve to hold a lid or ward off the intrusion of water. In his *Storia Antica di Como*, Monti relates what leaves little doubt as to the original use of these granite excavations. He says, that on the road which leads from Torno to Molina there are still (this is more than sixty years ago) great blocks of granite, remains of still larger pieces broken up by powder or chisel for building purposes, and the old people of the country tell how these had large excavations or niches, covered with lids of the same material, and containing human bones. They are then rightly named *avelli*. But whose tombs were they? To what epoch must we refer them? They appear to be unique instances in the archæology of sepulture, these granite sarcophagi, scattered on the hillsides of Como, so that no comparison can be instituted.

We may exclude them from Roman, Greek, or Etruscan origin, since the methods of burial employed by those nationalities present no points of resemblance to these granite troughs. The early Christians, too, buried their dead in the vicinity of a church. Are they the sepulchres of those Celts who, under the name Orobii, are said to have been the earliest settlers on the Lake? But elsewhere the early Celtic peoples buried their dead in *tumuli*, and show no trace of the use of the chisel. Remembering, then, the religion of the Gauls, and the probable trace of it in the *Pietra della Luna*, may we not assign these tombs to them with some show of likelihood? It is true that Gallic tombs of a very different sort have been found in Val di Vico, Malgesso, and elsewhere, which show a singular approximation to Roman usages; but a primitive people would naturally adopt, in the course of centuries, the customs of the civilised nations near them, and these strange granite graves may belong to a period long anterior to the influences of Rome.

Whatever the solution of the difficult problem, the experience of a visit to the whole locality will prove a de-

Photo by G. E. Thompson

PEONIES AT HOTEL FLORENCE, BELLAGIO

lightful one. The road, which we left at the bridge when we diverged to Negrenza, leads upwards to an airy pass over into the Brianza. Following its descent, we return to Torno easily in half an hour, a fact worth remembering by those who prefer to visit the tombs alone, and omit the *Pietra Pendola* at Mompiatto.

This lower portion of the Lake of Como is very beautiful, resembling a majestic river, a mile in width, flowing between lofty banks several thousand feet in height, richly wooded, broken by deep ravines, gloriously coloured and fringed by gleaming villages. It must, however, be admitted that this is not the universal opinion. I once heard one of my fellow-countrymen observe, with an air of entire originality, as we sailed along, that this part of the Lake was "nothing but a deep ditch." Presently, in another quarter of the boat, the same remark fell from another Englishman, and not long after a third volunteered the same interesting criticism. It seemed as though a jury might be empanelled, who would give this verdict unanimously against the lower arm of Como, and one began to reflect upon what evidence they could make the award. I then saw that they all carried the same guide-book, and I took occasion to borrow one for a moment's reference. The source of their inspiration was no longer a mystery. Their guide-book said that this part of the Lake of Como was "nothing but a deep ditch," and what could they do but shut their eyes to the glories around them and say the same?

For some miles above Como the shores of the Lake gleam with villas and glow with flowers. The fortunate of all nations seem to have pitched their tents in this Eden. Many of the villas are inscribed with a woman's name, which is mostly that of the founder's wife, Teresa, Giuseppina, Stefania, Carlotta. Close to Cernobbio Cardinal Gallio built a Villa in 1568, after designs by Pellegrino Pellegrini, an architect of Val Solda. He bequeathed it to his nephew Tolomeo, Duke of Vito, who in his turn gave it to the Jesuits, who owned it till 1769. After many vicissitudes of possession by the families of Odescalchi, Marriani, and Calderara, it was bought in 1815 by Caroline, Princess of Wales, wife of the future George IV., and named by her

Villa d'Este. She enlarged and enriched it, and for several years held a brilliant Court here. To her munificence is due the carriage road along the shore of the Lake, in place of the dangerous path, which was a serious menace to travellers, as is recorded in a Latin inscription by the wayside. In 1803 Napoleon I. spent five days here as the guest of General Pino, who upholstered the walls of one of the rooms for the Emperor's use in panels of yellow satin with the familiar N and the eagles, as at Versailles. This, the only relic of the conqueror's visit, is now used as a Breakfast Room. The extensive grounds, varied and picturesque, command many charming views of the Lake. Among their glories is a huge sycamore, probably the finest in the North of Italy.

The Villa d'Este is now one of the most attractive Hotels on the Lake of Como, and undoubtedly challenges comparison with the best in point of comfort, interest, and convenience. The visitor may wander for hours through its Park, which comprises a beautiful combination of Nature and Art, without even passing its gates.

Between Torrigia and Careno the Lake contracts to its narrowest limits. Above Torrigia rises Monte Bisbino, to the height of 4500 feet, a three hours' ascent from Carate or Villa d'Este, with a fine view in clear weather, and a small inn near the top. High up on its flank may be descried the mouth of a cave, known by the name of *Buca del Orso.* It is so called from the bones of the cave bear, *Ursus speleus,* which were found here in 1841 by Dr. Casella, who explored it to the distance of about four hundred yards. This is one of several similar caves in the vicinity of the Lake. Of these, the *Buca del Caldaiuolo,* above Cadenabbia, is famous for the hitherto insurmountable difficulties which it offers to a thorough exploration. The most important is the *Buca del Piombo,* near Erba, a vast cavern, which has been traversed to a distance of six hundred yards. Three distinct lines of masonry near the entrance seem to indicate that at one time it was fortified, and probably used as a place of refuge.

CHAPTER XIII

VAL INTELVI AND MONTE GENEROSO

"Among the sanctities of Nature, amongst glens, and green glades, and waterfalls, and towering rocks, and autumnal colours, and fallen leaves, and flashing springs."—T. Erskine.

The ascent of Monte Generoso from Argegno, by the Val Intelvi, forms one of the crowning exploits of the Lake of Como. Argegno is a small place of picturesque decay, which, three hundred years ago, P. Giovio described as a noble town adorned with a fortress, and private houses that could boast their towers. The Val Intelvi, he says, was planted thick with hamlets, and was famous for its sports of hunting and hawking.

Val Intelvi is said to be a corruption of Val d'Intelletto, or the Valley of Intellect, a name given to it on account of the number of distinguished artists, which it has produced. Nor does it seem unworthy of the praise, when we find that it gave birth, in the thirteenth century, to Adamo d'Arogno, the builder of the Cathedral of Trent; in the fourteenth, to Lorenzo dei Spazzi, architect of the Cathedral of Como; in the seventeenth, to Ercole Ferata, who restored the Venus de Medici for Cosimo III.; together with quite a host of architects, sculptors, and painters of no mean skill. But there can be no doubt, that the vicinity of the Lake of Como has given to the world from early times a remarkable list of men of high intellectual and artistic power.

This seems to be no extravagant claim, when we can enumerate among the sons of the Lake the two Plinies; Cæcilius, the poet and friend of Catullus; C. Atilius Septicianus, the grammarian; Benedetto and Paolo Giovio, Sigismondo Boldoni, Tommaso Grossi, Anton Maria Stampa, Leone Leoni, Tolomeo Gallio, Alessandro Volta, and a host of others too numerous to name. An Italian writer,[1] about the middle of last century, describes the neighbourhood of the Lake of Como as a district second to none in Europe for the genius and industry of its people. No territory of the same size can boast so many colonists abroad, or so much wealth at home. Each shore, or valley, has long had its children in Spain, France, Portugal, or Sicily. He goes on to enumerate the many kinds of scientific apparatus manufactured here, and exported to all parts of the world. And then, glancing at the merchants in wine, silk, and cloth; the architects, the builders, the house decorators, and various artists, who spring in shoals from the shores of the Lake of Como, he carries us back to the days of the Magistri Comacini, by pointing out how these trades combine in Guilds, travel far and wide, enact their own laws, and come near to constituting distinct republics. "One knows," he concludes, "that every Lake is fruitful in industry, but there is no instance in which any other has produced the same kind in the same degree."

The spirit of liberty also seems to have been fostered here. Napoleon I. was hailed as an apostle of freedom, but upon the declaration of the Kingdom of Italy, as an appanage of the Empire, in 1805, admiration turned to hatred. Passerini, the patriotic parish priest of the village of Ramponio, preached a crusade against the tyrant, who had so bitterly duped Italian confidence. He was arrested and beheaded at Como in 1807. These aspirations for independence received another blow when, after the peace of 1814, Lombardy became an Austrian province. In 1848 the Val Intelvi offered its victims on the Altar of Freedom. An insurrection, headed by Hendria Brenta of Varenna, speedily collapsed before a body of Croats, commissioned to pacify the district. The ringleaders were taken and shot at Camerlata.

The Val Intelvi is very beautiful. For an hour and a half we have the advantage of the carriage road on the right side of the ravine, which leads through S. Fedele to the charming summer resort of Lanzo. But we cross the valley to the left before touching S. Fedele, and after passing through some low-growing beech-woods emerge into the rolling, windy

[1] L'Entusiasmo, 1769.

mountain meadows, which never leave us to the very summit. Facility of access is now given by means of a Filovia, or tramcar, driven by an electric wire, but not running on rails, from Argegno to S. Fedele. The steering round the sharp turns of the zigzags is interesting. The car resembles an old-fashioned market-cart, with a cradle top, covered with cloth. It is supposed to hold sixteen, but several more, to say nothing of dogs and trunks, may be added, and melting moments be the result. No more delightful excursion could be made than that by this route to the familiar Hotel Belvedere, which lies twenty minutes beyond the village of Lanzo and its big Hotel Paraviso. The situation of the Belvedere is unrivalled. From its terrace, 3000 feet above sea level, you look down 2000 feet of wooded mountain to the whole length of the Lake of Lugano, and far away to the West to a stupendous wall of peaks and glaciers, towering above many ranges of lower hills, and culminating in the superb mass of Monte Rosa. For those who need stimulating air and a maximum of sunshine, no finer health resort could be found in Lakeland. For pedestrians the best return route is to Osteno, and thence by boat to Porlezza and by rail to Menaggio. Osteno is remarkable for its fine *orrido* or gorge, which can be traversed in a punt, while in the Parish Church there is a Madonna and Child of great merit, the work of Andrea Bregno (1411–1506).

There is a funicular railway, which descends from Lanzo to Sta. Margherita in a few minutes, whence the steamer may be taken to Porlezza. Tickets by the funicular railway are issued to visitors on very easy terms.

Good walkers will make the top of Monte Generoso in two hours, after crossing the Val Intelvi. It is quite possible to pass it unnoticed. For some distance the track lies just under the highest ridge of Generoso. A grassy slope slants away to a deep green valley to the left. On the right a bank of turf runs steeply up, with nothing to suggest that it is the top of a mountain. Here, however, is the summit of Generoso, and upon it you stand in the presence of one of those rare scenes, which intoxicate the senses and transport the soul. The best part of a mile beneath us, and almost at our feet, lies the Lake of Lugano. Beyond it rise the fainter and fainter lines of many mountain ranges. Delicate gauze-like mists veil the valleys, or float up to rest in silver wreaths of cloud upon the peaks. Towering over all, and filling half the round of the horizon, rears the mighty Alpine chain. With all its base wrapped in a robe of imperial purple, it flings its countless crests into the blue heaven, like the defiant arms of the mythic Titans. From Monte Viso in the far West to the Ortler Spitz in the distant East, the mail of ice is ablaze in the noonday sun. But Queen of all sits Monte Rosa, crowned with her diadem of five-fold peaks, and clad in the spotless ermine of her awful snows.

Another vision meets us as we turn. It is the rich Lombard plain, so blent with sky that of horizon there is none. White cities, villages, and towers gleam in the midst of its dark verdure. Silver streaks mark the windings of historic rivers. The lakes of Varese and Maggiore are dwarfed to the measure of a span. Far away our field glass shows the fretted pile of the Cathedral of Milan, and the horses that prance upon the Arch of Peace. A thousand strange memories throng the brain. From the dim days of Bellovesus the Gaul, six centuries before Christ, to the patriotic struggles of Garibaldi in our time, that plain has been diligently watered with the blood of conflicting humanity. We picture the fierce torrent of the early Celtic invaders, sweeping all before it. We hear the tramp of the Roman legions as they advance to conquer or resist, under such leaders as Scipio, and Marcellus, and Marius. We catch the glint of the arms of Hannibal as he marches on with his eye steadily fixed on the Rome he was never to see. Then we conjure up the shock of battle between the champions of Orthodoxy and the Arian heretics; or the factions of Guelph or Ghibelline locked in the deadly embrace of fratricidal war; or the struggles for territory between the sovereigns of Milan and the hardy Swiss; or the locust hordes of French or Germans who came to eat up

"that redundant growth
Of vines, and maize, and bower and brake,
Which Nature, kind to sloth,
And scarce solicited by human toil,
Pours from the riches of the teeming soil." [1]

[1] Sir Henry Taylor.

One of the charms of Generoso is, that all the nearer hills in the landscape are so richly clothed with wood as to give a softness to the scene impossible at a similar height on the Northern side of the Alps.

During the summer it is crowded by the Lombards and Piedmontese. The spring is the most delightful time of year for a visit, as then the whole mountain is a garden of flowers. There are now several Hotels on the mountain, and a funicular railway down to Capolago. But the descent through meadows and woods is sufficiently attractive to make it worth while to go on foot to Mendrisio, where we strike the S. Gotthard Railway and take train for Como.

There are two kinds of temper in which we may visit such cities of antiquity and art. We may merely be animated by the vulgar ambition to be able to say that we have seen what is famous, and enjoy the importance which a novel experience confers upon us in the eyes of the less fortunate. One has sometimes met people who are in open rebellion against the self-imposed tyranny of sight-seeing. They are worn out and confused by the churches and galleries through which they have raced. Much that they have seen has been mute to them. Boredom has marked them for its own. Yet they dare not relax their senseless toil, lest they should miss one object of note, and find themselves on their return home pitied by some supercilious friend, who assures them that they have missed the one thing, which made their journey worth while. They are in danger of adopting the method of the Chicago citizen, with whom it once befell me to hold the following conversation at the table of a Venetian Pension :—

"What have you seen to-day?" I asked.

"Waal! we've seen a palace," was the reply.

"Which palace?" I inquired; "Venice boasts rather a long list."

"Oh! I don't know the name of it," said the Western citizen. Then addressing his wife—

"My dear, tell this gentleman which palace it was we saw to-day."

"Oh! I don't know!" exclaimed the wife. "Auntie, dew you remember name of palace we saw this forenoon?"

"Deed I don't," said Auntie, in turn referring the query to an equally oblivious child, who with characteristic precocity offered to bet her bottom dollar upon the impossibility of remembering the name in such an old curiosity shop as Venice, where everything was out of repair and one place looked exactly like another.

"Waal," said the imperturbable father, "it don't matter much; anyhow I guess we've checked it off."

But there are many earnest travellers, who appreciate their opportunities and long to make the most of them. They are keenly alive to the dignity of the occasion, and only desire to profit by the wealth of History and Art which surrounds them. To such one or two practical hints may be useful. There is a preparation which is indispensable. The mind needs some equipment to enable it to seize, retain, assimilate and enjoy what it beholds. We may, of course, admire the stately, beautiful and picturesque in building, or the noble and harmonious in painting, without any knowledge of the people who called them into being, or moved up and down among them. But streets and towers, palaces and churches, pictures and statuary, gain vastly in interest and meaning, when they breathe with the passions and aspirations, the energy and hope, the life and power of humanity, and become interpreters of the thoughts and feelings of the ages, which have given birth to our own. Then they cease to be dead matter. They live.

Our first care should be to ascertain to what places we are going, and then, in a regular course of study, to acquaint ourselves with their historic landmarks. Nor is it difficult, with our wealth of Libraries and Literature, to discover the chief points of artistic interest in each city, and learn beforehand what we may of the men who created them, and of the influences which made those men what they were.

It is a good rule not to try to see everything. In sightseeing the ancient paradox holds true, which asserts that "the half is more than the whole." People find themselves surrounded by a profusion of objects catalogued in the guidebook, churches by the ream, pictures by the acre. They have no principle of discrimination as to their relative value, and conscientiously setting to work to see them all, end in

Photo by G. E. Thompson

NEAR PESCALLO

weariness, disgust, and disappointment, and really see none. The best plan of all is to master some leading rules of Art, and cultivate our taste and judgment under the inspiration of such writings as those of Mr. Ruskin, which have no equal for quickening appreciation, purifying taste, giving seriousness to the study of Art, and inspiring a love of the highest and the best. To see the best should in any case be our aim, or, if we see the worse, it should be to learn by contrast the dignity and worth of what is better.

It will be found a valuable aid to write out for ourselves in a portable note-book, in the course of our preparatory reading, the most noteworthy features of the cities to which we go, together with descriptions, criticisms, and historical episodes—in a word, to compile our own guide-book. Only those who have tried this method know the enormous increase of interest, pleasure, and instruction which it affords. Too often laborious Bædeker is allowed to spare us any previous inquiry or pains. But Bædeker is only a dry inventory of the contents of cities. He is of the most use before we set out, as an index to the subjects which we ought to read up. A valuable book to carry with us is Hare's "Cities of Italy." "But it takes up too much room," objects a lady. Then leave a dress behind. No? Then probably it matters little whether you carry Hare or not; in fact, whether you see anything or nothing. Mr. Hare resembles a sagacious master of ceremonies, who takes care to introduce the right guests to one another at the right moment. So, when he has led us to a palace, or church, or picture, he retires quietly into the background, leaving us face to face with some great master, who can speak with authority upon the particular work of art or point of history. So, in his delightful pages we talk with Virgil and Dante, Catullus and Shelley, Ruskin and Goethe, Street and Freeman, Ferguson and Perkins, Kügler and Mrs. Jameson, Gibbon and Milman, Arnold and Alford, Taine and Dickens, Lord Lindsay and J. A. Symonds, Vasari and Lanzi, with a host of others, able and willing to shed floods of light upon the fields of our research. Mr. Hare's readers will judge how far the criticism of the American was just, who said, "He is a clever fellow, but he slops over sometimes." After all, the royal maxim for every traveller to take to heart is, that "the eye only sees what it brings with it the power of seeing." To get and cultivate that power should be the first thought and the last.

> "It is the soul that sees; the outward eyes
> Present the object, but the mind descries."

That couplet stands on the title-page of some compact little volumes almost unknown to English readers. They are styled "Poems of Places," edited by H. W. Longfellow, and published by J. R. Osgood & Co., Boston, U.S.A. Four are devoted to Italy, and contain all the best Anglo-Saxon poetry that has been prompted by that inspiring theme, together with many translations from Latin, Italian, German, and French authors.

I have met so many travellers with minds almost a blank, and so grateful for any hints as to what they might advantageously read, with the best economy of time, that I venture to suggest the following books, as forming a useful foundation, and to be found in almost every library: Sismondi's small "History of Italian Republics," translated into English, supplies a general idea of the vicissitudes of the country; J. A. Symonds' "History of the Renaissance in Italy" deals with a period of the utmost importance, in his vivid and fascinating style; C. C. Perkins' "Italian Sculptors" and "Tuscan Sculptors" are a mine of enlightenment, both from the artistic and historic points of view. A lucid account of "Italian Painting," by Poynter and Head, or Mrs. Jameson's "Memoirs of Italian Painters," or Burckhardt's "Cicerone," will spare us much humiliation and self-reproach in Churches and Galleries, assist us in selecting the Pictures upon which to spend our time and energy, and put us into that sympathy with the several Masters, which comes of some small knowledge of their life and environment, their School, their relation to their times, their motive, and their aims. Mrs. Jameson's "Sacred and Legendary Art" would also give point and distinctness to many figures in the bewildering crowd of Saints, which look out from endless canvases and frescoed walls. If the story of but a few of the more popular subjects were mastered, it would be found of the greatest service, and largely increase the intelligence of our interest. Among the indispensable ones may be named the Four Doctors of the Latin Church, SS. Jerome, Ambrose, Augustine, and Gregory; the four of the Greek Church, SS. Chrysostom, Basil, Athanasius, and Gregory Nazianzen; SS. Sebastian, Christopher, Roch, Benedict, Francis of Assisi, Dominic, Anthony, Laurence, Vincent, Nicholas, Bernard, Catharine of Alexandria, Barbara, Agnes, Cecilia, Margaret, Ursula, Agatha, Lucy. An acquaintance with the legends of Joachim and Anna, parents of the Virgin Mary, and the marriage of Joseph and Mary, would throw a flood of light upon many quaint and beautiful pictures.

It may not be out of place here to note two abbreviated inscriptions, which often form a puzzle to the uninitiated. One is seen over every Church door, and consists of the letters D. O. M. They stand for *Deo optimo maximo*, *To the best and chief of Gods*, the universal formulary of dedication. The title was transferred to the Christian Deity from the Roman Jupiter, who, as supreme in rank and power among the old Divinities, was called *Optimus Maximus*. The other, S. P. Q. R., is seen upon monuments of the ancient Roman period, upon modern Roman municipal property, and in pictures which represent events of the ancient Roman era, pre-eminently in the Crucifixion. The complete phrase would be: *Senatus Populusque Romanus*, *The Senate and people of Rome.*

Let those, who propose to visit Italy furnish themselves but with the slender equipment here indicated, and they will ensure to themselves an unimagined increase of pleasure, and deliverance from that sense of tyranny which is inevitable, when we feel compelled to review a large number of objects that challenge our ignorance at every point, and fail to arouse in us any real interest whatever.

CHAPTER XIV

COMO

"The uncounted ages which man has polluted with his tears."
—RUSKIN.

AT Como our eye is sure to be caught at once by the conical hill behind the city. It is the Monte Baradello. Its commanding situation has endowed it with a history. Gauls, Romans, and Lombards successively recognised its importance, and crowned it with a powerful fortress. To its strong walls and towers the champions of Como fled to rally their valour, when for a moment they wavered in the first day's shock of their conflict with Milan, which lasted from 1118 to 1127 A.D. The duration of that war for close upon ten years, the long roll of allies banded against the devoted city, and the courage with which she kept them at bay so long, have caused a comparison to be drawn between Como and Troy, and even inspired a second Homer to sing the story of her struggle and fall. To Muratori we owe the first publication of his poem of two thousand and thirty lines, beginning—

> "Bellum, quod gessit populus cum gente superba
> Olim Cumanus,"

in the fifth volume of *Scriptores Rerum Italicarum*, p. 401; but in his preface he confesses that his colleague, G. M. Stampa, was its second father (*alter parens*), since its rescue from oblivion was due to his research and patience. Stampa himself says that he first stumbled upon a fragment of the poem in the Archives of the College of S. Peter at Monforte, and afterwards met with an older and more perfect copy, which he deciphered and restored.

P. Giovio assigns the authorship to Marcus Cumanus,

and says that the MS. was in his time most jealously preserved in the Archives of Como. Cumanus, however, is but an adjective used by some authors, who confused Como with the ancient Cumæ, so that Marcus Cumanus means no more than Marcus of Como, and who he was we have no means of ascertaining. Some attribute the poem to one of the great House of Raimondi. Be this as it may, it is the source from which we derive, through Corio and Calchi, the history of the episode. Its unclassical Latinity finds compensation in a vigour and reality, which leave little doubt that the writer was an actor in the stirring scenes which he narrates.

This war is typical of the suicidal frenzy, which drove the Italian cities at each other's throats on the smallest provocation, wasting the energy which might have repelled every foreign invader, and raised them into a powerful people, had it been conserved and united, instead of being squandered in internecine conflicts. The recital of some of the incidents of this war, as transmitted to us by the anonymous poet, will serve to invest with new life and interest many of the places now familiar to us on the Lake. Early in the twelfth century Milan cast longing eyes upon Como. A slight incident gave ground for picking a quarrel to one so interested in finding it. The rival Popes, Gregory VIII. and Urban II., had each appointed his own nominee to the See of Como. Landulfo Carcano, a Milanese, was the choice of the former; but the people of Como sided with Urban and drove Landulfo from their city. He took refuge at the Castle of S. Giorgio, at Agno, on the Lake of Lugano, and began to intrigue for the recovery of his bishopric. But the people of Como surprised the Castle by night, and in the fray killed two distinguished Milanese gentlemen. Milan flew to arms, spurred on by its Archbishop, who ordered the churches to be shut and the Sacraments suspended until the Carroccio had left the city.

The Carroccio was a ponderous waggon drawn by four white oxen in red trappings. In the centre rose a crucifix supported upon a globe, while above towered a lofty mast, from which floated the banner of the Republic. An altar for Mass, a chest of medicines and bandages for the wounded, and a band of martial music, completed the furniture of this singular vehicle. Their Carroccio was to each Italian State what the Ark was in old times to the Hebrews. It went forth with their armies, as the visible symbol of their political life, and so became the object of their most patriotic devotion. The flower of the troops, under the name of the Company of Death, were entrusted with its defence. Its presence inspired enthusiasm and courage. Its loss meant defeat and disgrace. In those days of very simple warfare the Carroccio had further advantages. It showed men where the commander was, where the disabled could find succour, where fugitives could rally in safety, and, in fact, formed the very heart of the army, which every soldier felt he must defend to the last drop of his blood.

Many instances might be quoted of the importance attached to the Carroccio. Arrigo of Monza is one of the heroes of Italian history, and as such is commemorated by a tablet in the cloister of the Cathedral of his city. When, in 1237, Frederic II. defeated the Milanese at Corte Nuova, Arrigo, captain of the Company of Death, succeeded in saving the insignia of the Carroccio and carrying them safely to Milan. Frederic, on the other hand, sent the captured car to Rome, with the following boastful epigram, placed in 1727 over the Senatorial palace upon the Campidoglio. Under Pope Benedict XIV. it was relegated to the Palazzo dei Conservatori close by, where it can now be found upon the right-hand wall of the second flight of stairs.

"Caesaris Augusti, Federici, Roma, Secundi,
Dona tene, currum, perpes in urbe decus,
Hic Mediolani, captus de strage, triumphos
Caesaris ut referat, inclita praeda venit,
Hostis in opprobrium pendebit, in urbis honorem
Mictatur, hunc urbis mictere jussit amor."

"O Rome, as the gift of Cæsar Augustus, Frederic II., keep this car for an everlasting honour in your city; taken in the rout, it comes a glorious spoil, to tell of Cæsar's triumphs at Milan; to the enemy's disgrace it shall hang, for your city's honour it is sent, love of your city bids me send it."

Those who visit Siena will find the masts, thirty feet high and more, of the Florentine Carroccio, taken by the Siennese at Monte Aperto in 1260, reared against the central piers of the Cathedral, while over the altar in the transept, next the Baptistery, is the great wooden crucifix from the same car, which failed to avert disaster from the hapless Florentines. It is related, that when Frederic Barbarossa ordered the Carroccio of the Milanese to be broken up after his victory in 1162, their grief was such, that at the sight of it his rough Germans were melted to unwonted tears.

In 1117 the fratricidal war began between Como and Milan, lasting with short intervals of varying success for ten years. To the aid of the Milanese came contingents from cities as far South as Bologna, East as Ferrara, West as Genoa and Pisa. But what cut Como to the quick was the ready help rendered to her foes by the people of the Lake, who almost to a village joined the Milanese.

At one time close siege is laid to the devoted city. At another, a fierce sortie repels the invaders, who retire disheartened for a time. Then the elated victors seize the respite for dealing a blow at their traitorous neighbours, whom they compare with Judas, and many a savage story of revenge still clings round town and ruin. It was a war of reprisals. To-day the bands of Como sack and burn Bellano, or Corenno, or Varenna, or Nesso, or Isola. To-morrow the troops of Lecco surprise the Comasque garrison in the Castle of Grato, and hang the unhappy captives from the walls to revive the spirits of the good folk of Lecco, as they watch the ghastly token of victory from their open *loggie*.

Nor is there wanting life and stir by water as well as by land. Large fleets are built and manned. Como has galleys tricked out with great bravery of flags and ensigns. The ships bear such names as *Alberga*, *Cristina*, *Grifo*, *Lupo*, *Scorrobiessa*, *Barbota*, *Ratto*, *Ganzerra*, and *Schifo*. Some are built for speed, and armed with iron prows to ram the enemy's craft. Others are broad of beam, for carrying wooden towers and novel artillery. The Pievesi introduce the use of a sort of naval Carroccio. A large boat is manned with twelve rowers and twenty-four soldiers, and over all floats a white banner, emblazoned with three red crosses, the standard of the Three Parishes. A crucifix surmounts an altar, and this conspicuous galley forms the centre of action for the entire fleet.

We may estimate the value of a ship from the conduct of Como, when in exchange for one which had fallen into her enemy's hands, she paid no less a price than the Castle of Dervio, which had been betrayed to her by its commandant. On one occasion the island of Comacina is fiercely beleaguered by the ships of Como and the Pievesi. The men of Perledo see the peril of their allies from the Torre di Vezio. Their galleys speed to the rescue round Lavedo. "When Greek joins Greek, then comes the tug of war," but this time victory rests with Troy.

Then again a great armada comes sailing up from Lecco, and is met by the fleet of Como between Lierna and the Serbelloni point. For the moment the ships of Lecco fly, but with nightfall they reissue from the harbour of Mandello, bent upon a novel stratagem, the patent of a clever Pisan whom they have on board. A hail of fiery darts, rendered more terrible by the darkness, pours upon the fleet of Como, and paralyses it with panic. The *Lupo* is taken, the *Schifo* is fired and sunk. Victory declares for the device of the ingenious Pisan.

At last, in 1127, the unequal contest had left Como exhausted, but her sons had no thought of surrender. Feigning a night sortie on the side of the town farthest from the Lake, they embarked their non-combatant population and portable property upon a fleet of boats, and during the confusion of the enemy, all escaped to the almost impregnable position of the Borgo del Vico, the quarter now studded with rich villas and gay gardens. From this coign of vantage they were able to make tolerable terms with their enemies, which were, nevertheless, entirely ignored when they had evacuated Vico and returned to Como.

The city and its neighbourhood were handed over to sack and ruin. We are not, then, surprised to find Como, a few years later, the devoted ally of the Emperor Frederic Barbarossa, when he took in hand the difficult task of humbling Milan. If she was Ghibelline before, the prospect of sharing in the effacement of her Guelphic rival would put an edge of passion upon her political sympathy. In 1159 the Emperor, enraged by the insolent defiance of his authority on the part of Milan, besieged that city, and when it capitulated under stress of famine in 1162, he utterly destroyed it, tearing down the buildings with iron hooks, and leaving its churches alone standing, in solemn protest, among the ruins. But Milan, aided by the cities of the Lombard League, rose again, like a phœnix from its ashes. More than this, she actively promoted the building of Alessandria, which formed a direct challenge to the Emperor, both as menacing his Ghibelline city of Paira, and taking its name from his bitterest foe, Pope Alexander III.

At last, in 1176, the tension became too great, and Frederic resolved to make one supreme effort to crush the League and efface Milan. The fortress on Monte Baradello lodged both Emperor and Empress on the eve of the battle, which was to decide the fate of Italy. The Emperor, largely reinforced by Germans and Ghibellines, met the Milanese, who had to rely mainly upon themselves, at Legnano, between Milan and Sesto Calende. The Milanese had organised a body of nine hundred horse, which they named the Cohort of Death, while the defence of the Carroccio was entrusted to three hundred youths of the flower of Lombard chivalry, all pledged to die rather than yield. When the vast array of the Emperor came near, the Milanese fell upon their knees and called on Heaven to espouse the cause of freedom. Frederic took this act of piety for submission to his power, but was quickly undeceived. The Milanese fought with the courage of despair, and by nightfall the proud Emperor was hiding for his life among the heaps of slain. A report of his death reached the Empress in the Castle of Baradello, but in three days he appeared again before its gates, a despised fugitive, bereft of his ambitious hopes, and only eager for an honourable peace. We shall find the crucifix used upon the Carroccio at Legnano hanging over the tomb of Archbishop Aribert in the Cathedral of Milan. He was the inventor of the Carroccio in the previous century, and successfully took the field on many occasions. His patriotism recalls the share borne by our own Archbishop Thurstan in the battle of the Standard, 1138 A.D.

It may be noted here, that the Church of S. Simpliciano at Milan was built by the Milanese as a thank-offering for this victory. Three doves flew from the tomb of three Saints, Sisimius, Martyrius, and Alexander, and perched on the mast of the Carroccio until the battle ended. They were believed to be the embodied spirits of those Saints, and to have contributed to victory by their supernatural aid. So in new forms the old legends repeat themselves, and we are once more face to face with the tale of the twin Dioscuri, who in the battle of Lake Regillus, mounted on their white steeds, wrested victory for the Romans from the Latins, and then were seen no more.

A century rolled on, and the Castle of Baradello became the scene of a ghastly tragedy. The Torriani of Val Sassina won the gratitude of the Milanese by their aid against Frederic II., and especially by the sympathy shown to the fugitives after the rout of Corte Nuova in 1237. At length, in 1259, Martino della Torre was made Lord of the People in Milan, a title which was also conferred upon him by Como and other cities. In the person of Napoleone della Torre, this power reached such a pitch of despotism, that the sympathy of the Guelphic faction, which he represented, was alienated from the family. The Pope had made Ottone Visconti Archbishop of Milan, to act as a check upon the growing power of Martino, who at once drove the new prelate into exile. The Visconti was Ghibelline, and in the time of Napoleone conspired with his party, many of which were in exile like himself, and prepared to invade the Milanese territory. Napoleone, underrating his enemy, allowed himself to be surprised by night and captured at Desio in 1277. He was consigned to the tender mercies of the people of Como, who imprisoned him, with three sons, a brother, and a nephew, in three iron cages, in the Castle of Baradello. Keenly sensitive to the ignominy of his position, exposed to the insults of the mob, tortured by vermin, with nails and hair like those of a wild beast, and bereft of the hope, which is the last stay of the unfortunate, the miserable captive dashed out his brains against the bars of his cage, August 1278. The others either died in their loathsome prison, or escaped by administering a bribe to their gaolers.

The fortress was destroyed by Antoine di Leyve, general of Charles V., in accordance with that jealousy of any relic of Italian power, which marked the Spanish régime. The solitary tower, which remains within a strong keep, is but a fragment of the fortress of Barbarossa. The summit of the hill on which it stands can be reached easily in half an hour from the railway station at Camerlata, and well repays the exertion by a magnificent view. The tower is popularly believed to have been accessible only by an underground passage. But it was entered by a door in its Western wall, at a considerable height from the ground, by means of a wooden ladder and platform, as in the case of many similar buildings, especially in the Engadine. The supposed subterranean approach proves upon inspection to have been a cistern for storing supplies of water for the fortress.

Tradition points out the slopes of Monte Baradello as the scene of the martyrdom of SS. Carpoforus, Esantus, Cassius, Severinus, Secundus, and Licinius. Fedele, another of their band, escaped, but was overtaken and slain at Samolico. These were all soldiers of the Theban Legion, and are said to have suffered in the reign of Diocletian, by order of Maximian, in the third century. The spot on which they suffered is known as La Salvetta, and is marked by a Chapel. At the foot of the Baradello lies the Church of S. Carpoforo, now the Parish Church of Camerlata,[1] but once the Cathedral of Como, from which it is about a mile distant. In early times it was the custom to plant the Churches at some distance from the towns, partly, perhaps, to escape the noise of common life during the offices of religion, and partly to avoid annoyance from Pagan curiosity, since we must remember, that for some centuries of this era a large proportion of the populations clung to the old Faiths. The tradition of the foundation of this Church on the site of a temple of Mercury is supported by the discovery in its neighbourhood of five stones containing dedications to that Deity, and a subterranean Chapel, unearthed in 1568, at the entrance of which was found the mutilated inscription, ... URIO SACR . . , of which the complete form is probably *Mercurio*

[1] *Ca-merlata*, "the fortified house," probably derives its name from the palace of the Podestà on the slope of Monte Baradello.

Sacrum. A piece of marble, sculptured with work of the best Roman period, is built into the apse.

It has been contended, that the present Church is the one built by S. Felix towards the end of the fourth century. But that it belongs to a much later period is proved by the discovery of a fragment of a sepulchral monument of the year 457 A.D., built into one of the oldest portions of the Church. S. Felix died in 391 A.D., so that the nave and aisles, which are the oldest part of the Church, could not in any case have been built less than seventy years after his death. But Tatti, a chronicler of Como, states, upon the authority of very ancient records, which he found in the monastery annexed to the Church, and which were accidentally destroyed while under his care, that Luitprand rebuilt the original small and ruinous Church of S. Carpoforo, on the same site and on the present plan, in the year 724 A.D. If this refers to the body of the Church, then it is probably true, since its whole style denotes great antiquity. The bell tower, the apse, and the chapel on the north side of the presbytery, are of distinctly later date. Comparison with other buildings of periods well ascertained would assign the tower to the eleventh century, the apse and chapel to the twelfth. On the outside of the apse we find the long, narrow, round-headed windows, the thin columns running from ground to roof, the cornice arches, and the minute ornament, which characterise the Lombard period.

Within the basilica, the presbytery and crypt form together an imposing feature. The former, raised high above the nave, is approached by two lateral flights of steps, between which a third conducts to the crypt, visible from the nave. The effect must have been very fine when the triumphal arch, now hidden by the roof of the nave, spanned the space above. Formerly a screen of ironwork closed this entrance to the crypt, to which access was obtained by a winding staircase from the chapel on the left. We find the crypt divided into nave and aisles by six granite columns of various design, worn with age. It follows the lines of the chancel above, except that the apse is broken up into three recesses, as we have already noticed in Sta. Maria del Tiglio at Gravedona, and other churches of the Lake.

Behind the altar a simple granite tomb holds the body of S. Felix, probably the first Bishop of Como, from 379 to 391 A.D., who received ordination at the hands of S. Ambrose (*Ordinatio quam accepisti per impositionem manuum mearum* [1]), and proved a successful antagonist of the idolatries, which still held their ground tenaciously in this part of Italy.

In an extant letter, S. Ambrose encourages Felix in his work, and congratulates him on his success. "You are waging," he writes, "a good warfare for your Master, guarding His trust and making interest on His money. . . . The harvest is plentiful, but the labourers few, and helpers are found with difficulty. But the old saying is true, that God is able to send labourers into His harvest. Among the nobility of Como, many have already begun to believe through your teaching, and He, Who has made believers, will give helpers."

In another letter, playful as a schoolboy's, the grave Archbishop thanks Felix for a present of truffles of amazing size. (*Misisti mihi tubera et quidem mirae magnitudinis, ut stupori forent ea tam grandia.*) But handsome as the gift was, it was no sufficient bribe to silence a just complaint against the neglect of Felix in visiting him. "And beware," he adds, "lest hereafter you find finer truffles of sorrow (*doloris tubera*), for this word has a double meaning; pleasant enough when it relates to a gift, but disagreeable when it is used of the body or the feelings. . . . See how strongly I feel when a joke pleases me. . . . It speaks badly for you, and no better for me, if you think, that gifts can atone for your absence, or that I can be bribed by them."

For the play upon *tubera* we may compare the Latin proverb—

> "Ubi uber ibi tuber;"

the equivalent of—

> "There is never a rose without a thorn."

It is a strange sensation to stand by this grave, and hear, as it were, the very tones, grave and gay, playful and earnest, which once rang in the ears of the dust that lies there,

[1] Letters of S. Ambrose.

cheering on a soul, that was fighting in the vanguard of the Christian Revolution.

S. Felix ordered his body to be buried in the Confessional of his Cathedral, near the bones of S. Carpoforo, which were reputed to lie there, though in the thirteenth century Arona claimed the honour of possessing them, and S. Carlo is reported to have removed them thence to Milan in 1576. In 1611 the reputed tomb of S. Felix was opened, when the remains of a body were found, with a chalice of glass and a pastoral staff. The latter, which is preserved in the sacristy, has a crook of bone fixed in a ball, and terminating in the head of a serpent biting a stag, which is pierced by a lance or sword. The stag is probably a symbol of Christ or the Church.

In ancient times S. Carpoforo was called the Church of the Seven Orders, perhaps, as B. Giovio conjectures, because, when it ceased to be used as a Cathedral in the fifth century, it was handed over to a College composed of the Seven Orders into which the Clergy were divided. The name of S. Carpoforo was given from the fact, that Bp. Felix here buried the relics of the six martyrs, with Carpoforo at their head, who suffered at La Salvetta. They are said to lie in a tomb, now hidden from sight, under the altar in the South aisle. The inscription upon this tomb is found in the records of an Episcopal visitation in the sixteenth century, and is as follows :—

"Huc veniens discat qua corpora sancta requirat :—
Hoc altare tenet: sex tanto lumine splendent.
Hic sunt Carpophorus, tum Cassius atque Secundus,
Et simul Extantus, Licinius atque Severus.
Hi spernendo viri mortem pro nomine Christi,
Nec metuendo mori, simul hic voluere reponi.
Ad talem numquam potuit quis cernere tumbam.
His Sanctis sanctus locus est multum venerandus,
Quem nullus laedat, potius sed dona rependat.
Extat et hic Felix divinis ductus habenis
Verbum divinum studuit qui dicere primum.
Comi namque bonus primus fuit ille Patronus :
In coelis Felix merito fit nomine Felix."

Learn, pilgrim, where you may find the holy bodies.
This altar holds them, six glorious lights.

Here are Carpoforus, and Cassius, and Secundus, and Extantus, and Licinius, and Severus.

These men, in scorn of death for the name of Christ, and fearless to die, were content to be laid here all together. Never could any one see such a tomb before. The spot hallowed by these holy men is worthy of much reverence. Let none injure it, but rather endow it with offerings. Here, too, is Felix, who was drawn by the cords of Divine love to first preach the Divine Word. For of Como he was the first good patron saint, and now in heaven, true to his name, he is happy indeed.

Here, too, is a Pagan cenotaph found in a wall of the church, by means of which one Lucius Sentius proposed to keep green the memory of himself and his family:—

V. F.

L SENTIVS
SEPTEMBER VI VR
SIBI ET SENTIAE RVFINAE LIBERT
ET CONIVGI OPTIMAE ET PIISSIMAE
ET SENTIO PROBO FRATRI SVO
ET SENTIO PROBO LIBE ET PROPINQVO
ET M CELERIENO MERCATORI
SORORIO SVO ET VERE VERENTISSEM
ET ATILIAE SATVRNINAE SORORI SVAE
ET BARBARAE NVTRICVLAE SENECTVTIS SVAE
ET L SENTIO ONESIMO LIBERTO
ET SERVANDAE

The inscription is merely an enumeration of the members of his family, whom L. Sentius wishes posterity to remember; but there is something pathetic in the phrase *nutriculae senectutis,* "the nurse of old age." The gentle Roman, in perpetuating the names of his dearest, refuses to forget the faithful servant, who had cared for the wants of his declining years. But Christian builders had small respect for any such memorial. The marble was good and suited their purpose, so without compunction they carved their symbolic hunting scenes on the reverse side, and made of it a fair stone to decorate a pulpit or a screen. But this, too, in turn fell a victim to change, and in some enlargement or restoration of the church was put to the mean use of a common building stone. And now once more the venerable marble comes to light, eloquent with that yearning not to be forgotten, which is the instinct of our race, and branded with the scorn felt by a dominant Faith for all, that was most sacred to men of another creed.

Ten minutes' walk in the direction of Como leads us to the old Basilica of S. Abbondio, which Freeman says wàs to Como what S. Ouen is to Rouen. Originally founded by S. Felix, it was at first dedicated to SS. Peter and Paul; but after the burial of S. Abbondio within its precincts it received his name. Abbondio was a Thessalonian, distinguished for learning, wisdom, and zeal, and an intimate friend of his predecessor in the See of Como, Amangius, by whom he was ordained Bishop before his death. In such esteem was Abbondio held by S. Leo, that he employed him as his Legate in missions of great difficulty to Constantinople, which he discharged with singular expedition and success. There is extant a letter of the famous Theodoret, Bishop of Cirus, to Abbondio, in which, after addressing him as "Dear Sir" and "Most Holy Brother," he congratulates him upon the aid he had rendered to religion by setting the mystery of the Incarnation in a clear light, and showing the unity of person and the two natures in Christ. In his own diocese Abbondio won great triumphs among both Arians and Pagans, and is even credited with the miracle of raising a dead youth to life again. He died in 468 A.D., when he was at once chosen to be Patron Saint of the city, and buried with great honours in the church, which was then named after him.

In the sixteenth century, during a process of restoration, the discovery of some remains of capitals, bases of columns, and inscriptions seemed to indicate the existence of an ancient temple. Before this restoration there was a porch in front of the church, of which traces may still be seen. Above it was a square chamber called "The Paradise," approached by two stone staircases, and from which a *loggia* or gallery was entered, which overlooked the church. This *loggia* still exists. The choir was divided from the rest of the church by a wall. This was all changed in 1586, in order to give more light to the church.

The Church of S. Abbondio is in the style of the Lombard period, built after one plan, with five aisles, vistas of tall columns and monolithic piers with cushion capitals, a Western gallery, an exceedingly rich and lofty apse, flanked on the outside by two bell towers of great height and beauty. The eaves, cornices, and towers are embellished by a telling decoration of red tile-work. The exterior of the apse shows some beautiful traces of antiquity. The single-light windows are decorated with carvings of arabesques, animals, and the vine symbolical of Christ. The door has a flowing spiral decoration round the arch, and symbolical animals form the capitals of the slight pilasters at the sides. The interior of the apse is curiously frescoed with Biblical subjects. For quaintness we may notice the angel, who approaches to warn the three Magi asleep in one bed, and the Temptation of our Lord by a devil of very humorous aspect.

In former times a singular procession took place in honour of S. Abbondio, the Patron Saint of Como. On his festival the bell of S. Giacomo called together the public officers, Guilds, and professions to the town hall, whence, to the sound of trumpets, the procession moved in martial order. First came the trumpeters, who excited the joy and devotion of the people with their festive strains. Next followed the flag of the porters, and then the carriers, butchers, and notaries. Seeing that rank was denoted by place in the procession, it would seem that notaries were held of small account; but the honour shown to the butchers was due to a splendid deed of theirs in repelling an enemy who, in 1333, had entered Como. Then came public officials, and the Podestà in the midst of his court. Upon arrival at the Basilica of S. Abbondio Mass was begun, and after the singing of the gospel, the Podestà and the officials advanced to the tomb of S. Abbondio and offered there twenty-six imperial lire, five pounds of wax, and their flag. Then the notaries presented the Saint with money and their own insignia. When the celebrant came to the offertory, he received the oblation of the other Guilds according to their dignity, and each gave wax, money, or its own standard. The ceremony died out towards the close of the eighteenth century.

The office of Podestà, or Mayor, in Italian cities was first created by Frederick Barbarossa. A foreigner was chosen, on the theory that he would remain impartial amidst their factions. He was elected annually, had several able lawyers for assessors, controlled the military force, held the power of life and death over criminals, and was responsible for his conduct to the Syndics at the close of the year.[1]

[1] Sismondi.

CHAPTER XV

COMO

"The Cathedral of Como is perhaps the most perfect building in Italy for illustrating the fusion of Gothic and Renaissance styles, both of good type and exquisite in their sobriety."—J. A. SYMONDS.

As we turn towards the city of Como, the Cathedral, crowned with its cupola, is the central object. Built of marble, richly mellowed by time, without and within, it takes high rank among the churches of Italy for artistic merit. Begun in 1396 and not completed until 1730, it is a happy harmony of different styles wrought out beneath many hands. It bears the stamp of beauty and dignity, and offers a wide field of varied study. Quarries of black marble at Olcio and of white at Musso, supplied the material, while among the architects we find the names of Lorenzo dei Spazzi of the Val Intelvi, the Rodari from the Lake of Lugano, Cristoforo Solari, and Lucchino da Milano. On the façade is a portrait of Cicco Simonetta, secretary of Francesco Sforza, who held Como in his Duchy of Milan in the middle of the fifteenth century. His statue is the fourth figure from the bottom in the second row from the Broletto, and shows a venerable old man wearing hat and beard, with a book and lion at his feet. The claim of Cicco to this honour was, that he got permission from the Duke to remove a portion of the wall of the citadel, and part of the Broletto, to admit of the lengthening of the nave by the addition of two piers of the white marble of Musso, together with the elaborate façade. When some one once spoke disparagingly of him to his master, Francesco is said to have answered coldly, "that so necessary was Cicco to him and the State, that were he to die, he should be obliged to have another made of wax!" Cicco was the brain of the regency, which governed the Duchy during the minority of Francesco's grandson, Gian Galeazzo. But Ludovico Il Moro, uncle of the little Duke, could not resist the temptation to seize the power; and as the able and loyal Cicco stood between him and his ambition, the usurper had to reach the prize across the dead body of the faithful statesman.

It is somewhat of a surprise to our Northern sentiment to find on either side the central door figures of Pliny the Elder and his nephew, Caius Plinius, the Younger. They are seated beneath canopies of rare workmanship, which "may be reckoned," says Symonds, "among the supreme achievements of delicate Renaissance sculpture." Under the statue of Pliny the Elder, on the left, is a relief of the first eruption of Vesuvius, in which his curiosity cost him his life.[1] He was in command of the Roman Fleet at Misenum. Going on shore to investigate the phenomenon, he seems to have met his death by suffocation or exhaustion. Of his voluminous writings, only "The History of Nature" has reached us. It is a quaint collection of eccentric natural phenomena, which he had himself seen, or learnt only by hearsay. It is quite devoid of any scientific method, and full of the grossest credulity. He briefly describes the intermittent spring at Villa Pliniana, and also repeats an old superstition, that the river Adda flows through the Lake of Como without mingling with its waters.

His nephew, Caius, whose effigy appears on the right, was a native of Como, a generous benefactor of the city, the wealthy owner of several villas on the Lake, a profound lover of its beauties; among numerous other dignities, Governor of Bithynia and Pontus, and in the year 100 A.D. Consul of Rome. As we look at this statue our uppermost thought is of the surprises of History and the strange irony of Time. We recall his famous letter to the Emperor Trajan, written from his province of Bithynia, in which he describes the progress of Christianity, its simple rites and gentle principles, asks for instructions in dealing with it, counsels moderation, and somewhat contemptuously expresses his belief, that such a superstition, harmless, if absurd, must

[1] For his nephew's graphic narrative of the incident, see Epist. vi. 16 to Corn. Tacitus.

speedily die of inanition, if left to itself. How astonished would the philosophic statesman be, could he see the Christian Religion housed in the splendour of countless temples like that of Como, and swaying a vaster empire than Rome ever ruled; still more, could he see himself raised to honour among the great men of that religion, with a magnificent breadth of toleration and sympathy, of which he set, by comparison, a faint though humane example.

Nor can we fail to draw a contrast between the patient fortitude enjoined by Christianity under all trials, and the brave despair, which Pliny so highly praised. He tells the story of a lady whose husband was afflicted with an incurable cancer. Wishing to show him how to escape from the tyranny of pain, she flung herself from the terrace of their villa into the Lake, bearing him with her in her resolute embrace. Part of the letter is worth transcribing, and runs thus:[1] "I was sailing lately upon our Lake with an old man of my acquaintance, who called my attention to a villa situated upon its shores, which had a chamber overhanging the water. 'From that room,' said he, 'a woman of our city threw herself and her husband. He suffered from an incurable ulcer, which caused him exquisite torture. Finding there was no hope of recovery, she advised him to put an end to his life, to which course she not only encouraged him by her example, but was actually the means of his death. For, tying herself to her husband, she plunged with him into the Lake.' Though this happened in the city in which I was born, I never heard it named before; and yet that this action is less renowned than that of Arria's,[2] is not because it was less remarkable, but because the person who performed it was of inferior rank." P. Giovio conjectures, that it was from a house built "on the site of the villa of Sigismondo dei Medici, at Corenno, that this double suicide was effected, since it answers so exactly to Pliny's description." He forgets, however, that the incident happened in Como itself, the city in which Pliny was born.

In another letter to Cornelius Tacitus[3] we have a glimpse of Pliny's practical patriotism, though the suspicion that he

[1] Ep. vi. 24. [2] Pliny, Ep. iii. 16. [3] Ep. iv. 13.

wrote with a view to publicity somewhat discounts our admiration of his generosity. The drift of the matter is this: Finding himself lately in his native town of Como, he received a visit from a youth, who told him, that he went to school at Milan because his own town of Como had no professors. Pliny proceeds to say how much better it would be for their sons to be educated at home, both for safety and economy. If the burden of expense were shared among a number, masters might be provided upon comparatively easy terms, when account is taken of the cost of travelling and the heavy outlay entailed by residence from home. He then offers to contribute one-third of any sum they like to raise for this purpose, and he does so on purely patriotic grounds, since he has no children of his own to educate. He would offer to bear the whole expense, but feels that it might be abused, as has been the case in other public foundations. Interest will whet the sense of responsibility. The result, he predicts, will be, that as they now send their sons to foreigners for education, so then, when they have established their school of professors in Como, foreigners in turn will come to them to seek for instruction. This is most likely the first historical record of a proposal to found a Proprietary School. Whether it was ever carried into effect there is no means of judging.

The rose window above the main entrance is one of the most beautiful in existence. The Northern and Southern doorways are a marvellous weaving in marble of a wreath of leaves and flowers, and grain, and creepers, and little birds. No one must fail to admire the frog carved upon the Northern doorway, as it is held by all the market women under the arcade of the Broletto outside, to be the gem of the building. Under the cornice of the roof, in place of the obscene gargoyles, with which we are so familiar in northern Gothic architecture, is ranged a troop of water-carriers, young and old, set firmly upon pedestals, and bearing on head or shoulders shapely jars, out of which the water pours to the ground. They are the work of Bernardo Bianco and Francesco Rusca. Entering the Church, we find a Baptistery attributed to Bramante, with eight columns in red marble, and a modern monument to Cardinal Tolomeo Gallio, one of the notable benefactors of Como. The nave is enriched with great tapestries, which screen it from the aisles. One of them is the banner of S. Alban, borne in great processions, and there are also windows depicting his life and story. In the left aisle is an altar of the Mater Dolorosa with a Burial by Tommaso Rodari, and an altar of S. Joseph with a statue of the Saint and a bas-relief by P. Marchesi, the last work of this distinguished artist.

The gems of the Church are some typical works of Luini and Gaudenzio Ferrari. Symonds[1] describes them as "an idyllic 'Nativity,' with fawn-like shepherds and choirs of angels, a sumptuous 'Adoration of the Magi,' a jewelled Sposalizio, or 'Marriage of Joseph and Mary,' with abundance of golden hair, flowing over draperies of green and crimson." To enter more fully into detail, over two altars, works of Luini and Ferrari, master and pupil, hang as pendants to one another, and serve to illustrate the respective characteristics of the two painters. The religious feeling is equally strong in both, but the sweet simplicity of Luini is in Ferrari replaced by ambitious composition, daring originality, and strong colour, which won for him from Lomazzo the praise of being one of the seven greatest painters of the world. In the North aisle the pupil has painted the Marriage of the Virgin, which is far from being one of his most successful works. There is a shrinking peasant bride, a timid bridegroom, the usual crowd of disappointed suitors, a scene full of life and movement and a glow of pleasant colour. But it fails to achieve the true success of arousing sympathy in the soul of the spectator.

Luini's Nativity, on the contrary, is one of his most beautiful works, a charming pastoral, which wins us at once by its idyllic simplicity. In the far distance we see the angelic message borne in the cold moonlight to the shepherds far afield, two of whom hasten to the tryst. In the foreground one of them with upraised hands recounts the story of his strange experience that Christmas night. Above, one of the master's exquisite choirs of cherubs discourses celestial music. So near can earth and heaven draw at the birth of a little child.

[1] "Sketches and Studies in Italy."

There is in the South aisle a rare piece of tabernacle work in gilded wood over the altar of S. Abbondio, which acquires new dignity from being flanked by two pictures of the same artists. Luini furnishes an Adoration of the Magi, quite inferior as a whole, but redeemed by those inevitable passages of grace and sweetness, which grew spontaneously beneath his brush. There is a divine charm in the Child touching the bald head of the old man, who kisses his foot. The youthful figure to the right is a beautiful creation. Noticeable, too, is some picturesque by-play between the pages, who remove their masters' hats.

Ferrari's Flight into Egypt on the other side, is one of his great achievements. The travellers are watched over, guided, protected, fed and worshipped by a crowd of lovely angels. One with golden hair, and upturned face full of holy light, and hand gracefully resting upon the neck of the ass, is as fine a fancy as ever took birth in a poet's brain. The Child alone, be it noticed, is conscious of the celestial world lying open all around to seeing eyes. While Joseph and Mary are lost in moody reverie, the Babe is in close and happy converse with the Angels. So true is Wordsworth's line, "Heaven lies around us in our infancy." The landscape full of deep shade, the tall waving palms, the floating forms, the divine faces, the harmonies of colour, and, above all, the intensity thrown into the whole painting, make this picture most noteworthy. We seem to be reminded here, as in a picture of Ferrari's master, Luini, at Novara, of the *motif* of Mr. Holman Hunt's Triumph of the Innocents. Farther Eastward is a rich piece of colouring by Luini of the Madonna, with SS. Jerome, Anthony of Padua, Nicholas, Augustine, and the kneeling figure of the donor, Carlo Raimondi of Como. The single child musician is one of Luini's most graceful conceptions. The *predella* beneath this picture has for its subjects, from left to right, S. Peter, S. Jerome at penance, S. John the Baptist and the Lamb, S. Jerome's Burial, and S. Paul. More to the West are two large frescoes, by Luini, of SS. Christopher and Sebastian, flanking some fourteenth-century reliefs.

Of the many statues inside the church, the most notable is that of S. Sebastian, in the chapel of the Madonna. The artist has contrived to invest it with a marvellous feeling of intense young life and manly beauty, which helps us to realise how this Saint has become the Apollo of Christian art. So perfect is this work, that although it was formerly attributed to one of the Rodari, an attempt has of late years been made to give the honour of its creation to no less a sculptor than Donatello. Rare in sculpture, S. Sebastian is a Saint upon whom every painter has tried his hand. His martyrdom is so often repeated as to arouse the Englishman's impatience, while the arrow-riddled body is described by the American as "an animated pincushion." The Italian, on the contrary, never wearies of this favourite Saint, and for two reasons: first of all, Sebastian, a martyr of Narbonne, in Gaul, in the third century, became a Christian while holding high office in the Empire. He first disclosed his Faith in defence of two friends, Marcus and Marcellinus, whom his eloquent plea saved from death in behalf of their religion; but only for a time, as shortly afterwards they were killed, and with them Sebastian was pierced by a shower of arrows. Left for dead, but wounded in no vital part, he was restored to life by Irene, the widow of one of his friends. Sebastian, however, was brave, and having publicly reproached Diocletian for his cruelty, he was dragged to the Circus and beaten to death with clubs. Sebastian then became the averter of pestilence, a high office in a land subject to terrible visitations of epidemic disease. Probably the idea sprang from the arrows of his martyrdom, which from remote times were the emblem of pestilence. The Psalms familiarise us with the fancy: "Thou shalt not be afraid of the arrow that flieth by day; nor the pestilence that walketh in darkness; nor for the sickness, that destroyeth in the noonday."

Apollo was at once destroyer and healer. His shafts inflicted pest and death, and he was therefore propitiated as the god, who could avert such disaster. Greek ideas survived in Christendom after Christian forms and names superseded those of the older mythology. How natural, then, for Sebastian to succeed Apollo. The fresh vigour of health glowing in his well-knit frame seems the antidote to disease. The arrows become a sign of the Saint's power as well as of his martyrdom. In a fine picture by Benozzo Gozzoli at San Gimignano, Sebastian is shielding the suppliant people from the plague-arrows, which fill the sky. In the great plague of S. Carlo in Milan, 1576, the last despairing appeal of the people was to the intercession of S. Sebastian, reputed to be a native of their city. They vowed to rebuild his church and keep a festival in his honour, which was done in the following year.

And then again Sebastian admits of a freer treatment than any other martyr. He is portrayed as an Apollo in the youth and bloom of his beauty, as well as in the nature of his office. Without doubt the undraped sensuous form, eloquent of manly virtue and noble suffering, has endeared itself to the susceptible nature of the South. He is the popular type of masculine beauty, courage, and piety, and among women there is a cult of S. Sebastian almost akin to passion in its fervour and devotion.

Near the South door is the bust of Benedetto Odescalchi, one of the two Popes given by Como to Christendom. He worthily filled the chair of S. Peter from 1676 to 1689, under the title of Innocent XI. He was an ardent reformer of ecclesiastical abuses, a direction in which his will outran his power. His life was embittered by his conflict with the Grande Monarque, who claimed rights over churches and revenues in France never before exercised by the Most Christian King.

To us it is more interesting to read from our notebook Muratori's[1] comment upon the arrival at the Vatican in 1686 of an ambassador from the Court of James II. of England. "It was," says the annalist, "a singular source of comfort to the Holy Father and to Rome, and was regarded as a gracious gift of Divine Providence, that after the lapse of a century, and in the midst of Great Britain's disunion, communications should be reopened with the Holy See."

It fell to the lot of Innocent XI. to extirpate the Quietist heresy of Michael Molinos, whose acquaintance many of us have made in the pages of "John Inglesant," if not elsewhere. "The seed of this pestilent error insensibly spread everywhere," says Muratori;[2] "but theologians, the Holy

[1] *Annali d'Italia.* [2] Ibid.

Office of the Inquisition, and a Papal bull effectually stamped it out." How powerful must have been the evil, which needed such tremendous engines to uproot it.

On the tomb of Benedetto Giovio, the historian already alluded to, is inscribed the following forcible epitaph :—

> "Quem invida mors vult esse mortuum,
> Historia, Patria, orationes et carmina
> Benedictum Giovium mori non sinunt."

> "Benedetto Giovio, whom envious death wishes dead,
> History, Fatherland, Prose and Poetry suffer not to die."

Close by, carved on a sarcophagus, are a mitre-staff and three fishes, the *lucio* of the Lake, and the canting emblem of the Lucini family of Como. Nearer the West is a miraculous picture of the Virgin, signed *Andrea da Passeris, 1502 A.D.*

In a line with the façade of the Duomo is the Broletto or Town Hall, built in courses of red, white, and black marble, 1215 A.D. Raised upon slightly pointed arches and octagonal pillars, it covers a fruit market, which always presents a lively scene. "In real beauty," says Street,[1] "it is scarcely inferior to any one building I have seen in Italy." The carved balcony or pulpit, which projects from the front, was used in old times for the promulgation of Decrees.

A short distance along the Corso Vittoria we reach the Church of S. Fedele, originally dedicated to Sta. Eufemia, probably dating back to the sixth or seventh century, used for a time as the Cathedral of Como. Although restoration has quite modernised the interior, the church retains some noteworthy features of antiquity. It is cruciform, has three aisles, and is vaulted throughout. The Tribune extends across the whole width of the church, and is raised upon pillars. The apse in particular preserves its ancient traits. Its form is that of the half of a decagon or figure with ten equal angles. On the outside the usual light columns or vertical string courses, which mark these Lombard churches, are carried from ground to roof, and a graceful Gallery running round the apse forms a delightful feature, which we shall find again in the Church of Sta. Maria Maggiore

1 "Brick and Marble Architecture in North Italy."

Bergamo. Within are two ambulatories, one above, the other on the level of the floor, but hidden by the choir stalls. There is no Confession under the Tribune, probably owing to the proximity of the Lake and consequent liability to floods. The tympanum of the North-Eastern door is triangular, and points to Byzantine influence. At one side of this door are some curious and very ancient bas-reliefs. One of the subjects is variously explained as Christ in Benediction, or Daniel in the Lion's Den; another, as Habakkuk carried away by the Angel; a third, which is the best preserved, is in the main idea common to two other churches, S. Pietro di Civate, and S. Giulio, on the Lago d'Orta. A Chimæra, half bird, half beast, probably represents Christ in His divine and human natures. In his grip is a gruesome-looking creature, like a long fish, with tail cleft into a trefoil, wings, a pair of fore-legs, and head well furnished with teeth. Below is a second of the same type, and the whole group is surrounded by vine-leaves and grapes. Was this a well-recognised symbolical expression of Christ and the Sacraments of Baptism and the Eucharist? or must we suppose it to be a portrayal of the Redeemer's victory over lower principles? Within the church, a dragon supports the basin of holy water, signifying the subdual of the power of evil to the service of religion. The capitals are sculptured with symbolical animals. In the Piazza in front of the church, at the S.W. angle, are some very old wooden houses, with the upper stories projecting on time-stained beams.

We pass on to Porta della Torre, a gateway surmounted by a five-storied tower, dating back to 1192 A.D. From the Promenade outside a good view is gained of the walls, which belong to various periods, from that of Barbarossa to 1858. Porta della Torre has associations of a recent time far dearer to Italian patriotism than any memories of earlier history. When France and Sardinia declared war against Austria in 1859, Field-Marshal Urban, of cruel memory, occupied Como with seven thousand Austrian troops. Garibaldi appeared at Varese with three thousand volunteers, defeated a large body of Austrians at S. Fermo, and after some hard fighting outside Como, entered the city by Porta

Garibaldi. Simultaneously the enemy's troops marched out at Porta della Torre, which consequently received the new name of Porta Vittoria.

Count Krasinski relates a curious instance in connection with this campaign. Garibaldi fought against great odds, and his temerity often exposed him to serious risks. Urban would have given the gallant patriot short shrift, had he fallen into his hands. Indeed, one supposes he would have had less compunction in shooting Garibaldi than that entire peasant family, executed by his orders without a moment's warning, for having a few ounces of powder in their cottage. That as it may, Garibaldi was in imminent danger of being surrounded at Cavellesca, a village in the mountains near Como, when a young lady of noble family in this locality, fired with patriotic devotion, undertook to warn him of his peril. She was successful, though at great risk to herself. This piece of heroism led to a visit from Garibaldi when the war was over. An accident in riding detained him at her father's house for three weeks, during which he contrived to fall in love with his preserver, made proposals of marriage, and was reluctantly accepted. The ill-assorted pair were married at Varese, where the romance was converted into a tragedy. Before the wedding-day was out a former lover appeared upon the scene, placed before the girl the incongruity of her alliance, offered her his own young hand and heart, and in fine persuaded her to elope with him there and then. It is said, that Garibaldi continued to be the hero of the truant bride in spite of her lapse, and that she sought a reconciliation, which was not unnaturally rejected.

The open space in front of Porta Vittoria, always full of life and interest, was the scene of a very touching incident in 1439. The immemorial state of Como had been one of internal feuds and subjection to external masters. In every quarter of the city rose fortified towers, not for the defence of the common interest, but as the menaces of one powerful family against another. The whole country groaned beneath this scourge of fratricidal dissension, until at last, under some common sense of the inordinate weight of the evil, the people of Como met in this open space, and swore upon the crucifix to quench their animosities in the blood of Jesus. This solemn compact is still commemorated on S. Lucy's day, though the time was all too short before it was forgotten in new discords. Abbondio Raimondi writes, that the inclination to compose their shameful civil strife was inspired by the preaching of the Blessed Bernardino of Siena, in 1438. He, however, died before his purpose was accomplished, though his work bore fruit the following year under the hand of another Brother of his Order. Near to this Piazza of Reconciliation is the Church of the Crucifix, interesting only as the home of a singular relic of mediæval credulity. A band of Flagellants visited Como in the fourteenth century, and left behind them a crucifix of cypress wood. It soon developed a miraculous power, which manifested itself in a variety of gracious influences, and it became the custom to carry the crucifix annually in solemn procession through the city. But in 1529, by some whim of the Commandant, the route was blocked by the heavy iron chain, stretched for defence across the bridge, which spans the Cosia. The ceremony was in danger of becoming a fiasco, when suddenly the great chain snapped and fell, "as by the touch of the finger of God," amid the wild enthusiasm of the populace. This fortunate coincidence won great glory for the Flagellants' crucifix.

Not far from the quay stands a statue by Marchesi of Como's illustrious son, Alessandro Volta, the experimental philosopher. The four words of dedication upon the pedestal are the eloquent expression of a people's homage:

"A Volta la patria."

Volta was born at Como in 1745, and died in 1827. This great apostle of science was reckoned to be a dull child, and was even in danger of being condemned to become a Jesuit. Happily he pursued another road, contributed largely to the world's knowledge of electricity, and will always be famous as the inventor of the Voltaic pile.

The approach to Como by water has lost much of its charm by the conversion of part of the ancient harbour into the Piazza Volta. In P. Giovio's map of the Lake, the port is depicted with a line of wall and towers drawn across the entrance, a work of considerable magnitude, and suggestive

Photo by T. W. M. Lunn

COMO

of a condition of society very different from that which exists at present. It should also be borne in mind, that after its destruction by the Milanese, the city of Como was built upon lower ground than formerly.

A funicular railway now scars the side of the hill to the E. of Como on which Brunate is built. It has become a popular resort for its salubrious air and fine view at once of the Alpine peaks and the Lombard Plain, each equally beautiful in its way. But it must be owned, that the development of Brunate has not increased the picturesqueness of Como or its outlook.

CHAPTER XVI

SARONNO

"A thing of beauty is a joy for ever;
Its loveliness increases."—KEATS.

PASSENGERS can reach Saronno in an hour from the Ferrovie Nord Station, a few yards to the E. of the quay at Como. It is conveniently visited *en route* to Milan, and is on no account to be missed, since it contains a feast of the Art of two great painters of the Lombard School. Turning to the left from the station, along the Varese road, we pass down a shady avenue of plane-trees, at the end of which a tall and graceful campanile towers above a shapely Bramantesque cupola. This is the Church of Sta. Maria dei Miracoli, and here Bernardino Luini and Gaudenzio Ferrari have left some of their finest works. The painting of the cupola is a masterpiece of the latter artist. He was born at Valduggia, in the Duchy of Milan, in 1484, and died in 1550. If report be true, several masters had a hand in the moulding of his genius—Giovanone, Scotto, Perugino and Luini. Raphael found him a worthy ally in depicting the great story of Psyche in the Villa Farnesina at Rome. His pupil, Lomazzo, calls him the eagle of his art, so strong is he in flight and so swift in execution. He also ranks him among the seven greatest painters of the world, and quotes him in illustration of the principle, that an artist should aim at becoming original, forming the whole of the composition in his own mind, and copying the individual parts from nature and truth. Like Lotto and Moretto, he was a devout Christian; so much so, that at Novara he was designated *Eximie pius*. The tone of his mind appears in his pictures, which are entirely confined to religious subjects. He excelled in expressing the feelings of piety, and "succeeded,"

Photo by T. W. M. Lund

IL SANTUARIO AT SARONNO

says Lanzi, "in portraying the minds even better than the forms of his characters." His finest qualities of work are seen in this unique cupola at Saronno, in S. Cristoforo at Vercelli, in S. Gaudenzio at Novara, and Sta. Maria delle Grazie at Varallo. J. A. Symonds[1] thus sums up his excellences and defects: "What Ferrari possessed was rapidity of movement, fulness and richness of reality, exuberance of invention, excellent portraiture, dramatic vehemence, and an almost unrivalled sympathy with the swift and passionate world of angels. What he lacked was power of composition, simplicity of total effect, harmony in colouring, control over his own luxuriance, the sense of tranquillity."

In the cupola at Saronno, from an infinite depth of softened glory, the Eternal Father bends in benediction. A wreath of little cherubs, delicate in tone and lovely in form, circle round the central figure. Full of free life and fearless in their childish glee, they seem to hint at the Eternal Power of renewal in the Ancient of Days, and His everlasting sympathy with what is young and glad and pure. Beneath the rosy-limbed children spreads another great circle of singers and musicians, all busy with the praises of the Mother of the Redeemer. Some sing from wide books or long scrolls, while others join the concert with pipe, or lute, or viol. The scrutiny of a keen eye may detect here and there some word of the ascending hymn. This part of the picture is splendid in its variety of form, its poetry of movement, and its harmony of rich tones. Although the composition contains one hundred and fifteen figures, the idea is conveyed of a throng without a crowd. A host of heavenly people fills the sky, but they are neither stiffly marshalled nor ungracefully packed. No casual glance will reveal the genius in this work. The spectator must be content to take pains to see it. The best point of view for surveying it in detail is from the gallery, to which the Sacristan is always ready to give access. Patient study will be well repaid, and those, who give it, will leave the church richer in their experience of spiritual beauty, and with a larger capacity for observation than ever before.

Below the cupola in the four angles are medallions, also

[1] "Lombard Vignettes."

by Gaudenzio Ferrari, of the Creation of Eve, the Fall, the Expulsion, and the First Tilling of the Earth. In the segments of the arches below the medallions the subjects are by Bernardino Lanini. His contribution consists of the Birth of Cain, the Sacrifices of Cain and Abel, the Murder of Abel, the Divine Remonstrance with Cain, Adam and his Family. The figure of Eve in the Temptation and the Birth of Cain are very beautiful. To Lanini also is due the charming frieze of Angels, Sea-horses, and fanciful designs, which runs round below the gallery. Still lower, so as to be easily studied, are SS. Christopher and Anthony, on either side of the chancel gates, and at right angles to them SS. Sebastian and Roch, by Luini. SS. Martin and George are by Cesare Magni, 1583. In the *atrium* before the High Altar, immediately on the left hand within the chancel gate, we find the first of Luini's great pictures. It is the Marriage of the Virgin. These are the espousals of no vulgar peasants, but the wedding of the Mother of the world's Redeemer. Mary is depicted as a woman of matchless dignity. Her stately grace, erect figure, and noble mien, suggest the highest type of womanhood. A look of exalted purpose and quiet strength gives a queenly quality to her face. The golden hair is bound by a simple wreath of myrtle. Such a Mother the Christ might well have had. One of the finest figures in the picture is that friend of the bride's, who stands to her left in a wonderfully painted, flowered robe, with a face of splendid beauty. The aged Joseph delicately places the ring upon Mary's finger, while the High Priest reverently supports her arm. Behind are the rival suitors, who, in face and action, betray their disappointment at the issue of the ordeal to which they submitted. One of them breaks a stick across his knee. The story goes, that when many lovers would marry Mary, the High Priest's aid was called in to determine to which of them she should be given. He ordered each to deposit his staff for one night in the Sanctuary of the Temple, and when in the morning that of the old man, Joseph, had alone shown signs of life and budded, the miracle seemed to leave no doubt about the husband decreed for her by Heaven. In many pictures of the Virgin's marriage, the indignant suitors not only break their sticks, but vent their spleen by belabouring Joseph with them.

Upon the opposite wall is painted a subject commonly described as The Dispute of Jesus with the Doctors of the Law. Such, indeed, has Luini, following the common tradition, represented that visit of the child of twelve years old to the Temple, when he was found by his parents, drinking in what he could learn from the official teachers of his nation, and losing nothing for the want of asking questions. Probably he was simply passing an examination, to which every Jewish boy of his years was subject, and it is certain that if his intellect was extraordinarily acute, his demeanour would be no less respectful. The artist has set the boy upon a raised daïs in the centre of the scene, and he has risen from his chair at the sight of his Mother entering with timid look and tender expostulation. A painful expression of age and precocious thought is thrown into the sharp, sad features of the child, which none the less wear a character of singular sweetness and beauty. The one hand extended with open palm towards his advancing Mother, and the other unostentatiously pointing upwards, are finely suggestive of the words, "Why did ye seek me; wist ye not that I must be about my Father's business?" In this picture Mary is a simple peasant woman; her attitude is full of abashed apology, not for appearing before her own child, but for intrusion upon this august assembly of Rabbis. In her face we read her love for her child and her gratitude for his recovery. The group of doctors is finely drawn and full of character; and it is said that the figure of the Rabbi with the long white beard, who occupies the last seat towards the screen and gazes out upon the spectator, is a portrait of Luini himself. The supercilious air of the old Pharisee next the child's chair, who barely tolerates the earnest argument of a younger man, and who would not be convinced by ten thousand, is quite inimitable.

As we approach the High Altar, the fresco upon the left-hand side represents The Presentation of Christ. This is, perhaps, the most remarkable picture of the series, from the subtle allegory woven through it. Again the scene is laid in the Temple. Upon the wall are dimly outlined three faded ghost-like frescoes. The uppermost is a medallion, supported by an exquisitely beautiful cherub, whose earnest look invites attention to its subject, namely, Moses holding the Tables of the Law, the eternal principles for man's life in the mind of God before man was made. Immediately below, upon two small panels side by side, are the Creation of Eve, and Eve after the Fall, a lovely nude figure, leaning wearily upon a hoe and looking out, with dreamy, pensive eyes, into the far-off promise of the future. On the pavement of the Temple below, that promise is being fulfilled. Simeon takes into his arms the child of Mary, a bright, wide-awake boy, and, in the spirit of the Seer, cries, "Mine eyes have seen Thy salvation." The seed of the woman is about to bruise the serpent's head. If by a woman came long ago the breach of the eternal Law, so now by a woman comes the power of its perfect fulfilment. By Simeon's side stands Anna, whose words also fill the Mother's heart with mingled hope and apprehension. The entire scene is full of life, colour, and movement. A buxom maiden trips across the floor with the offering of doves. A yokel enters with a lamb upon his shoulder. To our left is a noble group, with whom Joseph stands in earnest conversation. To the right, a boy holds Simeon's mitre. From a balcony above, happy-faced children look down, unconscious of the significance of the drama enacted below. Through the columns of the Temple is caught a glimpse of the Flight into Egypt, a hint of the bruising of the heel of the serpent's Conqueror. In the background rises the Sanctuary Church of Saronno, to represent, as it were, in prophetic vision, and by the painter's licence of anachronism, that vitalising Body of Christ at last firmly planted in the world to leaven and exalt it, against which Death has no power. No one can study this picture without feeling how deeply Luini, like other masters of his time, had entered into the spirit of the sacred writings of Jew and Christian.

The opposite picture of The Adoration of the Magi, is a noble instance of Luini's power, and is one of the most successful reproductions of the Arundel Society. A group of angel-choristers in the clouds, intent upon a scroll, a long procession of horses and camels winding down the mountain side, and laden with all manner of strange furniture and luggage, the rude shed with listening ox and ass, the splendid figures of two kneeling Kings, the exquisite beauty and brave apparel of the page who holds his master's turban, the proud form of Joseph with beckoning hand, the beautiful, grave Mother, who bears alone the heavy burden of her thoughts, and, above all, the bright, blessing child, compose a subject large and varied enough to give full play to the force and fancy of this great master.

A conspicuous feature of the two pictures, The Presentation of Christ, and The Adoration of the Kings, is seen in the Sibyls, which are introduced in the upper angles. Still higher, and best seen from the gallery, are the four Evangelists and the Four Doctors of the Latin Church, by the hand of Luini, in the following order: SS. John and Augustine, the latter holding in his hand his famous treatise, *Civitas Dei;* Matthew and Ambrose, Mark and Gregory the Great, Luke and Jerome. "S. Augustine concentrated all his genius on a great work, written under the impression of the invasion of Alaric, and intended to prove that 'the City of God' was not on earth, and that the downfall of the Empire need therefore cause no disquietude to the Christians." [1] In the small choir, behind the High Altar, are four of Luini's most perfect creations, SS. Apollonia and Catharine of Alexandria, with forceps and wheel, in token of the sufferings of their respective martyrdoms, and two angels in the character of altar servers. The one on the right of the spectator carries the *ampullini* or phials for wine and water, and the *fazzoletto bianco*, or white napkin; the other bears the *torribile* or censer, and the *navicella* or boat-shaped vessel for holding incense. These angels are kneeling, but their posture is unhappily concealed by the benches, which have been fixed in front of them. The Annunciation, painted upon glass, God the Father on the vault of the choir, and the Nativity in the cloister, complete this glorious gallery of the works of the Raffaelle of Lombardy.

In the archiepiscopal archives of Milan we find a detailed account of the origin of this Church of Our Lady of Miracles. In the year 1460, a little distance from Saronno, on the

[1] "European Morals," vol. i. p. 410; Lecky.

Varese road, stood a modest shrine, which sheltered an immemorial statue of the Virgin Mary, bearing on her arm the Infant Jesus. Overgrown with brambles, it seldom attracted notice from the passers-by. The chronicle points out how this neglect was turned to good account by God, in opening a fount of grace to the surrounding neighbourhood.

A certain Pedretto had lain bedridden for several years at Saronno, tortured by sciatica and hopeless of cure. One night, during one of his most violent attacks of pain, which wrung from him bitter cries, his wretched chamber was suddenly illuminated, and a majestic woman of celestial beauty stood before the sufferer and thus addressed him: "Peter, if you wish to be cured, go to the shrine on the Varese road, undertake to build a church in honour of the Virgin, and the means shall not be wanting." At these words fresh power took possession of his limbs. He rose from his bed, went straight to the shrine, and spent the rest of the night in fervent prayer before the neglected image. Next day, re-entering the town, he cried to all whom he met, "A miracle! a miracle! the Madonna of the Varese road! a miracle!" The people asked in amazement, "Is not this that poor man who was for years bedfast? How is it that we see him here of a sudden so well and happy?" And then he told his story, and all took up the cry, "A miracle! The Madonna has healed Pedretto!" In a few days the shrine was thronged by crowds of sick, who are said to have received the most unqualified cures. Pedretto took up his abode in a hut hard by, where he continually told his story, and begged alms for the erection of a church until the day of his death. The shrine was then protected by iron-work, which is still preserved beneath the portico at the side of the present church, and a small chapel was built at a short distance, which, in spite of restoration, repeatedly fell to pieces; by which token it appeared, says the chronicle, that the Queen of Heaven disdained an ordinary homage and desired a home unique in its glory, the more worthily to attest the splendour of her miracles. The first stone of a grand edifice was laid in 1498, amidst great popular rejoicings, but its progress was slow, and in 1576 it remained incomplete. In this and the following year Lombardy was devastated by the plague, and that frightful scourge revived in the Saronnesi the desire to finish the temple of their miraculous Madonna. Moreover, the project received an impetus from the sympathy of S. Carlo Borromeo, who was at that time Archbishop of Milan, and who visited Saronno during the plague, to comfort and aid the sufferers. The design for the completion of the present church required the removal of the ancient chapel, which enshrined the famous effigy of the Madonna. On the 10th of September 1581, S. Charles himself presided over the translation of the image, amid an immense concourse of fervent worshippers. It was borne through the gaily decorated town with much pomp of music, banners and numbers, and finally placed in its present position over the High Altar.

It is related, that S. Charles was anxious to celebrate Mass at this altar, but was obliged to defer his purpose until the following day, to admit of some necessary changes in its position. During the night the statue was placed in a corner beneath a veil to protect it from the dust made by the workmen. Within this veil, at the foot of the statue, the Saint concealed himself and spent the night unconscious of the outer world. In the morning the superintendent of the works having found him there, and begged him to pardon the disturbances of that noisy night, the Archbishop replied, that neither sound of hammer nor voice of workmen had been heard by him during the entire night. This incident is quoted as an instance of his singular power of contemplation and abstraction.

This church was endowed by Pope Alexander VI. with many privileges, which were confirmed by five successors on the throne of S. Peter. Among other rights it might give sanctuary to those who had made themselves liable to justice, and at the present time the church is known in the neighbourhood as Il Santuario, the complete name being Il Santuario della Beata Vergine. Unfortunately, history has left no authentic record of the life of Bernardino Luini. Vasari barely alludes to him as a painter of some merit. But there is a tradition at Saronno, that this famous painter was one of those who availed himself of the privilege of sanctuary, afforded by the Church of S. Mary of Miracles, in consequence of a homicide of which imagination alone can supply the details. The old verger loves to tell how it was during this time of asylum, that Luini occupied himself in painting the noble frescoes, which at once glorify S. Mary and attest the greatness of his artistic power. The story goes, that he received thirty *soldi*, or fifteen pence, a day, with meat and drink, from the Brethren of the little community, in return for his work, which is dated A.D. 1525, and that, upon quitting his place of refuge, he left, as a mark of his gratitude, the Nativity on the cloister wall, now carefully preserved under glass.

In language as just as it is beautiful, Ruskin[1] touches the pathetic fact of Luini's unstoried life, and compares his work with that of his reputed master, Leonardo. He says:

"The best examples of the results of wise normal discipline in Art will be found in whatever evidence remains respecting the lives of great Italian painters, though, unhappily, in eras of progress, but just in proportion to the admirableness and efficiency of the life, will be usually the scantiness of its history. The individualities and liberties, which are causes of destruction, may be recorded; but the loyal conditions of daily breath are never told. Because Leonardo made models of machines, dug canals, built fortifications, and dissipated half his art power in capricious ingenuities, we have many anecdotes of him, but no picture of importance on canvas, and only a few withered stains of one upon a wall. But because his pupil, or reputed pupil, Luini, laboured in constant and successful simplicity, we have no anecdotes of him; only hundreds of noble works. Luini is, perhaps, the best central type of the highly-trained Italian painter. He is the only man who entirely united the religious temper, which was the spirit-life of Art, with the physical power, which was its bodily life. He joins the purity and passion of Angelico to the strength of Veronese; the two elements, poised in perfect balance, are so calmed and restrained, each by the other, that most of us lose the sense of both. The artist does not see the strength, by reason of the chastened spirit in which it is used; and the

[1] "The Queen of the Air."

religious visionary does not recognise the passion, by reason of the frank, human truth with which it is rendered. He is a man ten times greater than Leonardo; a mighty colourist, while Leonardo was only a fine draughtsman in black, staining the chiaroscuro drawing, like a coloured print: he perceived and rendered the delicatest types of human beauty that had been painted since the days of the Greeks, while Leonardo depraved his finer instincts by caricature, and remained to the end of his days the slave of an archaic smile: and he is a designer as frank, instinctive, and exhaustless as Tintoret, while Leonardo's design is only an agony of science, admired chiefly because it is painful, and capable of analysis in its best accomplishment. Luini has left nothing behind him that is not lovely; but of his life, I believe, hardly anything is known beyond remnants of tradition, which murmur about Lugano and Saronno, and which remain ungleaned. This only is certain, that he was born in the loveliest district of North Italy, where hills, and streams, and air, meet in softest harmonies. Child of the Alps, and of their divinest lake, he is taught, without doubt or dismay, a lofty religious creed, and a sufficient law of life, and of its mechanical Arts. Whether lessoned by Leonardo himself, or merely one of many disciplined in the system of the Milanese School, he learns unerringly to draw, unerringly and enduringly to paint. His tasks are set him without question, day by day, by men who are justly satisfied with his work, and who accept it without any harmful praise or senseless blame. Place, scale, and subject are determined for him on the cloister wall or the church dome; as he is required, and for sufficient daily bread, and little more, he paints what he has been taught to design wisely, and has passion to realise gloriously; every touch he lays is eternal, every thought he conceives is beautiful and pure; his hand moves always in radiance of blessing; from day to day his life enlarges in power and peace; it passes away cloudlessly, the starry twilight remaining arched far against the night."

Once, as I sat opposite the Presentation, two peasant women, mother and daughter, came bustling up the choir, their trim dress and eager faces betokening some occasion of importance. They wore short blue gowns, with bodices and sleeves of white linen, and bright coloured kerchiefs of the Brianza crossed over the bosom. Their hair was brushed to glossy brightness, and the thick plaits were set round with a halo of silver pins. White stockings, wooden shoes, and red umbrellas completed their attire. Not a look did they bestow upon the glorious pictures of Luini, unveiled for our contemplation. After a few words in an undertone with the Sacristan, during which a fee was arranged and paid, they placed themselves immediately in front of the altar, and with faces full of rapt awe, fixed their eyes upon a blue curtain just above it. The Sacristan pulled a string, the curtain flew back, and revealed to view a Madonna in the shape of a great doll, bedizened with gaudy paint and tricked out in trumpery gew-gaws. This was none other than the effigy of Our Lady of Miracles. At once the woman and girl fell to their devotions with intense earnestness, the mother instructing the daughter how to approach the shrine. I know not what grace they came to ask, but there was that in their expression, which vouched for the reality of their conviction. A few brief minutes were allowed them for the sight of that precious image, and then the Sacristan drew the curtain back again in a business-like manner, in marked contrast to the pious air with which the simple women left the Church.

I could not fail to be reminded how often Art has been charged with the fostering of idolatry. So far is this from being the case, that it is difficult to find an instance on record in which the painting or sculpture of any great master has been credited with miraculous power, or resorted to for the purpose of adoration. Probably there are few objects of popular reverence more widely esteemed than the Bambino in the Ara Cœli at Rome, and the Black Madonna at Ivrea. Both are hideous, without the least pretension to artistic merit. Indeed it will be almost invariably found, that superstition offers no worship to creations of beauty, whether of art or nature, but to ugly fetishes of which the character can with difficulty be determined. The blurred and dingy canvas, the featureless doll, the shapeless lump of stone or bronze, these are the most popular *media* between earth and heaven, and the best trusted channels of Divine help and grace. The only instance I can recall of a master's work being held in reverence is that of a Madonna by Andrea del Sarto. The picture was bought in Rome by an Englishman, shipped for England, wrecked in the Mediterranean, washed ashore on the coast of the Maremma, near a small village, where it was placed in the parish church. Here it was accidentally found some years afterwards by the owner himself. The picture had then come to be regarded by the people as possessing marvellous powers, not because it was a great work of art, but a miraculous sign of the special favour of the Virgin, who had directed this likeness of herself to be carried to their shore.

Pedretto's credulity finds many parallels among the peasant folk of Italy, who devoutly believe that the Blessed Virgin manifests herself to her votaries from time to time. A curious instance of this belief came under my own notice and is worth relating. In a sunny island of Southern Italy lived a *contadino* whose industry and enterprise had amassed for him in the course of a few years a couple of thousand francs. When the Government seized and sold by public auction the Church lands, Antonio had the hardihood to purchase property to the extent of his savings, in spite of the excommunication threatened against any who should be guilty of the sacrilege. The result was, that with few competitors, he was able to buy at a nominal price, and became from that day a rich and prosperous man. But the ecclesiastical ban was issued, and for many years he was unable either to make Confession or receive the Blessed Sacrament. A devout Catholic, he felt his exclusion from these vital privileges to be a terrible disaster. Still, so little inclined was he to part from his good bargain, that he preferred to take his chance for the next world heavily handicapped as he was. With a large family, he had but one son, Costanzo, for whom he nursed a great ambition and many schemes. But the boy fell ill; the symptoms became most alarming; no food could be retained, and the doctor abandoned all hope of saving his life. It was Sunday morning, and it seemed as though before nightfall his dearest hope would be blighted. The Church and its consolations were closed against him, so he went into his vineyard, and there, to find relief, to use his own expression, he "talked with God." Presently a peasant woman came by, and calling to him from the road, invited him to take some plums from her basket. He declined her offer, but she became so importunate, that, to be rid of her intrusion, he helped himself to three of her plums, which he kept in his hand, quite forgetful of their existence while he continued to "talk with God." Returning home, he went straight to his son's bedside, when the lad said, "Father, what have you in your hand?" He showed the boy the forgotten fruit, upon which Costanzo cried out, that that was just what he was longing for. A plum was peeled and given to him, and from that moment recovery steadily began. Antonio then turned his thoughts to the kind peasant woman. He remembered, that while he knew every one upon the island, he had never seen this woman before, and he will tell you to-day, in softened tones and with mysterious gestures, that he has never seen her since. He takes her for the Blessed Virgin, and accepts her favour as a sign of pardon in a higher court than that of the Church on earth.

Those who are not "doing" Saronno in the shortest possible time, between two trains, would do well to wait for the last sweet Office of the day, when the church begins to grow dim in the gloaming. The religious instinct of the Saronnesi still remains strong, nor have their costumes and manners greatly changed since the days of Luini, Pedretto, and S. Charles. Suardi's picture of the Assumption of the Virgin will be rolled up in front of the organ, which will utter rustic strains. Whole families of peasants will kneel together in pretty groups upon the pavement, priests and choristers will flit across the scene with faintly shining tapers, and then the whole assembly lift their voices in the plaintive chant of some simple evening hymn. I have known people to travel a thousand miles with the ostensible purpose of studying the works of such unique masters as Luini, yet to have spent more time at Saronno in the purchase of its *amaretti*, or bitter almond cakes, at the railway station, than in seeing th e unrivalled masterpieces of Luini in the church.

The following piece of advice, proved by long experience to be sound and useful, is offered to young travellers who really wish to profit by the expense and trouble of their wanderings:—

Never be content to visit a great picture without sitting down before it, and writing as complete and accurate an account of it as would convey to an absent friend a fair idea of its subject and treatment. This simple plan saves us from a cursory inspection, quickens the power of observation, gives the eye time to detect many valuable details, which would otherwise escape notice, fixes the subject upon the memory, and generally enables us to make the work in some measure a permanent possession of our own.

No doubt it will be retorted, "But there are so many pictures to see, and only a limited time in which to see them; to act upon your suggestion we could not visit more than half-a-dozen pictures in a day, and must leave hundreds unnoticed." For my own part, I should say that it is far better to see even one picture really well, than to survey acres indifferently. To see, because others have seen, is a vulgar ambition unworthy of a lover of Art, and to wish to leave nothing unseen in an inadequate length of time is a kind of greediness, which is sure to meet with its due reward. Pictures are food for the mind, and a surfeit of them produces mental indigestion and nausea. The true gain of seeing is education, and that is an end never gained by any sort of cramming whatever. A few great works really mastered will fit us to see all others more intelligently, profoundly, and enjoyably, besides becoming a part of our very selves, an inalienable property of memory and feeling.

CHAPTER XVII

S. PIETRO DI CIVATE

"When you behold the harvests in the fields
Shaking with fear, the Po and the Ticino
Lashing the city walls with iron waves,
Then may you know that Charlemagne is come."
—LONGFELLOW.

LECCO is girdled by five distinct groups of mountains, each in itself majestic and beautiful. The dolomite ridges and the valleys which they command, will repay any pains which the geologist, the naturalist, and the lover of the beautiful will bestow upon them. The town of Lecco is mean and uninteresting, but it is worth remembering, that every September a dramatised edition of *I Promessi Sposi* is performed here for one week by a company of high talent, as a tribute to the memory of Manzoni, 1785-1873, who chose this insignificant town for the theatre of his famous tale. In the Piazza Manzoni is a statue of the writer by Confalonieri, on the pedestal of which are panels in relief of scenes from his great romance.

The fine bridge, Ponte Grande or Ponte Visconti, that spans the Lake at its narrowest part, was built in 1335 or 1336, by Azzone Visconti. It originally consisted of eight arches, magnificently fortified by towers, bastions, and drawbridges upon a scale worthy of the ancient Romans (*tribus inter se divisis exemptili ponte castellis et turribus*[1]). The First Francesco Sforza added more arches, while the Second demolished its defences. In 1570, floods and the débris of the old fortifications rendered engineering operations necessary. In 1609 the Count of Fuentes restored it, and in

[1] P. Giovio, *Descr. Lar. Lac.*

Photo by E. H. Gilpin

BRIDGE AT LECCO

Photo by T. W. M. Lund

S. PIETRO DI CIVATE

1798, during the Russian invasion, three arches were blown up by gunpowder. After crossing the bridge, a drive of half an hour along the Como road brings us to Civate, but there is now a railway, which can be more cheaply used, though the distance of the station from the village slightly lengthens the walk. An hour's journey on foot by a steep path up the Val dell' Oreo carries us from Civate into one of those solitudes in which the early Benedictines loved to place their homes. Upon a grassy knoll, at the edge of a deep gorge, stands a small chapel in the shape of a Greek cross. It is dedicated to S. Benedict, and is the original church of the little Brotherhood, which first settled here. It is now dismantled and disused. Desiderius, last of the Lombard kings, who married his daughter, Ermengarda, to Charlemagne, but died a captive exile in France, leaving his kingdom to become a province of the Frank emperor, had a castle in this neighbourhood. While hunting one day upon the mountains, his son, Adelchi, met with an accident, which struck him blind. In fulfilment of a vow, made on the spot, the king built a church to S. Peter, for the use of the colony of Benedictine Brothers. This church of S. Pietro di Civate was erected in A.D. 757, a few yards higher up the slope than the ancient chapel of San Benedetto. Local tradition says this was the second church in Christendom dedicated to the Apostle, S. Peter's at Rome being the first. It is approached by a flight of twenty-seven steps of red stone, which the pious people of the Brianza regard as peculiarly sacred. Prayers are devoutly said at every step of the ascent, as the Songs of Degrees used to be sung on the fifteen steps of the Temple Court at Jerusalem. This staircase leads to an external porch, pierced at the sides by arches, of which a portion has been unfortunately destroyed.

Passing through the door, we find ourselves in a vaulted portico of singular beauty and effect. It has three arches, which span the width of the little church, and open upon it. The vaultings are quaintly frescoed with subjects suggested by the Book of Revelation, the description of Eden in Genesis, Evangelists and angels, with explanatory Latin legends. At each side, as we enter, is a low screen decorated with bas-reliefs of symbolical figures in stucco or terra-cotta. The one to the right is a griffin, or combination of an eagle and lion, supposed to symbolise the divine and human natures united in Christ. On the left is a lion's body, out of the back of which grows a chamois, while the tail ends in a serpent's head. This chimæra is supposed to symbolise the triple empire of Christ over Heaven, Earth, and Hades. May it not represent the attributes of strength, swiftness, and wisdom combined in Deity? On the tympanum or wall above the arches of this portico is a picture of the woman in the wilderness described in Revelation xii. A huge dragon is prevented from swallowing a little child by S. Michael and his angels, who slay it with their spears. This picture has given rise to a superstition among the simple people, that a great serpent used to haunt this mountain, and feed on such children as it could find, and furnishes an instructive instance of how fables begin.

The columns of the portico are moulded spirally in stucco, and a rich band of foliage in the same material runs round the head of each arch. The little church, reached through this portico, is devoid of pillars or aisles. The windows are small, narrow, round-headed, and deep-set. In a picture on the left-hand wall, dated 1464, S. John is represented with a cup in one hand, from which he removes a serpent with the other, in allusion to the legend that, having had poison given him to drink, he first blessed it and then drank it without harm.

At the other end of the church stands the altar, beneath a Baldacchino or Ciborio supported by four pillars of stone. The canopy, in the shape of a priest's *berretta*, is of stucco, decorated with reliefs of Christ and the Apostles, SS. Peter and James, Christ and Angels, Christ crucified, and Christ risen. Within we read these lines, founded upon Revelation vii.:

Simplex turba Deum comitatur semper et agnum
Quæ licuit nullis cantat sibi cantica plectris
Hi veniunt agni stolas in sanguine loti
Ante Deum palmas ex omni genti ferontes.

A pure band always accompanies God and the Lamb, and sings the songs which were never known to other lyres. These out of every nation come before God with robes washed in the blood of the Lamb, and carrying palms.

The Baldacchino, like much of the stucco work, has been restored, but is an accurate copy of the original. The altar is, ecclesiastically, very interesting, being so placed, that the celebrant stands with his face towards the entrance of the church, as is the case with the High Altar of S. Peter's at Rome, and formerly of S. Ambrogio in Milan. This practice is in accordance with the use of S. Ambrose, to which the monastic Orders were subject in the diocese of Milan. The Ambrosian rite prescribed, that the Choir should not be placed behind the altar, but at the side, and consequently, says Sormani, there was no need for the celebrant to turn round, even at the *Dominus vobiscum*, since he had neither clergy nor people behind him.

Three steps, behind the High Altar, lead to the small Tribune with a low stone bench running round it for the Presbyters. In front of the altar the floor on both sides of the church is divided into rectangular spaces by bands of dark stone, giving the appearance of two ladders. These mark the graves of the monks. Two low screens fence off the flights of twenty-five steps, leading from each side of the church to the gloomy crypt or Confession, aptly called in Italian *Lo Scurolo*, or "dark hole," and anciently used by the religious Orders for retirement and meditation. On the right-hand screen are bas-reliefs of griffins holding fishes in their mouths, and lions among vines and grapes. The griffin and lion are both held to be symbolical of Christ. The composite character of the griffin portrays the union of the human and divine natures of the Redeemer. The lion represents Him as the glory of the tribe of Judah. The fish is a very ancient sign of baptism, and the vine recalls the chalice in the Eucharistic feast. Perhaps, therefore, these reliefs may be taken to represent the two great Christian Sacraments. But the fish is also used as an anagram to describe the Saviour's name, nature, and work. The Greek letters which compose the word ἰχθύς stood for Ἰησοῦς χριστὸς θεοῦ υἱὸς σωτὴρ, *Jesus Christ, Son of God, Saviour.* In very early times it was a secret symbol among persecuted Christians. The vine is an emblem of the life of Him, Who is the root or stock of humanity, according to the words, "I am the vine, ye are the branches." And so, possibly, in these reliefs nothing more is intended than an emphatic assertion of the dignity and character of Christ.

The crypt is usually under the High Altar, but here it is at the other end of the church, perhaps owing to the nature of the ground. The roof is supported by six columns, with debased Corinthian capitals. Behind the altar are two reliefs, of which the upper one represents Christ healing the paralytic, while below is the Crucifixion. Two saints stand at the sides with head reclining on hand. In front of each is a much smaller figure, which, in one case, carries a little bucket in his hand.[1] The simple and unsymbolical treatment of these subjects shows, that they belong to a later period than the eighth century, in which this Church was built, as the Resurrection and Passion were not so represented in this part of Italy until four hundred years later.

In a lunette to our left are figures of our Lord and two disciples. Upon a string-course (*fascia*) beneath are the words:—

Suppleat ut veterem non venit solvere legem,
Filius ecce Dei persolvere munera legis.

Lo! the Son of God came not to destroy the ancient law, but to fulfil the duties of the law.

This string-course, which, like the other reliefs and ornaments, is of stucco or terra-cotta, and perhaps not coeval with the building, formerly ran round the whole crypt, but much has been destroyed in the last twenty-five years. Near the stairs we used to read the following words suggestive of troublous times for the Church:—

Maria Virgo,
Salve, Regina, Mater, Populo succurre dolenti.

Mary, Virgin, Hail, Queen, Mother, succour thy people in sorrow.

---

[1] C. C. Perkins' "Italian Sculptors," p. 100.

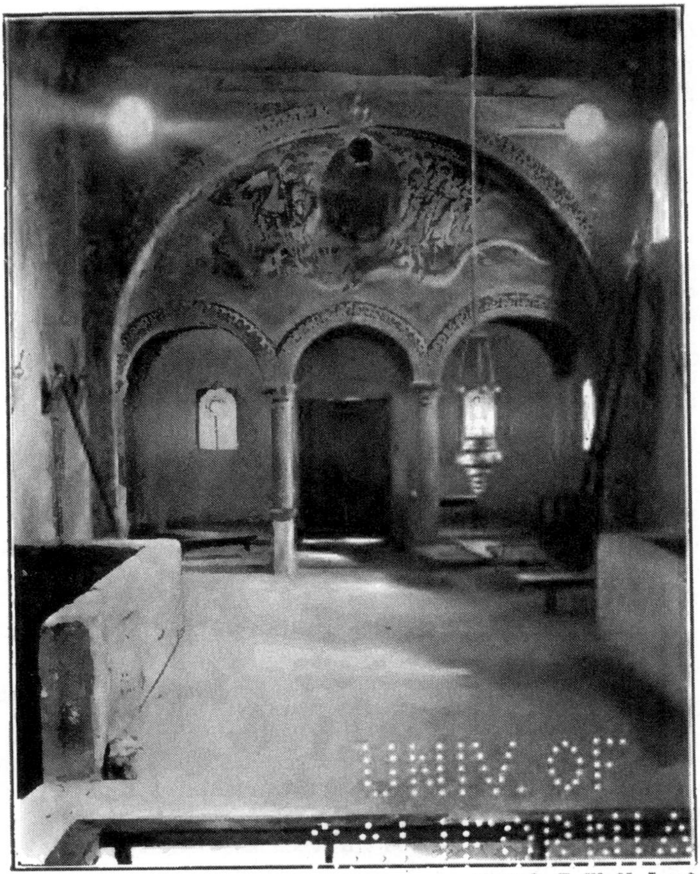

Photo by T. W. M. Lund

INTERIOR OF S. PIETRO DI CIVATE

Photo by T. W. M. Lund

LAGO D' ANNONE FROM S. PIETRO DI CIVATE

But they have been removed, and we now find above the window :—

> Virgine subnixa præfulget utraque fenestra.

And again :—

> Territus Hinc Hostis Fugiat Custodibus Istis.
>
> May the foe fly terror-stricken before those your guardians.

The remaining sentences are too fragmentary to be intelligible.

Among the relics which this church formerly claimed to possess, were the Keys of S. Peter and some rings of the chain, which bound him in the Mamertine prison. These were supposed to have the miraculous power of curing hydrophobia. On Ascension Day the people of Valmadrera visit the church, while the good folk of Civate make the pilgrimage on the Rogation-Days and the Feast of S. Peter. From the site of the Monastery there is a glorious view of the lakes of Civate, Annone, and Pusione, Monte Barro, the rocks of Lecco and the Lombard Plain.

Like Subiaco, Alvernia, Vallombrosa, and other Benedictine cloisters, S. Pietro di Civate was far removed from the world and well fitted for those, who wished to lead a life free from the trials of those turbulent times. Its seclusion sometimes brought strange and not always welcome guests to its hospitality. The chronicles furnish us with the portraiture of some of them.

In the latter half of the eleventh century a man of dignified bearing might be seen wending his way up the valley. His habit is that of an ecclesiastic. There is the play of a delicate sensitiveness upon a type of face, which bespeaks purity of purpose and the grace of patience. He is Arnolfo dei Capitani, Archbishop of Milan, who comes to seek an asylum from the intrigue and strife, which wrap the world in confusion and are a bitterness to his soul. The Emperor had nominated him to his See, but the Pope, resenting this usurpation of his pontifical rights, sent his Legate to deprive Arnolfo of the dignity. Without opposition, the Archbishop retires to the Monastery of S. Pietro. Here, in fasting and meditation, he waits for years, until the moment comes when the world has need of him again. At last another Pope, Urban II., needs the fire of such eloquence and sanctity as his to rouse the Lombards to a crusade against the Saracens. His fame has reached the Papal Court, and he is called out of his retirement in 1095 to resume the Archbishopric of Milan. But he does more than excite military ardour. By his wisdom and gentleness he reconciles parties and composes the strife of Guelphs and Ghibellines. Yet he cannot brook the burden of missions laid upon him by his master, the Pope. It was no part of the genius of such a nature to throw down the Papal gauntlet in the Courts of Emperors or mingle in base intrigues to secure a little more of power for the Church. The degradation of his tasks breaks his heart. Once more, a year after his reinstatement in his See, he comes to S. Pietro, but this time he is borne there to be laid to rest beneath its shadow.

A few years pass, and another priest presents himself at the Monastery door. He is bereft of nose and ears, while his right hand is seamed with deep red scars. This is Liprando of S. Paolo in Compito, who owes his mutilated visage to the cruelty of the heretic Nicolitaines and his own fidelity to the Church of his birth. The trophy of the scarred hand he won in the ordeal by fire, to which he submitted in the course of a long dispute with Grossolano, Archbishop of Milan, as a final test of the truth of his tenets. His courage and success availed him nothing, as his enemies were the stronger party, and held the burnt hand to be an invalidation of the miracle of his escape. From the bitter persecution which assailed him he fled to S. Pietro, but the ties of interest were stronger than those of hospitality. The Abbot, in fear of the Archbishop, excused himself from sheltering Liprando on the ground of his oath of fealty to his Superior, and the fugitive was driven forth again upon the world. Happily he found asylum in the Monastery of Pontida, where soon after he ended his days.

A century later there arrives another famous guest of misfortune. He, too, is an Archbishop of Milan, by name Leone da Parego. In his face and mien are written traits of physical courage, indomitable resolve, and the absence of all scruple in solving problems of difficulty. His eloquence had won for him the credit of a miraculous power of persuasion, and so he had been entrusted with the difficult task of finding an archbishop acceptable to the two conflicting parties in Milan. He sagaciously contrived to fail in his mission, and then, as a last resort, modestly proposed himself. He was accepted, and at once threw in his fortunes with what seemed to be the stronger party of the state, and upon the outbreak of civil war he led the nobility to the field, armed with his pastoral staff and sword. But his calculations were at fault. His army was defeated by the people under Martino della Torre, whom the Milanese had elected to be their head under the name of *Anziano della Credenza.* Then it was that Leone took refuge at Civate, where the Brothers were mostly of noble family. Misfortune, however, still pursued him, and the Torriani, having invaded the Brianza and taken the Castle of Civate, compelled him to fly to Legnano, where he died in 1251.

Four centuries elapse, and in 1574 S. Pietro is alive with a group of veıy different visitors. They are travellers, who pause for a brief space in the Monastery and spend their days in hunting the countryside. Crag and valley echo to the blast of their horns, the baying hounds fill the forest with their menace, and the falcons give small repose to flying game. By night there are many carousals, which make the Brothers rub their eyes and ask what new turn the wheel of fortune has taken. One day the master of this gay company returns from the chase with another capture than that of deer or heron. It is a young girl, famed for her beauty all the country round, who has fascinated him in the offer of a cup of water, as he passed her cottage, hot and faint. Such are her maidenly grace and courtesy, that he has offered to take her with him to France and enrol her among his Queen's women; for he is none other than the Third Henry of France, running away from his Polish kingdom with part of its *regalia* stowed away in his pack-saddles, to take the crown which death has snatched from his brother, Charles IX. The maiden has closed with the dazzling offer, but may too quickly mourn for her Lombard home in a strange land and amid the heartlessness of the life of a court. King Henry bids fair to prove but a sorry guardian for a beautiful peasant girl.

One more famous guest of S. Pietro we are permitted to see, and that the most distinguished of all. It is the Cardinal Archbishop, Charles Borromeo, who is visiting his diocese, as it never before was visited since the days of S. Ambrose, to uproot abuses and make reforms, and in the course of his herculean task reaches Civate, in 1571. With whatever feelings this particular community regarded his presence, it is conceivable that many houses and parishes which afterwards came to treasure the tradition of the saint's visit as their chief glory, would hate nothing more heartily in its reality; for the eye of that shrewd, thorough and holy man let little escape it, and he applied his remedies with no sparing hand. It is, however, left on record that at Civate, among other reforms, S. Charles was eager to revive the Ambrosian rite. The good people of Civate having been asked what else they preferred, made answer that they "wished to be either Roman or Lutheran," whereupon the wise Archbishop, considering the difficulty of the times, decided to let well alone.

A road leads over the mountain behind the Church into the Val Assina, and is said to be very fine.

There is a view worth the climb to see from the Croce or hill crowned by a cross above to the West.

Visitors should secure the key from the Sacristan, who lives in Civate, or they will make the pilgrimage in vain.

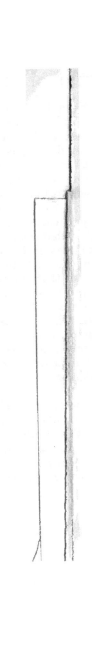

INDEX

O *

I

L

M

N

O

P

R

Printed by BALLANTYNE, HANSON & Co.

Lightning Source UK Ltd.
Milton Keynes UK
UKHW022050041021
391676UK00002B/110